MEREDETH TURSHEN

THE POLITICS OF PUBLIC HEALTH

RUTGERS UNIVERSITY PRESS
New Brunswick, New Jersey

Manufactured in the United States of America

Library of Congress Cataloging-in-Publication Data

Turshen, Meredeth
The politics of public health / Meredeth Turshen.
p. cm.
Bibliography: p.
Includes index.
ISBN 0-8135-1421-5 (cloth) ISBN 0-8135-1422-3 (pbk.)
1. Social medicine. 2. Public health. I. Title.
RA418.T915 1989
362.1—dc19 88-36976
CIP

In loving memory of my mother

CONTENTS

ACKNOWLEDGMENTS

I ENJOY READING authors's acknowledgments. Even when I skip a foreword or preface, I never miss the acknowledgments because they reveal something about the social relations of the book's production, which give important clues to what I am about to read. Of course, it is even more fun to reach the stage where one writes one's own note of thanks.

As befits one who believes in the economic importance of institutions, I begin by thanking Rutgers University, the Rutgers Research Council, the Department of Urban Studies, and the Graduate Program in Public Health of Rutgers and the University of Medicine and Dentistry of New Jersey–Robert Wood Johnson Medical School, all of which supported me while I did the research for this book. Special thanks to Bernard Goldstein and Michael Greenberg, director and codirector of the Graduate Program in Public Health, and to the students who listened to my lectures patiently (and impatiently) and challenged my ideas. I also wish to thank the Nuffield Institute for Health Services Studies of the University of Leeds at which I spent a sabbatical semester working on the book. Thanks to Carol Barker, acting director of the Nuffield Institute, and Shubi Ishemo for many stimulating discussions over delicious dinners of Scotch salmon.

My greatest debts are to my editor, Marlie Wasserman, who encouraged me and supported this book from the first tentative outline to the final version, and to my gifted reader, Evan Stark, whose generous comments were consistently positive, intellectually challenging, and most helpful in giving concrete guidance and direction. Dorothy Remy first suggested this work, which pulls together many of my ideas elaborated over twenty years in public health. And I thank Frank Popper for reminding me that revolutionaries don't speak in the passive voice.

Many people helped by sending me references or comments: thanks to Edward Allworth, Tony Astrachan, Rick Brown, Ron Caplan, Pierre Chaulet, Sally Cornwell, Ramana Dhara, Ray

Elling, the late Joel Gregory, Mike Greenberg, Nicki Hart, Malika Ladjali, Helen Lewis, John Lewis, Simon Messing, Josette Murphy, Michele Naples, Maggie Pearson, Spike Petersen, Rebecca Polland, Hélène Pour, Idrian Resnick, Len Rodberg, Jean Samson, Joe Scarpaci, Annie Thébaud-Mony, Rosemary Villars, Ingrid Waldron, and Dan Wartenberg. I thank Steven Feierman for his extensive comments on chapter five. My thanks to Michele Teitelbaum and Marilyn Campbell for fine editorial assistance. Special thanks to Cecile and Jerry Shore for rescuing me from the city heat at a critical moment in manuscript revisions.

A number of graduate students gave me technical assistance in the preparation of this manuscript: thanks to Battista Borio, Donita Devance-Manzini, Allan Lichtenstein, and Heather MacDonald.

Meredeth Turshen
Newark, NJ, 1 October 1988

THE POLITICS OF PUBLIC HEALTH

INTRODUCTION

What is public health? Is it preventive medicine? Government regulation? Free clinics? Rat control? Vaccination? The scope of public health is so broad that it encompasses all of this work plus sex education, food stamps for the poor, water fluoridation, and more.

In an era of rising medical care costs and in the midst of a threatened global epidemic of AIDS (against which the only preventive measure currently available is health education) and mounting deaths from cancer (of mainly environmental, preventable origins), public health is once more the focus of controversy. On one side are business and private medical practice, led in the 1980s by conservative administrations in the United States and Great Britain, arguing that the government should cut back its role in environmental protection and occupational health and safety while temporizing on the provision of medical care and health insurance. On the other side are shifting coalitions of environmentalists, labor unions, health workers, antinuclear and other public interest groups fighting for more government control of industry, including the health care industry.

This public/private confrontation is not a new phenomenon, as an examination of international public health history shows. From the radical transformation of English cities by sanitary reformers in the nineteenth century to the worldwide ecology movement of today, public health has attracted progressives and reformers, and its practitioners have often clashed head-on with the medical profession and with leaders of the business community.

This book is written in the progressive public health tradition: it criticizes the basic concepts and practices underlying conventional approaches to disease, draws on international—particularly African—and domestic illustrative material to demonstrate the limits of current approaches, and offers an alternative framework. Using contemporary and historical illustrations of the great moments and great debates in public health in the United States and abroad, this book analyzes the underlying principles that guide public health activists in their traditional mission of protecting communities and providing care to neglected groups. Addressed to community organizers and concerned citizens as well as health workers and students of public health, the analysis aims to provide a critical statement about the need for public health and an agenda for action.

The book is divided into four parts. Part One outlines current and alternative approaches to health. Chapters one to five focus on the methods of categorizing disease, theories of disease causation, and the practices that follow from these theories. The first chapter develops a new vocabulary and defines public health, preventive medicine, human ecology, and medical geography; it explains the differences between clinical medicine and public health, describes the scope of public health work, reviews conventional etiological theories, and outlines a new theory of disease causation.

Chapter two describes new tools for the study of disease. For all their diversity, public health disciplines share a common foundation in the nineteenth-century science of biology, the use of statistics, and the philosophical framework of empiricism and positivism. But if the etiology of disease lies in social relations of production, then public health needs a materialist definition of causality on which to base its policies and practice.

The third chapter examines public health policy. Each theory of disease leads to a different type of public health action or medical intervention. Progressive public health workers who believe that attacking the economic, social, and political determinants of disease is part of their job are concerned with housing, food, clothing, and income as well as health. A case history from the early part of this century—the discovery of the etiology of pellagra in the southern United States—illustrates the broad determinants of ill health.

The difficult issues of equity and access are discussed in chapter four. Public health work is carried out at many levels and in many institutions. As a rule of thumb, the higher the level of action, the more progressive the measure, because it reaches more people; but the higher the level, the less local communities can participate in or control public health programs. How the levels and institutions of public health are articulated determines the autonomy, flexibility, equity, and democracy of the system. Three models are described—those of the United States, the USSR, and the People's Republic of China—which represent three different economic, social, and political systems.

Chapter five selects women's health as a case study of the new approach to analyzing health and illness; it examines in depth three African countries—Algeria, Burkina Faso, and Tanzania—to demonstrate how health and disease are embedded in political economy.

Part Two outlines three conventional approaches to disease available to public health workers—containment, eradication, and cleansing of the environment—and analyzes their limitations. Chapter six describes two measures: the containment of disease agents in a limited space and the exclusion of disease from an area that is not affected. The first case history is a study of attempts to contain bubonic plague, which gave rise to extensive international quarantine regulations. The second study is of current attempts to contain dioxin, which proceed even though the public health field recognizes the limited effectiveness of containment.

The seventh chapter describes the nineteenth-century sanitary reform movement and its modern equivalents. When a hazardous agent has been disseminated in the environment, by accident, carelessness, or ignorance, the next step is to remove it, a costly and controversial procedure. Flying in the face of nineteenth-century laissez-faire economic philosophy, the sanitary reform movement in Britain used this approach to bring down the high urban death rates that marked the early phase of industrial capitalism. In this period, poverty was redefined and linked causally to population growth and environmental degradation—definitions that continue to shape policy today.

Disease eradication, which requires more than community planning and organization, is discussed in the eighth chapter. Without structural reform, these mass campaigns offer no lasting improvement in community health. Efforts to eradicate malaria failed because health service systems were not reformed and because agribusiness demanded increased use of pesticides, which undermined eradication efforts. A global mass vaccination campaign achieved total eradication of smallpox, but not lower death rates; Ethiopians no longer die quickly of smallpox, they die slowly of starvation.

Part Three changes the focus from conventional public health programs to progressive, non-medical approaches that offer new ways to conceptualize and tackle a wide range of issues. Four are discussed in as many chapters: preventive medicine, nutrition, mental health, and AIDS. Chapter nine examines preventive medicine, which is not always as successful as the global smallpox eradication campaign. Even if one disregards fiascoes such as the U.S. attempt to prevent an epidemic of swine flu that never materialized (while the vaccine killed, paralyzed, or injured thousands), other aspects of preventive medicine, such as the techniques of mass screening for early detection of disease, have been questioned on the grounds of doubtful efficacy and efficiency. The latest attempt to circumvent structural reform is the promotion of genetic engineering.

Chapter ten surveys nutrition and agribusiness. Most preventive measures, such as nutrition education, protect individuals; but only structural reform of agribusiness can protect the health and nutrition of the public. Public health nutrition began in the seventeenth century with the discovery that scurvy could be prevented among sailors by issuing them lime juice. The prevention of contemporary malnutrition is more complex and involves the entire international food system. A powerful food industry stalls reforms that would reduce nutrition-related diseases, and the "baby-killers" are still selling infant formula in the Third World[1] despite an international campaign to stop them.

It may actually be possible to prevent disease through social organization, and this is suggested in chapter eleven. Researchers have recognized the relation of social organization to mental illness since Émile Durkheim studied suicide in the nineteenth century. Subsequent studies confirm the relation of social class to mental illness. Nevertheless, public health has signally failed to protect mental health. The most radical approach to the prevention of this condition entails the reorganization of social relations. A number of attempts to treat mental illness in a community context are examined.

Chapter twelve considers AIDS, acquired immune deficiency

syndrome, which many people think of as the public health problem of the 1980s. Many of the issues discussed in this book arise in the case of AIDS: the limitations of clinical medicine, which has little to offer AIDS patients; the inability of U.S. health care to meet the needs of AIDS patients for jobs and housing, for drug rehabilitation, and for equitable care and humane treatment; the problems of a profit-motivated pharmaceutical industry; the reliance on unevaluated health education techniques; and unique questions of medical ethics regarding confidentiality, social control, and screening for a disease that cannot be cured. The chapter examines these issues in Africa where, under conditions of scarce resources, they become more acute and where the prejudices and misconceptions surrounding AIDS are thrown into relief.

Part Four looks to the future of public health. Chapter thirteen examines three basic issues in integration: research, training, and services. The integration of the social sciences in medical and scientific research is needed to solve complex contemporary environmental health problems. Interdisciplinary research presumes the integrated training of health personnel—not only that medical people will learn social science, but also that teams of health workers with different responsibilities (nursing, epidemiology, sanitation) will be trained together. With integrated training, there is hope that preventive and curative health services will be integrated, and that public health programs will no longer be based on single diseases (for example, tuberculosis) but on broad health problems (for example, living and working conditions).

The last chapter outlines an agenda for action. If death is due to nonspecific ill-being rather than a particular disease, if even the eradication of one disease means merely that people will die of something else, then public health workers need to revolutionize their field and the epidemiology that supports it. Concepts of social class, knowledge of political economy, and the goals of equity and access must inform not only public health work but all education. The conflicts between public health and private industry must be recognized as inevitable in the absence of structural reform. The empowerment of people through education and mass mobilization is the public health agenda for the year 2000.

PART ONE

New Principles for Public Health

Chapter 1

A NEW VOCABULARY

THE TERM *public health* is commonly used in two senses. The first sense is most easily described by the distinction between public and private services: public health most often denotes a set of resources—government services, or public services provided by a nonprofit agency. Or it means free medical care—free in quotation marks, of course; one does not pay a fee upon receiving a direct service, but the services must be paid for out of general revenue or earmarked taxes. Another way of looking at this type of public health is to specify its location or spatial context: these are services provided in a public space to which everyone is presumed to have access, but in practice in the United States only the marginalized use them.

The second and much more common usage of public health, and the sense in which the term is most often used in this book, is community health, in contradistinction to the personal health services of clinical medicine. Public health, in this sense, concerns a set of needs for protection from hazards that are rooted outside the individual; it embraces a wide range of community health services that affect large numbers of people—for example, epidemiological intelligence and vital and health statistics that are provided in the United States by the Public Health Service and the Centers for Disease Control and globally by the World Health Organization. In contrast, clinical medicine is typically practiced one-on-one with emphasis on curative care.

All kinds of combinations of public health and clinical medicine are possible, which seems contradictory. One can do public health work while employed by a private company; for example, in the context of a for-profit organization like Exxon or Nestlé one may practice one of the public health disciplines such as occupational health. Conversely, one can practice clinical medicine as a government employee; in the United States, for example, one may be a clinician with the Veteran's Administration or one may join the clinical medical service that the United Nations runs for its staff. The definitions, while clear, are used in confusing ways.

In addition to what public health is and where it is practiced, there are questions of how it is practiced and by whom. When public health work was limited to the provision of clean water supplies, sewerage, and garbage collection, it was easily distinguished from clinical medicine by the training of its practitioners. Public health inspectors were sanitarians, hygienists, and sanitary engineers, whereas physicians, surgeons, and nurses practiced medicine. Today the distinctions are blurred by the growing numbers of auxiliary personnel in clinical medicine (X-ray and lab technicians, dental hygienists and physical therapists) and by the assimilation of so many public health disciplines into clinical medicine—for example, occupational health, nutrition, and maternal and child health. Some would say public health itself has become a branch of medicine in the United States.

If what characterizes clinical medicine is one-on-one work, then the hallmark of public health is community action. Public health is concerned with factors that impact on health but are not normally associated with individual well-being—such as handguns, excise taxes, and highway speed limits. Yet a great deal of public health work does affect individuals; even when measures are planned on a community basis, they affect individuals or, even if they are directed at a group of individuals, they have their health impact by affecting a single individual. For example, sanitation, garbage collection, and street cleaning are community measures not designed to affect specific individuals or control single diseases, but they can have that ultimate effect. Upton Sinclair's novel *The Jungle* illustrates this point: the child of Jurgis Rudkus, the hero, falls off a makeshift sidewalk in a Chicago slum and drowns in a muddy street lacking drains that heavy spring rains have turned into a canal.

Another community measure not directed at a single individual and not singling out any particular group is legislation, such as the

1958 Delaney Clause that prohibits the use of carcinogenic food additives in the United States; this kind of regulation ultimately protects individuals from cancer. Mass vaccination campaigns, while planned on a community basis, are practiced on individuals. Even when clinical medicine deals with large numbers of people (as in mass screening for breast cancer), its concern is to identify and treat sick individuals. By contrast, even when public health targets individuals (as in tests for tuberculosis), its aim is to manage a problem that is identified as a threat to the community. These distinctions are important in planning programs and anticipating consequences of action.

René Dubos (1959; 1968) traces two streams of thought—the clinical, representing medicine, and the environmental, characterizing public health—back to ancient Greece, to Asclepius and Hygeia, respectively. Clinical medicine derives from the concern of the healer (Asclepius) with the individual, with the functioning of the individual body, with disease processes that take place within the body, and with interventions to alter the course of disease within the individual's body. Public health (or hygiene, from Hygeia) derives from community concerns with the environment and the interaction between societies and their environment, what is now called human ecology.

Public health is an interdisciplinary field and encompasses a number of disciplines including environmental health, occupational health, epidemiology, biostatistics, health education, nutrition, mental health, and health care organization and administration. Other disciplines of the social sciences have medical specialties that became part of public health, for example, geography, anthropology, sociology, economics, ethics, politics, law, and demography. Public health has a greater impact on our lives and affects many more of us than does clinical medicine, as the nineteenth-century sanitary reforms in Great Britain and the United States demonstrated. But, because clinical medicine, unlike public health, does not threaten vested interests, it and its technically dazzling disciplines (especially surgery) are more often in the news and get more good press, so that in our minds public health shrinks and becomes a narrow field. A review of the scope of public health will correct many misapprehensions.

The Scope and Origins of Public Health

A review could usefully begin by distinguishing clinical disciplines, such as preventive medicine, from public health disciplines, such as medical geography and human ecology. One way to distinguish them is by whether they act directly or indirectly on health status. Clinical medicine intervenes directly: acts are either surgical, chemical (as with drugs), electrical (electroconvulsive treatment), or physically manipulative (chiropracty). Public health intervenes indirectly using non-medical measures to affect health status. One function of public health workers is to monitor the environment for sources of potential ill health—for example, sanitarians inspect restaurants—or they alter a potentially harmful environment—for example, by fluoridating water or by monitoring the iodization of salt and the nutritional supplementation of food as in vitamin-enriched white bread.

To distinguish public health from clinical medicine in another way, plot the disciplines on a scale (see figure 1). Draw a straight line, representing a spectrum of states of health, with life or health at the left end and death at the right. Then distribute the disciplines along this spectrum according to where their practitioners intervene to affect health status. Somewhere near the middle is the onset of illness: this is where clinical medicine intervenes, at the moment of illness. Preventive medicine appears just to the left of clinical medicine; its practitioners apply a variety of tests to apparently healthy individuals in order to detect abnormalities at the earliest stages and prevent disabling conditions (for example, monthly blood pressure tests on pregnant women to monitor for hypertension and avoid toxemia).

The disciplines of public health appear to the left of preventive medicine. Epidemiology, the study of the spread of disease, may be placed next, and medical geography to its left; medical geographers map environmental and disease patterns, searching for unusual occurrences or factors that explain the patterns. Global maps of cancer have shown us the role of industrialization in that disease and have revealed interesting information about the role of diet, which showed up on cancer maps of Africa and China. Human ecology is to the left of medical geography, almost at the

Figure 1. *Selected Public Health Disciplines*

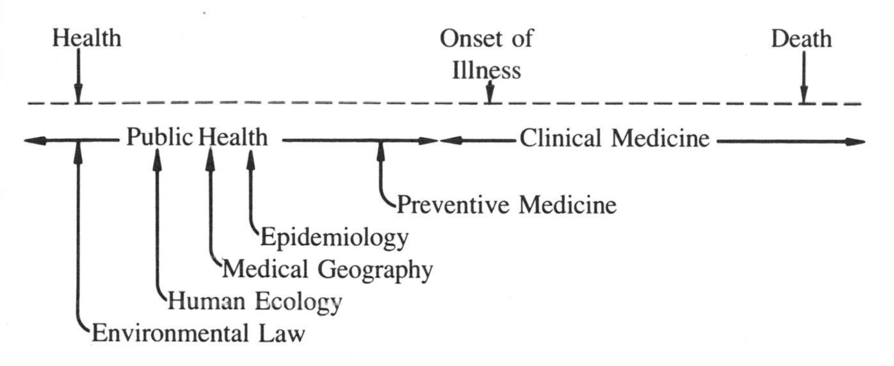

beginning of the scale closest to health. Human ecology, a recent field that grew out of biology and incorporated a lot of sociology and anthropology, is the study of the interactions of populations with their environment and the identification of potentially harmful interactions. Environmental law, which deals with legislation and regulations designed to conserve nature, might be placed last.

Public health is concerned with social organization—with what René Dubos (1968, 82) refers to as ways of life or what Jacques May (1954, 422), a prominent medical ecologist, called the culture that promotes and supports the survival of the group. Public health workers look at the interplay of social and environmental hazards; in traffic accidents, for example, they look at unsafe roads and unsafe cars, atmospheric and climatic conditions, and patterns of drug and alcohol abuse among drivers.

Because it represents direct action, vaccination is unlike other public health work. In order to protect communities from the spread of infection, public health workers administer vaccines that make exposed individuals immune to communicable disease. Logically, immunization belongs to clinical medicine, not public health. It became an important part of public health work in the nineteenth century because the poor could not afford vaccinations; the urban middle classes, threatened by epidemics, pressured governments to protect them by filling gaps in private medical coverage. Similarly, maternal and child health services belong to preventive medicine but have become part of public health because the poor could not afford obstetric and pediatric care and factory owners needed to ensure the birth of the next generation of workers (that is, the reproduction of the labor force).

Public health has a tradition of managing the physical environment which goes back hundreds of years to the first quarantine laws adopted in fourteenth-century Venice to arrest the bubonic plague, which was spread from rat-infested ships. Present-day public health practice in environmental management derives most immediately from the sanitary reform movement of nineteenth-century England, which improved urban sewerage, drainage, and water supplies. Management of the industrial environment, initially confined to regulation of the workplace, also occurred in this period. After the sanitary reforms were encoded in successive public health and factory acts that improved the lot of the poor in Great Britain and the United States, public health was depicted by conventional public health historians as a champion of workers and their families, a role that brought it into conflict with industry. Liberals like George Rosen (1958) portray public health heroically as government intervention to protect the working classes from the worst excesses of industrialization and urbanization. In this guise, public health has attracted well-meaning reformers from Edwin Chadwick, the architect of English sanitary reform, and Rudolf Virchow, his German counterpart, to the host of young professionals who flocked to the Carter administration in the late 1970s.

A more radical view of public health, the one adopted in this book, is that the working classes, in their confrontations with the business classes over such issues as housing, wages, and hours of employment, won industrywide regulations that are administered publicly (changes in a single factory or company can be managed privately). Workers and their families agitate for better working and living conditions; but the response to their demands, made palatable to business by various concessions, is a series of public health regulations and services. In effect, workers hope for profound economic and social change but get limited legislative reform. Ironically, there is compelling evidence that improved living and working conditions have had a far greater impact on health than public health and clinical medicine combined (McKeown 1976).

Industry has resisted—and continues to resist—public health

regulations. One example of industry's confrontation with government is the ongoing resistance to occupational safety and health legislation (others could be drawn from the regulation of alcohol or tobacco). U.S. corporations challenge the rules of the Occupational Safety and Health Administration in court as soon as they are promulgated. The 1978 cotton dust regulations to protect workers from bysinossis (brown lung disease), for example, were contested in the New Orleans Fifth Circuit Court the same day they were issued. Business has also used government control of public health to increase its hold over workers. Historically, it has used municipal public health administrations for social control and to reorganize the labor force, as in the measures taken when epidemics of cholera and smallpox occurred in nineteenth-century America. Health departments used the occasions to increase their powers and effectiveness. They were often opposed by the working class, who experienced the measures as extending control over their daily lives rather than improving their health and who were provoked to riot by the imposition of such public health measures as mass vaccination, quarantine, and hospital isolation in New Orleans, Milwaukee, New York, and elsewhere (Leavitt 1976; Stark 1977).

In the United States, clinicians and public health doctors have mediated confrontations between labor and management in situations that affect public health and industrial safety, sometimes on the side of business, sometimes for government, far less often for workers, their unions, or their communities. One common explanation of why physicians readily align their interests with business is that they are from the same social class as corporate leaders (see Turshen 1975, 86–100 for an analysis of the international evidence). Some Marxists believe that the medical profession is controlled by capitalists who reward doctors for their service to the highly profitable health care industry with money and prestige (McKinlay 1977). This approach emphasizes the class nature of the medical care system in capitalist societies (Navarro 1976). An alternative explanation is that, because it fails to address large social determinants of health, a medical approach to well-being is inherently limited (Stark 1982, Turshen 1977).

Even when public health workers testify on behalf of government or for unions in cases involving corporate challenges to the law or worker protests against company infractions, their testimony is a diversion from labor struggles because it shifts the focus from worker-management confrontations in the workplace to scientific disputes in the courtroom. And wealthy corporations can purchase the very best medical expertise. This process was astutely observed by Barbara Ellen Smith (1981) in her analysis of coal miners' pneumoconiosis (black lung disease). To win compensation, miners had to seize control of the definition of the disease from the medical profession—which was a political process and not a technical issue. Smith's analysis led her, correctly, to consider the theories of disease that are the premises of medical and public health work.

The Meaning of Health

Let us reflect for a moment on what we mean by health. A common source of confusion is the equation of health with health services or the equally mistaken assumption that health is primarily, or even largely, the product of health services. John Powles (1973), following the work of McKeown and Record (1962), compiled a useful graph that charts the fall of mortality in England and Wales, the dates of the introduction of effective medical cures such as antibiotic drugs, and the rise of expenditure on health services (see figures 2a and 2b). Clearly the steepest decline in mortality occurred in the nineteenth century, before medicine was established on scientific foundations, and few gains were made in the third quarter of the twentieth century despite huge investments in medicine. For example, the treatment of tuberculosis by streptomycin (the first effective TB therapy, which was introduced in 1947) contributed only 3.2 percent of the total reduction of deaths from that disease in the period 1848 to 1971 in England and Wales (McKeown 1976, 82). McKinlay and McKinlay (1977) came to similar conclusions in their analysis of data for the United States, and the thesis is now widely accepted.

There is no positive definition of health in the conventional literature. When one looks at the available definitions, including the WHO (UN World Health Organization) motto "Health is a

Figure 2a. *Mortality Trends in the United States 1900–1985, Contrasted with the Proportion of the Gross National Product Expended on Medical Care*

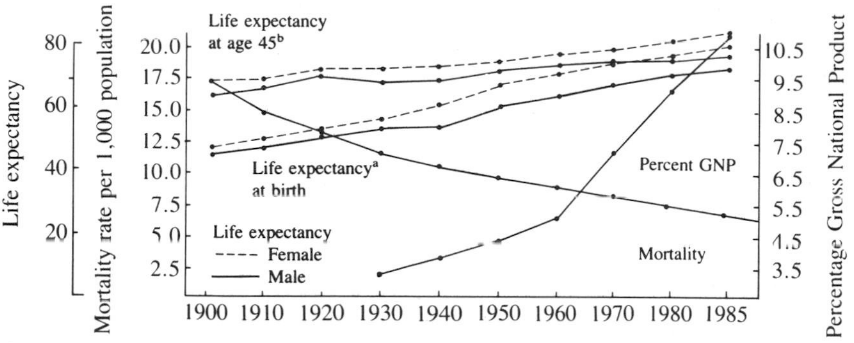

Sources: U.S. Department of Health and Human Services. 1988. *Vital Statistics of the United States 1985*. Washington, D.C.: U.S. Government Printing Office. Vol. II Mortality, Part A, Section 1, page 1; U.S. Department of Health and Human Services. 1986. *Health—U.S., 1986 and Prevention Profile*. Washington, D.C.: U.S. Government Printing Office. Table 89, page 183.

[a]From 1900 to 1929, data for death registration states; from 1929 data for United States.
[b]Whites only.

Figure 2b. *Mortality Trends during the Last Century, England and Wales, with Recent Expenditure Trends*

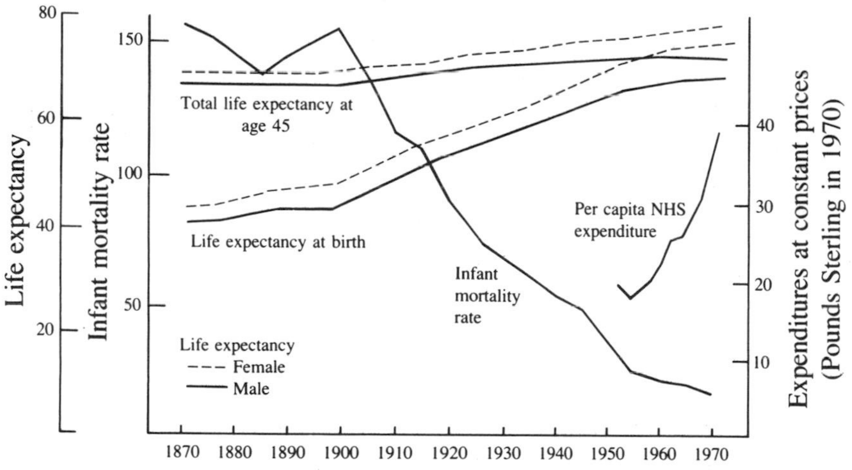

Source: J. Powles, "On the Limitations of Modern Medicine," *Sci. Med. Man* 1. (1973):2.

state of complete physical, mental and social well-being and not merely the absence of disease or infirmity," one finds health described in terms of the absence of disease or disability or in terms that are general, descriptive, subjective, individual, and unmeasurable. If one cannot define health, one cannot measure the success or failure of efforts to improve health.

If there are no acceptable or globally recorded measurements of health, there are several of disease, some of which have been in use for more than a century—incidence (the number of cases over a period of time), prevalence (the number of cases at any one point in time), age-specific morbidity (the numbers of cases in an age-group such as infancy), and age-specific mortality (the numbers of deaths in an age-group). England and Wales have registered the cause of death since 1838. The central and critical contemporary question for public health workers is whether a relationship exists between documented falls in disease-specific mortality (that is, the conquest of specific diseases, of which the most spectacular example is the global eradication of smallpox) and improvement of health. The question is crucial because, despite medical and technical advances, the evidence of persistent and widespread ill health worldwide is persuasive.

Powles (1973), McKeown (1976), McKinlay and McKinlay (1977), and others explain the fall in mortality before 1950 in terms of the improved diet and hygiene that accompanied rising standards of living in England and the United States. They arrive at their conclusion by examining disease-specific mortality in order to assess the factors that contributed to the fall in death rates. Their purpose is to identify the relative role of medicine (immunization and therapy), which they find to be very minor. But this method is misleading because it gives the overall impression that the aggregate fall is the sum of these parts (drops in the leading causes of death), when in fact the parts are interchangeable and do not, in this sense, account for lowered total death rates.

It is not only that specific diseases are not always accurately diagnosed. Tuberculosis, for example, is a poorly defined constellation of symptoms with multiple causes. McKeown (1976, 31) says, "there must be doubts about the diagnosis of tuberculosis at a time when it was not possible to X-ray the chest or identify the tubercle bacillus." And in the conditions obtaining in many parts of the Third World, or given the summary diagnosis offered to minorities in many advanced countries, such doubts must persist.

Nor is it only that the particular composition of the death rate is specific to a society in a given historical period. What people die of is associated with the kind of work they undertake, with social stratification, and with the organization of everyday life. For example, E. P. Thompson (1968, 352) writes of early nineteenth-century England that "The industrial town-dweller often could not escape the stench of industrial refuse and of open sewers, and his children played among the garbage and privy middens." As could be expected, infectious diseases contributed heavily to child mortality in these circumstances.

The type of disease is a separate issue from the burden of mortality and morbidity. If English and American mortality rates fell in the nineteenth century because standards of living improved, then, very simply, high mortality is due to low or falling standards of living. The radical conclusion to be drawn from the work of McKeown and his followers is that mortality is not disease-specific. What the distinction between types and numbers of deaths comes down to is the underlying cause of health or illness.

Conventional Theories of Disease Causation

There are many theories of what causes disease; five contemporary theses are discussed here: the theory that germs are responsible; that disease is the result of genetic abnormality; that lifestyles dispose to illness or health; that diseases have multiple causes, many of which are rooted in the physical or psychosocial environment; and that health and disease are socially produced. They are discussed in turn.

Germ theory, the first biomedical theory of disease causation, is relatively recent; it dates from the late nineteenth century. Before the 1880s there was no microscopic evidence linking specific bacteria or viruses to particular diseases. Louis Pasteur (1822–1895) and Robert Koch (1843–1910) identified such agents and established the foundations of the germ theory. Stated simply, the germ theory of disease holds that external, discrete, and specific agents are responsible for disease, and that, in general, diseases are short-lived, self-limiting, and acute conditions. It follows from this theoretical premise that cure is based on killing or eliminating the disease agent, by exterminating it or by rendering it harmless. And prevention is based on cutting contact between the host and the disease agent or on rendering the host impermeable, a state known medically as immunity.

This etiological picture rests on a limited definition of disease. It encompasses the clinical and spatial aspects but ignores the psychosocial and historical dimensions. The original epidemiological work on cholera by the English physician John Snow (1813–1858) in the late 1840s addressed the way the infection spread, which allowed sanitary engineers to interrupt it, but said little else about its nature. Koch's identification of the cholera vibrio in 1883 told us little more, although it did enable individual medical attention to improve. It is questionable whether knowing which particular microorganism "causes" cholera explains very much about the nature of disease, why it occurs or whom it attacks. For example, the germ theory sheds no light on the nineteenth-century cholera epidemics in Zanzibar observed by James Christie, which claimed the lives of 20,000 to 30,000 Africans living in squalor while none of the 60 well-off Europeans on the island were affected (Davies 1959). The germ theory tends to confuse the treatment of a disease with its cause, a common error of biological reductionism.

Popularized by Pasteur, whose work was widely known, the germ theory generated tremendous excitement among the bourgeoisie; it gave them the (false) sense that they were now able to control disease, which was consistent with their technical mastery of the environment gained during the industrial revolution (Hobsbawm 1975, 258). In fact these early discoveries improved diagnosis but had little impact on disease, which did not yield till biochemists developed antibiotics many years later. The ascendancy of the germ theory inaugurated what has been called the "bacteriological era," which lasted for approximately fifty years. It was a time of discovery, glorified in conventional histories of medicine that usually ignore the social context of these discoveries and what that context says about the nature of the discoveries themselves.

The social context of the rise of medicine based on the germ theory of disease—the period from the 1880s to the 1930s—was one of enormous change in Europe. From an economy that had been dominated at the beginning of the nineteenth century by agricultural production on family farms with an emphasis on community and cooperation, Europe was transformed by the industrial revolution and the wealth extracted from colonial possessions into a radically different world dominated by industrialism, urbanism, individualism, and competition. The germ theory of disease was very much a creature of its times. It affirmed individualism by focusing on disease processes within each individual. It upheld the moral cynicism of competitive industrialists who popularized a corrupted version of Darwin's theory that only the fittest survive. Health was now an individual, and no longer a collective, responsibility.

Evan Stark (personal communication, 1988) points out that the germ theory became popular only after manufacturing was being superseded by new systems of mass production and workers were overcoming the early problems of industrialization through their struggles. This was after improved living and working conditions had effectively controlled infectious disease. The context for the rise of medical solutions and explanations was the prior decline in mortality. Medical efficacy was discovered when it was already largely irrevelant.

During the bacteriological era, earlier theories of environmental causes of disease (for example, miasmatism, which held that pestilences were spread by an unhealthy atmosphere corrupted by noxious emanations [see Tesh 1988, 25–32 for a review of this theory]) were set aside as unscientific and fell away from public view. The accomplishments of the sanitary reforms of mid-nineteenth-century Britain were forgotten—that is, the state withdrew funding from the medical department—and public health was regarded as less glamorous than the search for the "magic bullet," the cure for each newly discovered disease (Macleod 1967). Industrialists gained the upper hand and consolidated their control of the labor force; they were assisted by a rising standard of living, which was subsidized by exploited labor in the colonies. Berliner (1985, 82) points out that germ theory became consistent with the social and political status quo, which it defended; it gave business a way to improve the resilience of the work force without social reforms intimately linked to other theories such as Rudolf Virchow's (1985) social medicine, which entailed revolution and the overthrow of the existing social order.

After World War II, which had given impetus to surgery and the manufacture and diffusion of antibiotics that were effective in controlling infections, it became clear that the germ theory failed to explain adequately the chronic diseases that were now the leading causes of death in the industrialized countries. Researchers were unable to find single causative agents of these conditions and turned their attention back to environmentalism. A new theory of multifactorial disease causation was introduced, which did not so much abandon the germ theory as add a new concentric circle of explanations around it. In the epidemiological triad of interacting host, agent, and environment, environment was redefined as both psychosocial and physical, agents became multiple, and the host was the subject of research on how disease acted in the body at the cellular level, as the new science of immunology became an important field of study. Because the theory also multiplied scientific uncertainty, probabilistic notions of relative risk replaced the specific etiology of germ theory. The theoretical advance that multifactorial causation represents enlarged the scope of clinical and public health intervention: with many more factors implicated as causes, there were many more opportunities for action.

In general, industrialists are less comfortable with multifactorial theories of disease than with the germ theory because they are implicated as responsible for many of the environmental conditions now identified as etiological factors (Tesh 1988, 55). One response is a new emphasis on the biological foundations of disease, supported by advances in genetics. Industry supports genetic research, which identifies individuals who are supposedly hereditarily vulnerable to toxic environments. A number of large companies support laboratories doing research on this "gene theory" of disease, which shifts responsibility for illness back to the individual. In 1983, Dow, Exxon, Du Pont, IBM, Eli Lilly, and other multinational corporations sponsored a major conference on genetic variations in susceptibility to disease, a field called "ecogenetics," at Cold Spring Harbor, New York (Hunt 1986).

Looking back over the past thirty years, it seems that there has been remarkably little progress in cutting mortality from chronic diseases, especially when compared to earlier progress in reducing mortality in the nineteenth century or to the large amounts of money spent on medical care and research since World War II (Powles 1973, see figures 2a and 2b). The leading causes of death in the industrial countries, which are cardiovascular and cerebrovascular diseases, can be neither prevented nor cured, although medicine can ameliorate some of these conditions and can reduce associated physical pain. What we lack is a model of health and disease that more adequately represents reality. Although environmentalism opens our eyes to factors such as diet, environmental exposure to toxic substances, the importance of the workplace and occupational history, it is inadequate because it does not address the power relationships of race, class, and gender that dominate our everyday lives. Multifactorialists can discuss income, race, and class only as personal characteristics; they have no way to look at group characteristics or at social structures and conceptual systems.

Some environmentalists, in the face of this failure, invoke a catchall explanation: the problem lies in the way people live (Calkins 1987). Lifestyle theories of disease causation became popular with analyses of stress by Hans Selye (1956), which were followed by studies linking smoking to lung cancer and by research into the relation of stress, diet, and exercise to heart disease. Lifestyle theorists such as John Knowles (1977) hold each individual responsible for his or her health; illness is the result of irresponsible behavior (failure to exercise; overindulgence in rich, fatty foods and alcohol; smoking; promiscuous sex; and so on). This analysis gave rise to the now widespread belief that by changing individual habits one can dramatically reduce the risk of dying from heart disease and cancer. The only empirical evidence for this belief is that smokers who quit smoking reduce their chance of developing these diseases. Lifestyle theories also engendered holistic, self-help health movements (Salmon 1984).

E. P. Thompson (1968, 230) points out in another context that discussions of standards of living often pass into discussions of ways of life, although the two are not the same; "The first is a measurement of quantities: the second a description (and sometimes an evaluation) of qualities." From the lifestyle viewpoint, prevention is no longer the work of industrial hygienists or sanitary engineers but of health educators who can bring about behavior modification. In social work and sociology, this response is known as blaming the victim (Ryan 1976). Victim blaming is particularly popular with conservative governments as it relieves them of the burden of caring for those unable or, in their words, unwilling to protect themselves.

A New Theory

A new theory of disease called "the social production of health and illness" has gained wide acceptance internationally in progressive public health and social science circles. This theory claims that mortality is nonspecific, that overall community health is not affected by the elimination of any one cause of death. The specific diseases named as causes of death on death certificates are expressions of particular historical circumstances, and these circumstances are more important to understanding ill health than the clinical or biological information related to specific diseases. For example, the 1967–1979 smallpox eradication campaign does not appear to have improved health in the Third World (infant mortality is actually rising in some African countries), nor was the development of a vaccine against smallpox responsible for falling death rates in nineteenth-century England.

According to this theory, health and disease are products of the way society is organized, of the way subsistence is produced as well as surplus, and of the way subsistence and surplus are distributed among the members of society. (Surplus is that part of what is produced that is not needed for subsistence. Industrial profits, land rent, and bank interest are all forms of surplus. People can use surplus to make themselves into something new or different, such as artists or musicians.) Disease and health are products of the relationship between the producers of wealth and the owners of the means of production, as well as between producers and the distributors of goods and services, because the distribution of resources vital for health—such as housing, food, or leisure—is a function of the relative power of different groups. Health and disease are also products of the organization of procreation, child rearing, and socialization—the reproduction of social life and economic organization. And, as Stark points out (personal communication, 1988), the role of politics in managing relations among groups and in negotiating differences is also key. Thus to study public health is to study disease in the context of these relations over time.

It follows from this theory of disease that fundamental social reorganization—the reorganization of production relations, including changes in the way surplus is distributed in societies—is imperative for prevention and cure. The focus of disease shifts from the host or the individual to social classes defined in relation to production and to the way production is organized.

Although it is non-medical, this theory acknowledges the role of bacteria, parasites, viruses, and other agents of disease, most of which have existed since the beginning of history. But the expression of a specific disease, whether communicable or non-communicable, from the storehouse of possible diseases, and the particular group or groups of people who contract it, are historically specific phenomena. In *The Political Ecology of Disease in Tanzania* (1984), I described in detail the historical development of epidemics in East Africa; the cumulative effects of European exploration, wars of conquest, and the slave trade at the end of the nineteenth century were devastating epidemics of old and new diseases (old in the sense of indigenous such as smallpox and new in the sense of imported such as rinderpest). The research persuaded me of the overwhelming role of non-medical factors in epidemic disease.

Epidemics, then, are events linked to precise forms of social organization affected by specific circumstances. The dimensions of an epidemic are revealed less by its physical appearance in demographic space than by its historical development, its common social history. Even though victims of chronic diseases do not die in physical proximity in a short span of time, they die nonetheless in epidemics from identical causes stemming from a complex, but identifiable, source (Stark 1977). Disease varies from place to place, less because of climate or geography than because of the way work and reproduction are organized and carried out in those places. This theory of disease causation specifically rejects any notion of determinism, whether biological determinism, which reduces disease to physiological processes and confuses treatment with cause, or teleological determinism, which defines phenomena in terms of functions or roles or ends.

One of the most difficult concepts of this new theory of disease causation is nonspecific mortality, the idea that the specific causes of death can change without influencing the total number of deaths. Medical and public health workers are so conditioned to think in terms of disease-specific mortality and morbidity, of the International Classification of Diseases, and of death certificates specifying primary and secondary or contributory causes of death, that the idea of nonspecific mortality is difficult to grasp. It challenges the foundations of biomedical science because it implies that much clinical research, treatment, and prevention of disease do not bring about the improvement of health. In fact it makes a hash of most medical education and argues for the need to find new ways to teach about disease and health.

The best-known evidence for nonspecific mortality is the Inter-American Child Mortality Study in which Puffer and Serrano (1973) found that the eradication of measles by immunization made no change in total child mortality, only in what the children died of (which may be the same as or different from what was written on their death certificates). Skeptics point out that the study was conducted in conditions of extreme deprivation; when standards of living fall below subsistence levels, even the best health services appear to make no impact. They question whether these findings are applicable to affluent populations. I believe they are, because I believe that chronic illness is a product of social factors of production common to many countries. And good health services can have an impact even in the midst of war and famine, as current events in Mozambique show (Cliff and Noormahomed 1988). Significantly, the theory of nonspecific mortality shifts the question from what causes disease to what causes ill health.

Causes of Ill Health

It is public health dogma that people in the South, which comprises the countries of the Third World, suffer from infectious diseases, much as Europeans did a century ago, whereas today chronic diseases afflict the industrial countries of the North.[1] This doctrine is the public health version of modernization theory, which was first advanced by political scientists. According to modernization theory, Third World countries are underdeveloped because they are culturally traditional and economically backward. The public health version holds that as "backward" countries develop, they too will experience the chronic diseases associated with later stages of industrialization and urbanization. That modernization theory is patently flawed has been demonstrated by the Hungarian political economist Tamas Szentes (1971) and the Latin Americanist Andre Gunder Frank (1971), among others. In this book I show that the public health version is equally faulty.

Not only have diseases such as schistosomiasis, leprosy, venereal disease, and tuberculosis been wrongly labeled (they are chronic conditions, not highly contagious diseases like measles), but chronic disease has reached epidemic proportions in the Third World. Epidemics of occupational accidents, injuries, and illness would probably be found to occur more commonly in the South than in the North, if anyone kept track of them, as would hypertension and diabetes. Chronic malnutrition is the South's equivalent of the chronic diseases of obesity so widespread in the North.

Underlying these epidemics North and South is the modern phenomenon of stress, and it is a neocolonialist attitude to believe that only "civilized" northerners suffer its consequences. Stress is closely associated with social disorganization and family breakdown, problems as common in the Bantustans of South Africa as in the ghettos of New York. Alcohol consumption and cigarette smoking are strategies for survival under stress, albeit potentially self-destructive ones. These strategies, which are falsely portrayed as habits of individual choice in the North, have spread so rapidly and are now so prevalent in the South as to reveal clearly their epidemic character. They are not the only indications that chronic disease afflicts countries in the South as well as those in the North. The threatened epidemic of AIDS, acquired immune deficiency syndrome, in which the body is unable to fight infection as a result of chronic malnutrition, repeated infection, antibiotic resistance, and the HIV virus, is important in east and central Africa as well as New York and San Francisco.

Stress is largely a response to capitalist social relations; it is an expression of our reactions to the extraction of surplus value from all social activity, not only from production at the workplace. Since the introduction of migratory labor systems (which transported male workers from their homes to work sites far away, sometimes in other countries, leaving behind the workers' families to scratch a living from their farms), this extension of extraction has been characteristic of capitalist development in Third World countries. Proponents of the economic theory of dualism, which is the economist's version of modernization theory (dualists hold that Third World countries have two economies, a backward hinterland and a modern enclave), have denied the negative effects of migratory labor systems, claiming that it was good for "backward" countries with unlimited labor supplies to develop modern sectors such as mining. The failure to understand the nature of capital's strategy has led radicals to overemphasize processes like proletarianization (which turns self-sufficient farmers into wage laborers) in their analysis of twentieth century developments in the Third World and thus to overlook, until very recently, the exploitation of women—and almost to miss the crisis of social reproduction, which has affected women primarily (Turshen and Barker 1986).

Comparable phenomena associating stress and migration with disease have been documented by Cassel and Tyroler (1961) and Eyer and Sterling (1977) in industrial societies. Cassel and Tyroler studied the health effects of the dramatic social and cultural changes that accompanied rapid industrialization in North Carolina. They found that recent migrants to an industrial milieu are likely to manifest increased rates of psychological, somatic, and social ill health. Eyer and Sterling, examining national data for the United States, found that capitalist social organization, through intensified, conflicted work and the destruction of cooperative, supportive forms of social community, causes excessive mortality among adults.

In the twentieth century, economies have reorganized and changed from competitive capitalism to monopoly capitalism, which is characterized by the introduction of such mass production techniques as the assembly line and the formation of large multinational corporations; and organized labor has consolidated in legislation such gains as shorter working days, improved wages, workplace safety and health, and restricted child labor. The response of industrialists was to incorporate reforms (such as the eight-hour day) by intensifying the effort required at work. Industry responded positively to workers' demands for goods and services in order to orchestrate consumption, family life, and leisure according to the same standards of productivity applied in factories (Stark 1977). When working-class families became strong enough to refuse to absorb the daily costs associated with family maintenance, which industry passed off to them, government was called in to provide the necessary goods and services. The dates of the introduction of this policy around the world vary: late nineteenth century in western Europe, early twentieth century in North America, and post-World War II in Asia and Africa. (The dates in Latin America vary: 1930s in the countries of the southern cone, post-World War II elsewhere.)

The historical and international perspective on economic and social change adopted here is important because it helps account for the transition to modern chronic diseases. In the past, international interest was limited to the geographical spread of contagious diseases such as plague and cholera, and historical studies focused on the impact of disease on society (McNeill 1976). The social production approach to analyses of ill health depends critically on an international as well as a historical context because the very process of change is international in nature. It is interesting that AIDS is the first disease that will be researched in a historical and international perspective.

The independence of Third World countries in the two decades following World War II posed a new problem for capitalists: for the first time capital was no longer identical with the state, in the sense that they were now of different nationalities. Except in South Africa and Namibia where virtual identity is maintained, capitalism has been forced to accommodate a variety of economic and political organizations in the Third World, from transparent puppet regimes and open market economies (such as Liberia, Zaire, and Bantustans such as the Ciskei) to opaque nonmarket economies and one-party states (for example, Algeria, Angola, Guinea, Mozambique, and Tanzania). A single strategy that could be applied in all cases has been difficult to find, hence the rapid turnover of unsuccessful approaches (known in economic circles by such clichés as "import substitution," "redistribution with growth," and "basic needs"). With the loss of state identity, capitalism could no longer command the repressive force it wielded in the colonial era; even the most transparent of puppet regimes can balk and be recalcitrant. On the other hand, capitalists have learned to deflect struggle from themselves to the state, so that in many countries, especially where 20 to 40 percent of the people are unemployed, confrontations take place between workers and the state.

The postcolonial state inherited certain functions relative to the provision of health and social services that were assigned by social capital in the era of capital's identity with the state. After independence, Third World people looked to their governments to provide the care that colonial regimes had withheld; for example, many Third World countries considered it a matter of national pride to maintain colonial standards of medicine and surgery while desegregating government hospitals—even when the costs consumed their health budgets, the medical care was inappropriate, and hospitals served only a fraction of their population (Turshen 1984). In countries in which the indigenous private sector was impoverished—as it sometimes deliberately had been by the colonial regime—the postcolonial state was forced to provide a greater range of services to a larger population than in countries in which the private sector flourished. The money for this expanded social sector came from underdeveloped private enterprise and cut into profits. In this sense, the very size of the postcolonial state may be related to capital's problem of preserving profit.

When statehood dissolved the merger between colonial governments and capital, it also obscured the prior confrontational relationship between colonized people and colonial capitalism. After independence, people came to believe that health and social policies were the products of the new government planners, rather than the fruits of labor's struggle with capital. Inevitably, discontent with living and working conditions took the form of protests against the new regimes rather than fights with foreign companies. And in countries with parastatal corporations (in which the government is a shareholder—sometimes the only one), the role of overseas capital was even more obscure.

Popular Resistance

Confrontations about control occur throughout the social arena with equal intensity; it is arbitrary to limit the focus of inquiry to the factory, plantation, or mine. Strikes and work stoppages are not the only forms of struggle, nor are work sites the only places where struggle occurs. Bus and school boycotts, rent strikes, and food riots are all instances of struggle. Direct appropriation is another and it takes several forms: squatting, beggary, and theft. Resistance is clearly demonstrated in black markets, illegal migration, flight, and refused cooperation. Public health and medical services have not escaped their share of protest, but often popular resistance in the health sector is not recognized as such.

In the colonial period, quarantine measures were used, ostensibly to arrest the spread of disease, but ultimately to control the influx of workers. To resist quarantine was to resist unjust arrest. Colonial health officials justified residential segregation on the grounds that a *cordon sanitaire* (the ring thrown around an area to keep out all infection) was needed to control disease, but in fact ghetto concentrations simplified the task of the police, as is still obvious in South African Black townships today. Violations of the *cordon sanitaire* were acts of resistance. In colonial Mozambique, the links between health care, the military, and the police were direct and explicit: health care was dispensed by the coercive arm of the state. To reject medical care was to reject colonialism.

Epidemics and famines are manifestations of crises of social reproduction as experienced by their victims; the crises are brought about by the profit imperatives of capitalism. Today, in many parts of the Third World (especially Africa) for a combination of historical, economic, political, and ecological reasons, the profit squeeze has caused living standards to fall below subsistence levels. The gains of an earlier cycle of struggle for political independence, which brought higher standards of living and better health in the first two decades following World War II, are now largely lost. What for capitalists is a crisis of profit is experienced by working-class families as reduced income, fewer goods, and poorer services, including public health and medical care. Class conflict is inevitable in these circumstances. The response of capital and of the states it has coerced is to use the crisis to reorganize and discipline labor by invoking repressive police powers of arrest, inspection, and fines, and to increase control of the work force by strengthening the public health administrator's use of invasive regulations. In documenting the health effects of the crisis, we need to respect people's modes of organization and to recognize that their struggle for health is ultimately a struggle for freedom.

This chapter summarizes and shows the limits of biomedical theories underlying conventional public health approaches to disease. It contrasts clinical medicine with public health, internal disease processes with external hazards, and individual medicine with community concerns. It offers an alternative framework, which focuses on the differences between the broad social aims of public agitation—often rooted in trade union activities—and the relatively narrow vision of the conventional public health response to demands for better living and working conditions.

A new theory of disease causation called the social production of health and illness puts public health, not only in historical perspective, but also in an international context. While insisting upon the historical specificity of both infectious and chronic disease epidemics, this view advances the notion of nonspecific mortality—that is, it separates the cause of death from total mortality. The concept of nonspecific mortality is used to reinterpret the work of McKeown and his followers and to explain why the elimination of any one cause of death does not affect overall health.

The next chapter will examine the methods used to study disease, which are associated with conventional public health approaches. The methodology common to the different public health disciplines unifies the field. New methods are needed, however, to put the new theory of social production into practice.

Chapter 2

NEW TOOLS
FOR THE STUDY OF ILL HEALTH

MY INQUIRY into the nature of ill health is an examination of the methodological foundations of medicine and public health, as well as a study of theories of disease causation. The first part of this chapter explores the philosophical rationale for scientific methodology: How do we know what we know? How do we know whether what we know is true, or how do we test the truth of our knowledge? At issue here is the nature of causality. The new theory of the social production of illness and health described in chapter one requires a redefinition of causality. Marxist critiques of science advance a new definition based not on empiricism and positivism, which are the bases of natural science, but on realism and materialism.

The second part of this chapter concerns the methodology of categorizing populations studied in public health. The question here is, how do we organize knowledge and classify data? The methods of multifactorial causation—the static enumeration and statistical manipulation of population characteristics and environmental factors—are contrasted with those of historical materialism, which posits a dynamic relationship among classes of people and between people and nature over time. Concepts of social class are discussed, and the notion of entitlements is introduced so as to include Third World populations in the analysis.

Challenges to Positivism

Philosophers, feminists, social scientists, and lay persons are challenging empiricism and positivism. Some philosophers reject the empiricist division of truth into two categories—synthetic (grounded in fact) and analytic (independent of matters of fact)—because facts cannot be separated from their meanings; they also reject reductionism, which is the belief that every statement is equivalent to some logical construction of immediate experience (Quine 1953, 20). Feminists find the positivist physical sciences hostile to gender analyses, in part because there is no critical tradition in the philosophy of science (Harding 1986, 34–35). In Harding's view (1986, 250), "A maximally objective science, natural or social, will be one that includes a self-conscious and critical examination of the relationship between the social experience of its creators and the kinds of cognitive structures favored in its inquiry."

Factory workers and farmers are saying that they know something about the physical world even though they cannot express themselves in scientific language. Two examples illustrate this point: factory workers dying of angiosarcoma (a rare form of cancer of the liver) in the early 1970s linked it to the production of polyvinyl chloride long before company physicians acknowledged the connection (Doniger 1978); and farmers with cattle dying of poisonous PBB (a chemical flame retardant) linked the deaths to contaminated feedstock long before public health officials did (Chen 1979; Turshen 1980). In environmental health, there have been strong clashes between people who are assumed to have no factual knowledge, such as housewives, and people who are assumed to have verifiable knowledge, such as scientists. Of the dozens of examples that illustrate this point, the residents of the chemically contaminated Love Canal area of Niagara Falls, New York, are easily the best known. Lay people, claiming that there are other ways to know about the world than by rigorous experimentation and measurement, are relying on experiential knowledge—an appeal to direct experience for "true data"—which is also empiricist. These challenges are important because they ask scientists and public health workers to lay aside intellectual prejudices against people of another class, race, or sex and to recognize other sources of knowledge.

With the development of science in Third World countries and as Third World people reclaim their own heritage from the depredations of colonialism and racism, many other knowledge systems are gaining world attention. No longer can all scientific medical knowledge be equated with biomedical knowledge. The rehabilitation of Chinese, Ayurvedic, and other so-called traditional medical systems challenges the primacy of biomedical science (Bannerman, Burton, and Wen-Chieh 1983; Salmon 1984).

These challenges raise questions about the basis of knowledge in health. Public health draws upon engineering, statistics, and biology and is therefore grounded in pragmatism, positivism, and empiricism. Its practitioners work, not from a fixed body of public health theory, but by trial and error, revising as they proceed, with theories borrowed from other disciplines. Because there is no theoretical or critical philosophical tradition in public health, its practitioners are relatively unquestioning about the theories they borrow. For this reason the debates about empiricism and positivism are important to public health.

Natural science is the foundation of clinical medicine and, together with engineering and bacteriology which developed at the end of the nineteenth century, it became the basis of modern public health. At the same time, the social sciences were emerging and, using the methods of the new field of statistics, were finding expression in preventive medicine and public health practice (Porter 1986). Many surveys of living and working conditions appeared in the 1830s and 1840s—what Hobsbawm (1962, 45) calls the great stream of literature on the social effects of the industrial revolution in Europe and America; these social studies gave impetus to the sanitary reform movement.

The relation of natural to social science can be viewed in several ways. Hobsbawm (1975, 261) suggests that, up to the end of the nineteenth century, most of the social sciences (anthropology, linguistics, sociology, economics) shared a basic framework of research and theory with the natural sciences in the form of evolutionism, the liberal belief in progress. "The study of human society was a positive science like any other evolutionary discipline from geology to biology," according to Hobsbawm (1987, 269). A divergence appeared within the natural sciences between those conscious of linear progress, such as medicine, and those that were revolutionized, such as mathematics and physics. The revolution, which divorced science from intuition, marked a break with empiricism and the formal and axiomatic bases of natural science.

More commonly, authors see a split between the natural and social sciences; Bernal (1954, 693) reports that the British Royal Society refused to recognize social science as science, reserving the term for natural science. The split is said to be based on different methodologies, and it is ironic that so many social scientists should aspire to conform to the positivist principles of certain natural sciences, which were jettisoned by mathematicians and physicists at the beginning of the twentieth century.

Marx also challenged positivism and considered himself a scientist; his intention was to give a scientific account of social change. In a passage on Darwin (Bottomore and Rubel 1963, 79), Marx wrote, "The inadequacy of the abstract materialism of natural science, which leaves out of consideration the historical process, is at once evident from the abstract and ideological conceptions of its spokesmen, whenever they venture beyond the bounds of their own specialism."

As public health draws heavily on the social sciences (the more so since epidemiology includes psychosocial factors in multifactorial explanations of disease), it confronts the question of whether its researchers can continue to use the positivist methodologies of clinical medicine, engineering, and biology. Naturalists say that society can be studied in the same way as nature because the same positivist principles apply to both branches of science. The antinaturalist tradition of hermeneutics (the art of interpretation which aims to disclose an underlying coherence or sense in a text whose meaning is unclear) is in disagreement because the subject matter of society is radically different. Some Marxists say there is no difference between the two positions because they both accept a positivist account of natural science and share an empiricist ontology (Bhaskar 1979).

The empiricist outlook may be defined as the belief that knowledge can be gained through the assembly of rigorously observed and tested data, which are enumerated and statistically manipulated; empiricist social science takes concept formation to be the mapping of empirically observed regularities. Empiricists also believe that data can be free of theoretical assumptions, a belief that has been challenged in empirical terms and on ontological grounds (Myrdal 1969). Realistically, it is impossible for data to be neutral because, from the very first days of data collection, the researcher makes a selection. Data collection cannot cover the universe, and in the process of selection the researcher makes value judgments, which may include the unexamined assumptions of his or her socialization (for example, the biases of race, gender, and social class). Intentional or not, value judgments cannot be excluded from the data collection process or from the process of framing research questions. The conclusion drawn is that science is not neutral, and users of research findings need to inquire into the values of researchers.

The ontological argument against the neutrality of research data is that scientific research, like all other enterprises, is influenced by the society in which it is carried out (Hobsbawm 1987, 251). It does not respond only to its own internal logic, as positivist scientists and philosophers would have us believe. Economic organization determines the path of scientific research and discovery. Not only the means used by natural scientists in their research, but also the ideas guiding their theoretical approach are conditioned by social events and pressures.[1] Elsewhere I have described the history of economic influences on the development of public health (Turshen 1977).

Clinical medicine, engineering, biology, and statistics share the philosophical framework of empiricism and positivism, which use a specific notion of causality. Simply put, the positivist rule is that cause precedes effect and that there is a constant conjunction of cause and effect or a regularity of succession among events (Bradford Hill 1961; Rothman 1982). Positivists explain the world in terms of operational laws, using statistical techniques as detectors of lawlike regularities in data and as a neutral language in which to express the regularities that they find. Social scientists using a positivist approach try to imitate the natural sciences. Scientists want to detect regularity in order to assert control over our environment, which the expectation of repetitive behavior enables us to do. The ability to make predictions is the real test of a discipline for positivists. In the hierarchy of social science disciplines, economics is at the top because it makes the most use of statistics, frequently finds regularities, and is the most lawlike. The same criteria are used to rank experimental psychology above social psychology. This ranking is spurious, as is the objective of making the social sciences like the natural sciences. Why should quantitative information a priori be more valuable than qualitative information?

Marx had a radically different understanding of causality, which may be one reason his methodology is wrongly considered weak. Marx grounded his analysis in the social relations of production, transcending the disjunction between efficient and final causes (Gould 1980, 69–100). Ollman (1976, 16, 131) notes that Marx rejected the rules of temporal precedence and constant conjunction because he saw all conjunction as organic. Reciprocal effect predominates and has logical priority over causality; laws are concerned with patterns of reciprocal effect. In a Marxist ontology, nature and society are both open systems. Natural scientists construct closed systems for purposes of experimentation, and often the results are so useful that we forget they are only approximations of reality, not reality itself. Social scientists cannot experiment in this way and must deal with open systems in which invariant empirical regularities do not obtain.

Drawn to its logical conclusion, the idea of open studies of social systems is radical and far-reaching. Some Marxists assert that we must discard theories of causality and law based on Hume,[2] statistical models of explanation, deductive and inductive theories of scientific development and criteria of confirmation, and theories based on Karl Popper's scientific rationality and criteria of falsification (Bhaskar 1979, 127–128). This leads them to insist that the criteria for the rational confirmation and rejection of theories in social science cannot be predictive and must be exclusively explanatory. Although this dismissal would seem to leave Marxist social science methodologically weak, the conclusions are persuasive. Because social systems are open, historicism (in the sense of deductively justified prediction) is untenable. Qualitatively new developments are constantly occurring in society, which social scientific theory cannot be expected to anticipate.

The Influence of Engineering on the Biomedical Model

The biomedical model, the increasingly disputed paradigm of clinical medicine, emerged in the twentieth century as the logical synthesis of operational verification by measurement, clinical study and experimentation, and evaluation according to engineering norms (Turshen 1977). Scientists, beginning in the seventeenth century with Galileo, Descartes, and Newton, conceived of nature in mechanistic terms; biologists applied this conception to individual living organisms, regarding them as machines to be taken apart and reassembled (McKeown 1971). Physicians and surgeons used this mechanized framework to investigate the mechanical troubles of the human body and to intervene therapeutically. Currently, the rapid development of medical technology and the extensive use of machinery in diagnostics, surgery, and rehabilitation are reinforcing the centrality of engineering in the biomedical model.

McKeown (1976) alleges that medical science and services are misdirected because they rest on the erroneous assumption that health is based on internal intervention in a machinelike human body; he asks us to shift attention from internal to external disease-causing processes. Powles (1973) also is critical of the engineering analogy, noting that it focuses medical attention on the individual; he regrets the failure of evolutionary theory, historical demography, and medical ecology to influence medical theory, and he wants us to pitch analysis at the level of populations rather than single organisms. Capra (1983) argues for an ecological systems view, a resolution of the Cartesian mind-body split, and holistic healing.

Situating this debate in Marxist political economy, Stark (1982) contends that a medical approach abstracts illness and health from the historically specific struggles in which they are constituted and views them as natural by-products of some immutable process outside concrete social activity. He rightly directs our attention to capitalist social relations, arguing that illness is socially constituted; that class, race, and gender relations are implicated; and that epidemic disease reflects capital's capacity to turn a crisis in social relations of production into a crisis of working-class conditions.

Engineering is not only important in biomedical theory, it has dominated the practice of public health since the nineteenth-century sanitary reform movement in Great Britain, which owed its success in part to hydraulics. Sanitary engineering and the maintenance of public works have become central tasks of public health services in most municipalities. Community awareness of the dangers of toxic wastes has recently reinforced this task. Industrial hygienists, responsible for factory inspection and the health of the work force, require a knowledge of mechanics; they believe that the prevention of work-related death and disability is best accomplished by redesigning loud, vibrating, leaky, unguarded, or otherwise hazardous machines.

The Contribution of Biology to Public Health

Biology is the basis of most public health disciplines and many of the medical sciences. It is the study of living things, including molecules, neurological systems, and biological development. Until the twentieth century when it became an experimental discipline, biologists proceeded by observation and description. Writers like Lewis Thomas (1974) romanticize biology by using it as a metaphor for the whole world ("the earth is like a single cell"); this hyperbole promotes a false impression that biology can solve complex social problems (Luria 1974). But both biology and the clinical medical paradigm are too limited, too narrow in their methods and approach to the study of disease, to solve problems that require at the very least a historical and sociological understanding of the relation between the whole and the part, between subsystem and global system (Enzensberger 1974; Levins and Lewontin 1985). In its current reductionist version, in which the properties of complex wholes are explained in terms of the units they comprise, biology has had a retrogressive effect on public health.

Biological determinism, which sees behavior as the inevitable consequence of the biochemical properties of cells that are determined by their genes, has warped our concepts of disease and disease processes. It has harmed public health in such fields as mental health and prison health, where it advances genetic explanations of disordered behavior and criminal behavior (Lewontin, Rose, and Kamin 1984; Taylor, Walton, and Young 1974). Branches of public health that depend on behavioral sciences for intellectual direction, as for example health education, are particularly vulnerable to the fallacies of biological determinism because, in the words of its critic Stephen J. Gould (1981, 20), "it holds that shared behavioral norms, and the social and economic differences between human groups—primarily races, classes, and sexes—arise from inherited, inborn distinctions."

The fallacy of reductionism is the crux of scholarly critiques of sociobiology, which is a biologically determinist explanation of human existence (Gould 1978; Thompson 1982; Levins and Lewontin 1985). The influence of sociobiology is particularly noxious in public health programs for maternal and child health. Feminists point out that there is a distinction between sex, which is biologically determined, and gender, which is culturally defined, and that one cannot derive culture (women's behavior) from biology (female reproductive organs). The social characteristics that E. O. Wilson and others (see Caplan 1978) attempt to derive from biological traits are neither inevitable nor immutable, according to feminists (Fooden, Gordon, and Hughley 1983). Because public health depends so heavily on a knowledge of cultural patterns and social organization for the planning of disease control programs, the critique of sociobiology must be assimilated to both theory and practice.

Vital and Health Statistics

Statistics is the shared methodology of public health disciplines; the use of statistics is central to the practice of public health and separates community health care from clinical medicine. Both pure and applied mathematics are usually portrayed as technical fields untainted by social values or ideology. This portrayal of statistics is at least misleading, if not politically mystifying, because knowledge assessed and presented statistically is not automatically objective. Radical critics of the "neutral" view show that data are socially produced in specific circumstances (for example, under the influence of a funding agency and a research institute), for specific reasons (government use in planning social programs, for instance, hardly an apolitical act), and with techniques developed and transformed in historically specific ways (Irvine, Miles, and Evans 1979).[3]

The field has political origins: the development of vital and health statistics is tied to a significant turning point in European history when Europe emerged from feudalism, entered the capitalist era, and formed the first industrial nation-states. Vital and health statistics began in the fifteenth century in the period of mercantilism with the exploration of global trade routes, the beginning of international competition among countries, and the seizing of the first colonies. The emergence of state finance and the extension of taxation in the seventeenth century gave rise to a field initially called "political arithmetic" by its founder, the English physician and political economist William Petty (1623–1687). On the basis of his work in Ireland, which was England's first colony, Petty noted that national governments required information about their populations not needed by feudal lords. For example, governments needed to know how large their population was because the strength of a nation was judged by the size of its armed forces; it was also important to know the physical quality of its fighting men. The registration of vital statistics had formerly been the job of the church in Europe, but when governments began to be interested in the health of their populations, the collection of statistics extended beyond the registration of births, deaths, and marriages and became the responsibility of civil authorities (Porter 1986).

With the industrial revolution beginning in the mid-eighteenth century in England, the labor force became the focus of statistical analysis. Governments wanted to know, in addition to how many people they governed and men's fitness for armed service, about people's ability to work in factories and to reproduce at a rate that would provide a new generation of laborers. And so from 1801 the government took regular censuses in the United Kingdom, and by 1851 it had worked out a classification of the population based on occupation. From 1911 the registrar general, in decennial census reports on occupational health, used five social grades or classes, which are occupational categories.

The government categorized vital and health statistics according to social class because it saw a marked relationship between poverty and illness, as well as between poverty and illness and social unrest. Poverty has long been, and still is, a subject of inquiry in Great Britain. Researchers readily demonstrated inequalities in health in the 1830s and 1840s, even though they used crude statistical methods: the best known studies are Chadwick's report on sanitary conditions (Flinn 1965) and Frederick Engels's exposé of working-class conditions in England (Hobsbawm 1969). A recent contribution is the Black Report, which the conservative government of Margaret Thatcher tried to suppress (Townsend and Davidson 1982).

The determination of inequalities in health and inequities in health care requires a concept of social class for the dual purposes of measurement and remediation. Although the United States followed Great Britain's lead in many other aspects of public health, it chose race and income instead of class as the main categories of its health reporting system. The choice of category, like the choice of social indicators (for example, literacy, mortality, life expectancy), reflects the political preoccupations of a society and may even represent a government's deliberate construction of political debate on its chosen terms. Nectoux, Lintott, and Carr-Hill (1980) claim that governments use social indicators for purposes of social control. Miles (1985, 78) points out that some indicators divert public attention from the causes of problems to their symptoms and thus influence responses.

The next section tries to clarify the definition of social class and to indicate other ways to categorize populations. These methodological issues are important questions underlying not only the presentation of vital and health data, but also the reorganization of public health services.

Statistical Classifications Used in Public Health

The most common statistical division of the population used in the United States is income. This limited economic criterion has little to do with the notion of economic or occupational class. The

United States Department of Health and Human Services uses Census Bureau data on income not only to plan health services, but also to calculate the cost of social welfare programs. (This is a traditional use of statistics; the British government has used demographic data to estimate the costs of poor relief since the seventeenth century.) Income is an indicator applied to populations living in poverty, which are presumed to have higher rates of illness. Scott (1981), in his review of concepts and measurement of poverty, demonstrates the arbitrary nature of poverty lines, even when bundles of subsistence goods are substituted for cash income. He notes, for instance, that the poverty line in the United States is between ten and seventeen times higher than that in India, although both pretend to be absolute. He also explains how easy it is for researchers to show poverty to be declining or increasing over time.

The second proxy for social class most frequently used in the United States is race, which is a political category (masquerading as a biological classification) that has become more refined over time; many more racial and ethnic groupings are distinguished today than thirty years ago. There is, biologically speaking, only one race, the human race, and no biological justification for the creation of subspecies of *Homo sapiens* (Gould 1978, 231–236). The very fact of the proliferation of racial groupings in recent U.S. censuses is evidence of the political rather than the biological nature of these divisions. Fredrickson (1981, 96–97) underscores this conclusion when he points out that the United States is the only country to have used the arbitrary device of classifying all descendants of mixed unions with their Black progenitors; even the racist South Africans created an intermediate status ("coloureds"), and, in the East Indies, the Dutch gave the same legal and political status to offspring of Dutch males who married Asian women as to children of European couples.

Income and race shift our focus away from the causes of poverty to individual characteristics that the government can use to frame policy or manipulate so as to blame the victims. In contrast, the categorization employed in the United Kingdom by the registrar general is based on five social classes. At the top is class I, which consists of professionals including physicians, engineers, architects, and scientists. It also includes large employers and directors of businesses. Next is class II, which is simply called "intermediate"; it consists of lower professionals such as teachers, pharmacists, social workers, authors, owners of small businesses, managers, and farmers. Social class III is divided into manual and nonmanual skilled workers. The nonmanual skilled workers include artisans and white-collar jobholders such as office and clerical workers. Manual skilled workers include supervisors (for example, in factories) and transport workers.

Social class IV consists of partly skilled workers, including semi-skilled factory workers, agricultural laborers, and service workers. (Notice how far down the scale service workers are; service work is the largest growing occupational field in the United States.) Social class V consists of unskilled workers and includes laborers, domestic servants, and casual workers. Casual workers are people who take part-time, temporary work and thus never qualify for many company benefits. Workers in this category receive minimum wages and have no job security.

The categories used by the registrar general present several problems. First, they really describe job status, not occupation in the sense of an economic class. The word *status* is used in its sociological derivation in two different senses: status as esteem (meaning prestige and property) and status as lifestyle. Although esteem, prestige, and property tell us something about social, political, and economic situations that affect people's health, they are value judgments rather than objective criteria. They reflect people's relative standing in society, a changing phenomenon that is culture-bound. The concept of lifestyle, which encompasses people's living habits including eating, sleeping, drinking, and recreation, is as poor a basis as status for decisions affecting health because neither lifestyle nor status explains the etiology of disease.

In addition to these general objections, the registrar general's categories present some very specific problems. First, married women who work take the occupational classification of their husbands, it being reasoned that family incomes are pooled; as a result, a woman who is a clerical worker and whose husband is a teacher is counted in social class II, not III. Interesting historical evidence challenges the assumption that the family's living standards are set by the husband: Laura Oren's (1973) study of working-class women in England showed that married women have a lower standard of living than their husbands because they have fewer luxuries and less leisure time.

Unmarried women are classified independently, even if they still live at their family home; thus a young unmarried clerical worker living with parents who are both teachers is counted in social class III, not II. Domestic servants are categorized in social class V, whereas the wife of a teacher who remains at home and does domestic labor but is not paid for it is counted in social class II. The classification of women is arbitrarily based on their marital status rather than their occupation. As 50 percent of married women are in the paid work force in many industrialized countries, a significant proportion of the population would be miscategorized under this system.

There is no category for owners of capital, that is, people who do no work to earn an income, their wealth being sufficient to provide their wants; they are lumped together with large employers and salaried directors of businesses as professionals in social class I. All self-employed people are categorized in social class II, which comprises such disparate occupations as writing, farming, and owning a small business. The existence of large groups that do not fit the five categories exposes the inadequacy of the system.

Additional problems arise in trying to use the system in underdeveloped countries. If 80 percent of the population lives by farming, social class II loses its meaning. If household income is not pooled, as it is not in most of sub-Saharan Africa, the classification of married women according to their husband's occupation is meaningless. If most physicians, engineers, architects, and scientists are salaried employees of the state, it is meaningless to lump professionals together with directors of companies and owners of large businesses in social class I.

Although the system of occupational classes used by the U.K. registrar general to show inequality is flawed, it is an improvement over the common categories of race and income used in the United States and, with modification of the classification of married women, could usefully be adopted in the United States. However, underdeveloped countries should turn to another source for a system better suited to societies not based largely on wage labor.

The trend in most underdeveloped countries is to substitute two program concepts for social class: one is target groups and the other is at-risk populations. In practice, both concepts are used to delineate biological groups, that is an age-group (for example, infants, the elderly), a sexual group (for instance, mothers, homosexuals), or a clinical group (based on a particular disease much as hospital wards are organized). Sometimes an occupational group is designated as the population at risk, but it is not an occupational group in the sense of economic class. Sometimes an income group is designated; we talk of targeting the "poorest of the poor." These categories are reductionist because they reduce people to a single biological or economic trait; and because they are one-dimensional, they are inadequate for public health programs that are serious about attacking the social causes of ill health.

Another tendency, especially prevalent in research based on theories of multifactorial causation, is to enumerate biological, economic, and social characteristics called variables—for example, age, sex, income, education, occupation, race, marital status—and then manipulate them statistically to find correlations. Here a statistical technique—for instance, regression analysis—substitutes for theory about the relations between (to take an obvious example) female sex and low income.

In contrast, the Marxist definition of class is dynamic because it includes a theory of power relations; it is also comprehensive because it includes economic, social, political, and historical characteristics, as well as a notion of their interrelations. It uses the concept of occupation but in the sense of economic class, which is based upon one's relation to the conditions of production in a given society. Marx's empirical investigations led him to conclude that in capitalist society, there is a class that owns and controls industry and the conditions of production and another class of workers and producers who, in order to survive and to support children, have no alternative but to work for wages. Between these two major classes he found intermediate strata of professionals, shopkeepers and owners of small businesses, self-employed farmers and artisans, civil servants, army officers, intellectual workers, and so on, which have grown in all twentieth-century capitalist societies. Theorists find it very difficult to categorize these middle classes (Poulantzas 1973; Wright 1978). Nonetheless, the Marxist concept of class remains a highly useful analytical tool in industrial societies.

Social Class in Nonindustrial Societies

The applicability of Marx's class analysis to Third World societies has been the subject of bitter debates (see, for example, Cohen and Daniel 1981, 75–163). Amartya Sen (1981), who is Drummond Professor of Political Economy at Oxford University and professor of economics and philosophy at Harvard, suggests a new approach to the problem of social classification, one which is compatible with Marxism and facilitates the disaggregation of large occupational categories in nonindustrial societies. It is important to health planners because it enables them to identify groups at risk of ill health with indicators more precise than income or biological variables.

Using the concept of entitlements, which provide the wherewithal to exchange for commodities in a private ownership market economy, Sen posits five types: trade, production, labor, inheritance, and transfers. Trade-based entitlements are those obtained by trading something one owns; production entitles one to own what one acquires by arranging production using owned or hired resources; one's labor power gets trade and production-based entitlements; inheritance entitles one to own something previously owned by another; and transfers are state-provided social security entitlements. A person's exchange entitlements depend on his or her position in the economic class structure as well as the modes of production in the economy.

Sen details the influences that determine people's exchange entitlements: (1) what they can earn by selling their nonlabor assets and how much it costs them to buy what they want (trade); (2) what they can produce with their own labor power and resources or resource services they can buy, and also the cost of purchasing resources or resource services and the value of the products that can be sold (production); (3) whether they can find employment, and if so for how long and at what wage rate (labor); (4) the value of what one is legitimately given by another after taxes, etc. (inheritance); and (5) the social security benefits they are entitled to (excluding charity, which is a nonentitlement transfer) and the taxes, etc. they must pay (transfers). Transfers are of great importance in socialist economies, as are systems of guaranteed employment at wage rates that can procure basic needs.

With this categorization, one can differentiate a peasant from an agricultural laborer in terms of ownership, as well as distinguish the landless laborer from the sharecropper according to the use of labor power: the landless laborer is employed for a wage, while the sharecropper will do the cultivation and own a part of the product. In terms of vulnerability to the diseases of poverty, these distinctions are critical, for they enable governments to pinpoint the economic and social institutions at the base of ill health. If food prices rise, for example, peasants and sharecroppers will be less at risk of malnutrition than landless laborers; landlessness may be the problem to attack here. Similarly, those who sell services (barbers or cab drivers) or handicraft products (shoemakers or artisans) are more exposed to market vagaries and food price rises than peasants and sharecroppers, even when the typical standard of living of the former is no higher than that of the latter. Here a social security system (or safety net) might provide protection against famine.

It may be possible to mesh the two systems; the U.K. registrar general's five social classes may fit into Sen's second category of production entitlements. If so, the new system could be adopted by all countries, which would facilitate comparative studies. The system would be a compromise, however, with the Marxist concept of economic class because occupation is not an adequate proxy for the organization of work; a list of occupations is static, whereas the organization of work (both paid and unpaid) supplies the dynamic of power relationships. A system that combines British social classes and Sen's entitlement categories would continue to obscure the social relations of production that determine "who shall suffer from what and how seriously" (Stark 1982, 60).

Chapter 3

PUBLIC HEALTH POLICY

THIS CHAPTER EXAMINES public health policy, in contrast to previous chapters on theory and methods. The argument made is that the proper focus of public health work is the restructuring of the social relations of production, because health and illness are ultimately determined by economic, social, and political organization. Medical care is so specialized, and in the United States so privatized and split off from social welfare, that the links between health and economic, social, and political organization are often obscured from public view. Effective attacks on the ultimate determinants of ill health entail fundamental economic, social, and political reorganization. This chapter provides the connections between public health theory, methods, and policy.

Public health policy, in the sense of government decisions to provide personal health and community services, engenders a set of controversial questions about the role of the state, not only in regulating the private health care industry, but also in creating and maintaining major health institutions. Since the mid-1970s, conservative governments in industrial countries have criticized and cut back the budgets of the institutions of the welfare state, including variants of national health services (Gough 1979). The International Monetary Fund and the World Bank forced many Third World countries to follow suit by making cutbacks a condition of their assistance. The health institutions of the welfare state have been attacked from the Right and Left. On the Right, the questions about state intervention are framed in terms of individual responsibility for health and the functioning of free markets. On the Left, the questions range from whether ill health is inherent in the capitalist system to whether any government under capitalism can intervene effectively (Polack 1971; Thunhurst 1982).

According to Renaud (1975), state intervention in health has specific limitations imposed by the contradictory position of the state in capitalist society: government must meet the health needs produced by capitalist industrial growth in a way that legitimizes the capitalist system. Social reorganization is effective but destabilizes the system. Legislative reforms are less threatening but also less effective; they can mediate the determinants of disease, and progressive social policies do promote health (Sidel and Sidel 1984). Indeed, the reform of public policies affecting housing, food, clothing, and income, for example, can have a dramatic impact on the health of selected groups, at least in the short-term. But, as we shall see, reforms have limited redistributive effects and do little to close the gaps in mortality between the highest and lowest social classes.

An example of the impact of public policy on health may be drawn from the housing sector. Housing conditions are closely associated with health status, and housing tenure correlates with mortality (Hart 1985, 1986). In Britain, people in all social classes who live in houses they own experience lower mortality than people who rent apartments in public housing. If the housing problem is framed in this way, the Thatcher government's current policy of selling council housing to tenants may correlate with improved mortality in the group now renting houses; it will do nothing for apartment dwellers and less for the growing numbers of homeless. The real issue here is the quality of housing and the need for diversity in public or publicly subsidized housing.

Housing quality includes problems of climate control, numbers of people per room, and shelter for the homeless. Inadequate heating, or a form of heating that is too expensive for the occupant to use, is a factor in hypothermia (dangerously low body temperatures) in elderly people with limited means; energy policies that subsidize the poor can overcome this problem. Overcrowding, defined as more than two people per room, can facilitate the rapid spread of respiratory and other contagious diseases; the availability of ample low-income housing can reduce their incidence. Overcrowding and its opposite, isolation, can also produce adverse psychological reactions: the issue is cultural, social, and psychological. In Great Britain, living in high-rise apartment houses has deleterious consequences for families and may give rise to mental illness (Thunhurst 1982, 21–23). Lack of any housing is the most harmful to health of all; homelessness is now a problem of national proportions in Great Britain and the United States (Erickson and Wilhelm 1986). Of course it has been a problem for decades in Third World countries such as India. The solution is not the provision of temporary shelters, but the provision of low-cost housing and family support.

These needs contrast sharply with the public health approach to housing, which usually involves inspection and enforcement of various regulations. The conventional methods employed in public health tend to reduce complex social causes to proximate physical hazards and to create specialized subgroups to manage those hazards. It follows from this approach that the standard evaluation involves an examination of each public policy sector and a review of the role of public health workers in the formulation and implementation of related public policies, but this procedure tends to segregate specialized public health workers such as housing code inspectors. An alternative approach adopted here takes the social production theory and methods described in chapters one and two as starting points for an alternative public health practice, which allows the integration of housing with other determinants of health so that all public health workers see housing as their concern. This alternative practice also facilitates the evaluation of the impact of each public health or medical intervention on the health of the public.

Disease Theories and Public Health Action

Let us return to the germ theory of disease, which was an outgrowth of Louis Pasteur's commercial work for the French wine, beer, and silk industries (Hobsbawm 1975, 258). The search for the causative agents of the diseases ravaging those trades led Pasteur to look for preventive measures (Dubos 1959, 218); in fact, it would have made no economic sense to search for a cure.

Initial work in the late nineteenth century based on the germ theory of disease was in preventive medicine, in the search for vaccinations, inoculations, and antitoxins. It was not until 1909, with the work of German bacteriologist Paul Ehrlich (1854–1915) on a remedy for syphilis, that germ theory was successful in finding a medical cure, an event that inaugurated the era of searches for the "magic bullet"—a specific cure for each disease. Eventually, germ theory gave clinical medicine a scientific foundation for surgical, electrical, and chemical curative procedures, but in the bacteriological era the focus remained on the biology of single, causative agents of disease (Berliner 1985, 79–91).

Research in clinical medicine still pursues these two avenues—preventive and curative measures. Unfortunately implementation is usually divided, with preventive work falling to public health and curative work reserved in the United States for the private sector.[1] Even in countries in which governments nationalized medical services, the split between preventive and curative services is preserved.

Preventive and curative medicine, concerned as they are with disease processes in individuals, have limited physical impact on the health of the public.[2] Because curative medicine intervenes after disease is established to alter the course of a single episode of disease, its health effects are more circumscribed than those of preventive medicine; at best curative measures can restore the health of the individual. Preventive medicine can prevent an episode of disease, and a very good vaccine confers protection for five or more years against a specific disease. In this way, preventive measures can reduce disease-specific mortality, but they may do so without improving health: overall death rates may remain constant, as they did in Latin America after a comprehensive measles vaccination campaign (Puffer and Serrano 1973). When vaccination campaigns are mounted by public health workers on a community scale, they affect community health by restricting the circulation of infection.

Theories of multifactorial disease causation often lead to action on several fronts at once, action that may combine public health, preventive, and curative measures. The clinical measures taken to deal with cardiovascular disease, for example, may include bypass surgery, the insertion of a pacemaker, and chemical intervention with drugs to control blood pressure and cholesterol levels. Measures to prevent heart disease might be, but rarely are, the reorganization of work to reduce extremes of heat, cold, and noise; excessive speed and long hours of work; exposure to toxic chemicals such as nitroglycerin; and the redesign of machines to alter prolonged standing, bending, and squatting. When these preventive measures are mandated and enforced by government, they become part of public health. Clearly then, multifactorial theories do not necessarily lead to individualistic solutions.

Environmental and germ theories of causation are compatible, as an example drawn from infectious disease epidemiology demonstrates. The cholera vibrio may be the proximate cause of cholera, in the sense that no case of cholera develops in the absence of the bacteria, but such environmental measures as good sanitation, fly control, food hygiene, purification of water, and pasteurization of milk confer protection that is more effective than the currently available immunization. These environmental measures will also affect other bacterial infections at the same time, which is no small bonus.

Multifactorial causation and risk assessment, its associated methodology, are most frequently linked with environmental approaches to community health (Greenberg 1987). Environmentalists reason that if 80 percent of cancers are environmental in origin, then ridding the environment of carcinogens is the best way to prevent this disease. They follow germ theorists in seeking to identify specific chemicals such as vinyl chloride monomer as the cause of specific cancers such as angiosarcoma (a rare cancer of the liver). They diverge in their solutions: while germ theorists search for a specific, causative virus and the corresponding "magic bullet" cure, environmentalists rely on market mechanisms, voluntary professional standards, or the government to eliminate carcinogens.

Theories of multifactorial causation that implicate lifestyles in the etiology of disease usually lead to recommendations for behavior modification (Gotsch and Pearson 1987). Health educators believe that informed people can be motivated to adopt and maintain healthful habits. In the case of cardiovascular disease, behavior identified as contributing to heart attacks includes type-A personality, smoking, lack of exercise, overeating, and a diet high in polysaturated fats. The behavioral approach is to teach people at risk of heart disease the appropriate skills that will enable them to refrain from self-defeating practices.

Health education for the purpose of behavior modification is concerned with the individual, even when the educational sessions are organized in groups or when mass media are used to convey the message. If exhortation fails, laws may mandate the desired behavioral change (for example, requirements to wear seat belts or raising the legal drinking age to twenty-one years). Behavior modification becomes a public health measure when the coercive power of the state, never very far below the surface, is invoked.

Many health education campaigns fail in part because lifestyle theory is unable to explain why people adopt unhealthy habits (blaming them for their ignorance does not constitute an explanation) or why they fail to change them. The theory does not question its assumptions that people choose their lifestyles and that they are equally free to change them. Connections between lifestyle and social differentiation by race, class, and sex are noted or labeled rather than used for their explanatory powers.

The behavioral approach to cardiovascular disease presents an interesting comparison with the environmental approach because it entails a reengineering of the individual rather than the environment. It suggests that we change individual reactions to stress, rather than investigate the organization of work that is stressful; that we educate workers to wear protective clothing, rather than redesign machines that emit hazardous substances; that we alter individual eating habits, rather than restrain the food industry from supplying a diet high in polysaturated fats; that we exhort people to exercise, rather than end supports (such as tax breaks for oil companies) to the automobile industry, which forces a sedentary life upon us by continuing to oppose the redevelopment of the mass transit system it destroyed; and that we campaign against smoking, rather than stop subsidizing the tobacco industry, which resists medical evidence associating tobacco use with disease.

The fourth theory discussed in chapter one, the gene theory of disease, identifies faulty genes as either the direct cause of disease (as in Tay-Sachs, a disease that results in mental subnormality and spastic paralysis thought to be caused by an inborn error of fat metabolism) or the indirect cause (as in exposure to toxic chemicals that cause cancer in workers with alleged genetic defects). The gene theory may lead to genetic screening programs at workplaces and the placement of susceptible workers in jobs in which they are not exposed to hazardous substances, to genetic counseling at family planning clinics and recommendations for artificial insemination or abortion, and perhaps to genetic engineering (surgery to repair genetic defects during pregnancy or just after birth). The first two measures are preventive, the third is curative. None requires changes in work organization, work relations, or the reengineering of the work environment—structural reforms that would have a lasting impact on all workers, not just single individuals.

In summary, public health programs based on these four theories of disease causation share a focus on the individual, who is sometimes labeled as bearing class, racial, and sexual traits, but is not analyzed as a member of a dynamic economic class. The sick individual or group suffering the same illness is the unit of analysis in curative and preventive medical programs. These theories are also disease-specific, in the sense that they describe the etiology of specific illnesses but not of ill health in general. Curiously, environmental measures that entail a community approach predate the development of these theories and rest instead on miasmatism, a general theory of ill health that was discarded as unscientific. (Miasmatists believed that marshes and swamps produced poisonous and airborne substances that caused fevers.) Miasmatism informed Britain's successful sanitary reform movement that began in 1845 and declined after 1875, before the germ theory of disease was developed.

A single example will sharpen the contrast in these four approaches to public health. According to the germ theory of disease, malaria is caused by a parasite and one should try to kill this disease agent in its human host, an individualistic approach that is currently being pursued in pharmaceutical research sponsored by the World Health Organization and others (WHO 1985a). The second line of attack for germ theorists is to kill the parasite together with its insect vector, the mosquito, which became feasible with the development of insecticides such as DDT. In contrast, lifestyle theorists emphasize the need to change human behavior in malarious, mosquito-infested areas, for example by promoting the proper use of mosquito netting on beds (Gillett 1975). Gene theory presents a third contrast; it underlies the approach adopted in studies of parasite resistance to drugs and mosquito resistance to insecticides, as well as mosquito susceptibility to parasites (UNDP/World Bank/WHO 1986). The environmental approach, the fourth contrast, was tried long before the invention of DDT; it deprives the mosquito of its habitat by draining pools of stagnant water, by filling in ditches and open drains where water collects, and by draining or eliminating swamps and marshes.

Individualistic approaches are class biased and unable to address broad economic, social, and political determinants of health such as development. In the case of malaria, Ackerknecht (1945) shows the fundamentally social character of the disease and notes the correlation of economic development (especially the building of railroads, the growth of cattle breeding, and the increase in wealth), social progress (better housing), and the end of migration, with the disappearance of the disease in the Upper Mississippi Valley in the nineteenth century. So long as etiological theories are disease-specific, not even environmental approaches that are community-oriented will solve the underlying problems that lead to ill health. This statement needs elaboration. Chapter two on methods for the study of disease discussed different concepts of social class; now is the time to use those concepts and demonstrate the relation between social class, ill health, and public health practice.

Poverty, Inequality, and Ill Health

Because there are no data on mortality by class in the United States, it is necessary to use statistics from Great Britain. British studies show that the poorer health experience of the lower occupational groups applies at all stages of life (Townsend and Davidson 1982). The evidence systematically relates the risk of death to social class at every age. Inequalities in health correlate with social class: the highest death rates are found in social class V and the lowest in social class I. These differences have not declined over time. Similar although less complete findings are reported for France (Desplanques 1984). The ways in which this correlation is explained profoundly affect public health practice because each explanation implies a different programmatic response.

The first explanation is that the relationship between health and inequality is a statistical artifact; health and class may both be artificial variables and the relation between them of little causal significance. In this view, the failure of health inequalities to diminish over time is explained by the reduction of the proportion of the population in social classes IV and V, and the failure to reduce the gap between classes is counterbalanced by the shrinkage in the relative size of the poorer classes themselves. Were this view accepted as the basis of public health practice, there would be no need to change policy because general health improvements would continue to trickle down and social class V would eventually disappear. This account is incorrect because the poorer social classes have not contracted sharply, and the relatively poor progress in health applies to much larger sections of the manual occupational classes than just unskilled workers (Townsend and Davidson 1982, 113). In addition, the pattern of the gap between professional and unskilled households—largest in the first year of life and smallest at retirement ages—contradicts the artifact explanation (Hart 1986, 234).

A second explanation is that natural or social selection might account for the upper classes being healthier and the poorer classes being sicker. Crudely stated, this version assumes that one's health determines one's class position. If occupational class is a filter that sorts human beings and if health is a major basis of selection, then social class I might have the lowest rate of premature mortality because it is made up of the strongest men and women in the population and, conversely, social class V which contains the weakest people might have the highest death rate. In this view, health is a genetic property, a more or less fixed characteristic of individuals, that is not affected by social and economic environment. Public health practice based on this view ranges from the direct intervention of eugenicists and Nazis in an attempt to improve the genetic pool to benign neglect on the grounds that government policies cannot change human destiny.

Unfortunately for Social Darwinists there is little evidence that ill health is strictly reflective of class. One can think of many members of the upper classes who suffered chronic disability—historical figures such as Henry VI of England (1421–1471) who reigned for forty years despite mental illness and Franklin Delano Roosevelt who was president of the United States for eleven years despite a crippling case of poliomyelitis. In the United States illness can reduce a manual worker to the ranks of the unskilled, but this decline reflects the failure of health and social services rather than some personal trait. No innate physical characteristics of brain or body destine men and women in social class V to live the shortest lives and reap the most meager rewards (Townsend and Davidson 1982, 113).

The view that afflicted people drift to the bottom of society appears in studies of severe mental disorders. That argument is debunked by Dowd (1984, 102) who notes that it amounts to a castigation of schizophrenics for their social incompetence. Dowd contextualizes hypotheses of drift and selection in the larger controversy over the relative importance of nature (genetic factors) and nurture (psychosocial factors).

A third explanation of the correlation between health and social class is that group culture or the individual behavior of social class members might explain mortality experience. This version is termed the "culture of poverty" or "transmitted deprivation" and is usually applied to the poor alone. Stark (1982) calls it "social genetics" because it implies that one set of social factors or experiences automatically produces another without historical or willed intervention. According to this explanation, health behaviors represent biological and social adaptations that persist even when the environment changes; they pass as outmoded ideas and old-fashioned practices from one generation to the next. In this view, child abuse can be explained by the fact that the parents were abused in their childhood, and the illegitimacy of children can be explained by the illegitimacy of their mothers, and so on. The implication is that the beliefs and values of the poor are static, autonomous, and dependent on conventional values or orthodox beliefs, that culture uniformly molds individual personality, that the motivations acquired in childhood do not change in later life, and that childhood experiences in the family become encapsulated in the personality and are projected into the institutional structures that pattern adult behavior and beliefs—all of which is wrong (Leacock 1971). Public health practice based on this view tries to reeducate the poor and break the cycle of behavior transmission rather than give people the means to rise out of poverty.

Evidence from anthropological and sociological studies of the poor refutes the assumptions of this explanation. Studies show that the process of adaptation continues actively throughout an individual's lifetime, and cultural norms and definitions of roles are constantly redirected or reinforced by the institutional structures within which individuals function. For example, if the culture of poverty thesis were correct, the poor would have resisted such new ideas as the practice of family planning, but the historical evidence is to the contrary.

Another version of this third explanation emphasizes individual behavior; it holds that good or bad health is embedded in socially distinguishable styles of life associated with and reinforced by class. The use of lifestyles as a predictor of mortality experience is seen by its adherents as more positive than the culture of poverty thesis because lifestyles can be changed with education. Although lifestyle explanations emphasize individual rather than group behavior, they are based on the same assumptions as the culture of poverty. In addition to the criticism of those assumptions that I have discussed, some of the behavior that makes up lifestyles cuts across social class (for example, high carbohydrate diets, smoking, and nonparticipation in sports); some is considered in isolation from other aspects of life (for example, manual workers who enjoy spectator sports rather than active participation may have to exert physical strength and agility in their jobs); and some is explained less by ignorance or personal tastes than by limited access and resources.

The fourth explanation of the correlation between health and social class uses a multifactorial theory of disease to emphasize the role of economic and associated socio-structural factors in the distribution of health and well-being. It focuses on the direct influence of poverty or economic deprivation in the production of variation in rates of mortality. A relationship between material deprivation, disease, and death is now well established. Historical evidence from the industrial revolution in England bears out the accuracy of this observation, and the relationship holds true today. Studies in the United States repeat this finding.

Material subsistence needs cannot be defined uniquely and unambiguously in terms that are independent of the overall level of economic development in society. On the one hand, people may have too little for their basic physiological needs as well as social needs. On the other hand, poverty is a relative concept, and those who are unable to share the amenities or facilities provided within a rich society, or who are unable to fulfill the social and occupational obligations placed upon them by virtue of their limited resources, can properly be regarded as poor. They may also be disadvantaged relative to the risks of illness or accident or the factors that positively promote health (Townsend and Davidson 1982, 115).

The fourth explanation stresses occupational class as a multifaceted concept; in addition to the variables most readily associated with socioeconomic position—income, savings, property, and housing—there are many other dimensions that exert an active causal influence on health. At work, people encounter different material conditions and amenities, levels of danger and risk, degree of security and stability, association with other workers, levels of self-fulfillment and job satisfaction, and physical or mental strain. For example, shift work is known to be associated with stress-related diseases (Baker 1980). In Great Britain 25 percent of manual workers do shift work, while only 5 percent of professionals and managers do so (Blane 1982).

A historical case study—the first of many scattered throughout this book—illustrates the limits of the multifactorial theory of disease, explanations of health and social-class correlations based upon it, and the public health practices that flow from it. The case reviewed here is the discovery of the cause of pellagra, a disease associated with anemia, dermatitis, nerve and spinal cord changes, loss of muscle control, and mental confusion.

Case History of Pellagra

Few contemporary researchers employ the multifactorial approach as consistently and thoroughly as did Sydenstricker and Goldberger in their studies on pellagra (Kasius 1974; Terris

1964).[3] In that era, when everyone's model of disease was informed by germ theory, pellagra was thought to be a communicable disease. (Eventually pellagra was identified as a lack of vitamin B, particularly niacin, which is occasionally seen today in cases of advanced alcoholism.) Together with G. A. Wheeler, Sydenstricker and Goldberger looked not for a specific infectious agent but at the condition of the afflicted population. They studied cotton mill workers in seven villages of South Carolina and considered a remarkable range of economic and social variables as relevant to ill health.

They looked carefully at the population which to others was undifferentiated, and they saw differences between people whose income was twelve dollars a month and those whose income was twenty dollars a month—that's how low the incomes were and how narrow the range of income. They considered not only what money could buy (that is, what food was available in stores, which is part of the question of what constitutes diet), but also the ways people supplemented what they bought. They studied peddlers who went from house to house selling bits of things, an activity we hardly see any more but which is still very common in Third World countries.

They inspected what was in the stores, found out what people could grow themselves, and studied the quality of the soil in order to determine the quality of the produce that came out of it so as to calculate exactly what nutrients home produce contributed. They also took account of seasonality, which is too often ignored even in the Third World. Seasons are important because there are hunger periods just before harvests when the incidence of disease rises (Turshen 1984, 62–64).

A few researchers thought the cause of pellagra might be rooted in diet but dismissed the idea. Sydenstricker, Wheeler, and Goldberger, applying the careful methodology described in what came to be a total of fifty-four articles for this project, studied everything about the population before eliminating anything. They found a close correlation between the absence of protein, large amounts of maize or cornmeal in the diet, and cases of pellagra. The conclusion that pellagra is caused by a dietary deficiency, which is in keeping with the germ theory of disease, is of less interest than the methodology employed by Sydenstricker and his coworkers. In terms of public health practice, the discovery led to the possibility of eradicating the disease with the distribution of vitamin B.

The unfortunate consequence of the reversion to germ theory was the eventual elimination of a disease without altering any of its economic, social, or political determinants. For example, if wages were raised, several ills of poverty in addition to poor diet such as poor general health status, might have been addressed simultaneously. Or, if the millworkers had been politically empowered—say through unionization (a goal still resisted in the 1970s, see Conway 1979)—several related economic problems might have been addressed. In the end, Sydenstricker, Wheeler, and Goldberger did not challenge the concept of disease. Vitamin replacement may solve pellagra, but it leaves untouched a host of other problems.

Implications for Public Health Policy

What conclusions for public health policy can we draw from this analysis? The 1980 British Working Group on Inequalities in Health concluded, "While the health care service can play a significant part in reducing inequalities in health, measures to reduce differences in material standards of living at work, in the home, and in everyday social and community life are of even greater importance" (Townsend and Davidson 1982, 173). The British National Health Service (NHS) provides everyone with free medical care—at home, in the general practitioner's office, and in the hospital—yet in forty years of operation it failed to change the relative levels of health in the five social classes. In some respects, the health experience of unskilled and semiskilled manual classes (class V and IV) deteriorated relative to class I throughout the 1960s and 1970s. Clearly the benefits of medical care are distributed unevenly in Great Britain, and the NHS has had a minimum redistributive effect.

One possible inference is that public health workers should be advocates of the communities they serve; they need to protect and defend poor and neglected groups in those communities, but they will not serve these groups well if they induce dependency. The Working Group recommended a comprehensive antipoverty strategy for Great Britain that may be applicable in the United States and elsewhere. It includes full employment, a fairer distribution of resources through restrictions on inherited and accumulated wealth, and an overhaul of the educational system so that it produces self-dependent people with high levels of individual skills and with less need of advice and supervision from professionals. The group also recommends a policy for families and children that adopts as a national goal the abolition of child poverty, and it makes a radical proposal to increase direct cash grants to mothers and families. The Working Group's priorities for the community are a comprehensive disability allowance, improved working conditions, and improved housing.

To implement this strategy is not only to serve as community advocates, but also to attack the ultimate causes of disease. As the Working Group points out, measures to reduce material inequalities, which are the root cause of inequalities in health, necessarily entail undertaking structural reorganization. One job in public health is to design and promote the structural reorganization that will effect change in communities.

The social production theory of health and illness explains the findings of the Working Group better than the other four theories. In terms of public health policy, the theory of social production leads to structural reforms, to basic changes in society and in the way social life is organized. It also leads to community solutions, in part because it helps people find common cause by relating their individual ills to social conditions. By helping people recognize that there is a common social basis for individual health problems, public health workers can encourage them to join forces in seeking solutions.

The theory that illness is socially produced emphasizes the importance of community analysis, the importance for both communities and epidemiologists to look at ultimate causes of illness and disease, and the importance of using analysis as a popular tool, as a means of empowerment. When the British Working Group on Inequalities and Health speaks of reforming education so that it makes people self-dependent, they are speaking of the same issue—of overcoming helplessness.

Chapter 4

EQUITY AND ACCESS

EQUITY AND ACCESS are first principles of justice: they give meaning to the notion of universal equality beyond the political realm (as in the declaration that "all men [*sic*] are created equal") by extending it to the economic and social realms. In the context of human rights law from which these notions arise, economic, social, and cultural rights—the right to employment and fair working conditions, the right to a standard of living that ensures health and well-being, the right to social security, special rights of motherhood and childhood, the right to education, and the right to participate in the cultural life of the community—are considered second generation rights. In contrast, first generation civil and political rights are the prohibition of slavery, freedom of thought and religion, the right of every accused person to a fair trial, and the rights to life, liberty, and citizenship (Zalaquett 1981). The United States alone continues to debate whether health care is a right or a privilege; other economies, both open market and planned, accept that it is a right of citizenship, although not all can afford to provide free care to everyone.

In conventional public health practice, equity refers to the fair distribution of health services and equal access to them. In this chapter I use the concepts of second generation human rights to extend conventional health interpretations to include not only access to goods and services—in the broad sense of material conditions that promote health—but also equal access to the means of production (resources such as land, raw materials, and factories) and equal rights to participation in social decision-making so as to exert control over essential resources. Underlying this shift of focus from health services to the means of production is the belief that the economic formation—that is, the social relations of production and the forces of production—determines both current disease patterns and present health services. The social relations of production comprise the socialization of both capital and labor. The socialization of capital ranges from very little in a free market economy with a dominant private sector to a great deal, as in a non-market or planned economy with a dominant public sector. The socialization of labor also covers a range—from free labor markets typical of laissez-faire economies in which class differentiation is pronounced, to workers' control of the means of production in a classless society. The forces of production, which are predictors of the limits and possibilities of health care systems, range from low to high levels of resources and technology. These differences are illustrated with case studies in three countries in chapter five.

Access must mean more than obtaining medical care. As we saw in chapter three, the British National Health Service improved health but did not close the gap in death rates between social class I and social class V. Access to resources, work or social security, and education should be a part of the meaning of health equity. Participation in public health should mean that both users and providers can influence decisions affecting health and well-being, the types of service offered, and the priorities assigned to them.

Equity and equality of access are issues whenever high costs are barriers to health care. Planning is thought to lower costs by reducing waste, which is the result of competitive and overlapping research and the duplication of facilities and personnel. With the savings, governments can provide services in unprofitable geographic areas (for example, rural areas with low population density and inner-city areas with high rates of poverty) and to people with rare or chronic conditions requiring expensive or long-term care beyond their means.

Equity and access are more complicated issues when the definition of health care is broadened to include environmental health. Land, water, air, forests, factories, and raw materials are among the resources that constitute the means of production in every society. The arrangements to protect some of these resources (such as air) and to guarantee access to others (such as water) vary markedly from one mode of production to another. Such variations are clear in Native American testimony; Indians and Europeans held opposite attitudes toward land and nature:[1]

> In the New World, whites cleared the forests and cultivated the ground, slaughtered wild game in massive quantities, mined the earth's gold and silver as if they would never end, and began peopling villages and towns blocked out after those in their homelands. Yet the Indians viewed themselves as the earth's grateful occupiers and custodians, not as its owners and engineers. Defining land as a commercial product like sugar or gunpowder, the whites measured it, bought it or stole it, fenced it, tilled or built upon it, with an abandon that horrified Indians. At the same time the colonists, whose society was founded on private ownership and consolidation of personal riches, looked disapprovingly at the Indians' custom of sharing land in common (Nabakov 1978, 85).

State intervention to regulate individual ownership of essential resources has been necessary since the early days of capitalism. The lack of success in ensuring the vital minimum—clean air and water—in industrial countries 140 years after the first public health act was passed is apparent in today's ubiquitous pollution battles. The problem is that the logic of capitalism, which is private profit, and the long-term conservation of the environment, which can only be managed collectively, are mutually exclusive categories (Turshen, Barker, and O'Keefe 1988).

Equity and access, as defined here, entail participation as an element of political systems. Democracy is an issue whenever high levels of expertise exclude the general public from decision-making. The level at which planning is carried out and the priority assigned to expertise and participation determine access. Unplanned systems are necessarily undemocratic because decisions are in private hands with no public contribution possible beyond consumer choice. The United States exemplifies a demand-driven system in which organized consumers have been able to wrest important protective legislation from the government. In planned systems, opportunities for participation vary according to whether the planning model is centralized (as in the USSR) or decentralized (as in the People's Republic of China).

How equity and access are organized in the public health services of countries with differing economic systems is the subject of this chapter, which looks at two service models: planned and unplanned. It is not my purpose to compare these examples but to assess them on their own terms. In order to evaluate equity and access in various economies, it is necessary first to situate current public health practice in a global context and to see what public health work actually consists of and where it is done.

Public Health Practice

Public health is understood broadly as practiced at many levels: by the individual (one-on-one health education, for example); by the family (where most of us first learn personal hygiene and acquire eating habits and ideas about nutrition); and by government institutions, including international agencies. Conventionally, public health work is carried out in the community, sometimes called the locality or municipality—depending on whether it is rural or urban—and in county, state, and federal governments (or provincial bureau and national ministry, depending on the political organization of the country). Above the national level or institution, there are regional arrangements involving several countries, for example, the European Economic Community, the Organization for Economic Cooperation and Development, and the Organization of American States, which do public health work. Finally, international public health is carried out by global organizations such as the World Health Organization (WHO).

When one talks about the levels at which public health tasks are performed, one necessarily indicates the institution that actually does the work. Most public health work is done in government bureaucracies: departments of health, the U.S. Public Health Service, and national ministries of health. Public health is taught in universities and medical schools. Some multinational organizations that do public health work (such as WHO) are staffed by international civil servants. Public health work is also carried out by nongovernmental organizations (some of which are bureaucracies, too); for example, the International Union Against Tuberculosis, known for its Christmas seals, has national chapters composed of state and local agencies. The fact that public health workers are often bureaucrats gives a certain character to the work and the profession and sets off both from the entrepreneurial practice of private medicine.

The mechanisms of public health include policy (for example, policies that affect the family such as housing policy); legislation including state and federal laws (in the United States, workers' compensation is an example of legislation at the state level, Medicare and Medicaid are examples of federal laws implemented at the state level, TOSCA [Toxic Substances Control Act] and FIFRA [Federal Insecticide, Fungicide, and Rodenticide Act] are federal environmental laws); and regulations, which may be bureaucratic elaborations of legislation but are sometimes measures adopted by administrative fiat. The mechanisms also include the legal and judicial framework, that is, the mechanisms of enforcement. The successful implementation of regulations often depends on police powers of arrest, imprisonment, and fines.

One could do public health work at any of the levels or in any of the institutions described, but in terms of impact on the public—measured by the number of people affected—which level, institution, or mechanism matters greatly. One rule of thumb is that, as far as legislation is concerned, the higher the level at which laws are passed, the more people will be encompassed under the regulations, and in that sense the more progressive the rule will be. Thus one would press for federal workers' compensation to replace state laws because more workers would be covered more adequately by federal law (U.S. National Commission 1973). On the other hand, the lower the level of autonomy, the greater the degree of democracy and flexibility.[2] And sometimes, under repressive right-wing regimes, local initiatives are the only progressive action possible (Ray H. Elling 1986, personal communication).

The reason for adopting regulations at the national or international level—especially laws, conventions, or treaties that have police powers of enforcement—is to equalize regional disparities in public health. Uniform European laws adopted by the European Economic Community equalize disparities in occupational and environmental conditions between the older, industrialized, unionized countries such as Great Britain and the more recently industrialized and urbanized members such as Spain (Jaumont, Lenègre, and Rocard 1973). International laws would equalize disparities between the Third World and the industrial countries.

This equalization is accomplished in several ways. Uniform national and international laws stop industry from moving to areas of limited regulation in order to avoid the higher costs of strict enforcement (Castleman and Navarro 1987). For example, the U.S. South owes its industrial growth to the relocation of factories before the passage of national legislation on clean air and water and occupational safety and health (Watkins and Perry 1977, 41). Or, to take an international example, restrictions on the asbestos industry in the United States motivated its removal to Mexico, which an international convention banning asbestos production might have prevented (Butler et al. 1978, 24–28). Similarly, current concerns about the export of hazardous wastes by private firms located in industrial countries with strict laws to African nations with no protective legislation illustrate the role of international power relations in issues that affect national health and safety (Castleman and Navarro 1987).

Uniform international laws also give an impetus to national legislation that might otherwise have been postponed or never adopted at all; for example, several Third World countries, members of the International Labour Organisation (ILO), have adopted restrictions on child labor to conform with ILO conventions (Mendelievich 1980). In this case, the international regulation carries no powers of enforcement, but the national ratifying legislation does. Prosecution is another matter however.

International conventions were first adopted in the fourteenth century to protect public health by checking the spread of disease, in that instance bubonic plague. Similar conventions are still in force today, and WHO operates an epidemiological intelligence unit to monitor a number of notifiable diseases such as cholera. WHO's powers of enforcement are weak. It has happened that a country refused to acknowledge an outbreak of cholera, and WHO used its regulation of notifiable diseases to disclose the epidemic against that government's wishes. Sometimes WHO's only power is to threaten a country with expulsion from the organization on the grounds that it is not upholding one of the treaties it signed when it became a member—not a threat one would want to invoke too often. Most of WHO's work is advisory, and the organization has no way to enforce the measures it recommends.

The ILO, which has adopted many conventions affecting worker safety and health, also has no way of enforcing the measures it recommends. In fact, often it cannot persuade governments to ratify many of the conventions adopted by its governing body, a tripartite organ composed of representatives of labor, management, and government. Many ILO conventions are never ratified by governments including the United States, which regard them as an infringement of national sovereignty.

The level at which public health work is done and the way in which work at various levels is coordinated raise fundamental issues of equity, equality of access, and democracy. These issues are played out in the two main models of health care: planned and unplanned. Unplanned health care is private medical care subject to capitalist market forces, and it is usually also regulated by government; for example, all private hospitals in the United States are legally required to provide the same standard of satisfactory patient care as public and nonprofit or voluntary hospitals. No public health service, in the sense of government provision of health care, is unplanned, although the public sector may represent the smallest part of available services.

The next three sections of this chapter lay out the models of planned and unplanned health care in the United States, the USSR, and the People's Republic of China. Each section begins with a description of health services in order to evaluate the population's access to medical care and the equity of the system. This is followed by a description of occupational and environmental health protection in order to address access and equity in the larger sense that I have outlined. The sections end with an assessment of mortality experience.

Unplanned Health Care: The United States

The organization of health care delivery in the United States is difficult to describe because health services are unplanned and medical care is carefully protected as a nonsystem. Most industrialized countries have a ministry of health that plays a central role in financing and operating health services. In the mixed market and planned economies of western Europe, such ministries often provide the framework and create the structure within which the various components of the system function, even when they do not directly operate the entire system (Jonas 1981, 6).

In the United States, the government neither operates a system of health care delivery nor finances health care in its entirety (Jonas and Banta 1981, 313); in fact the U.S. government is less involved in health care than the governments of most other industrialized countries, mainly because the private sector has successfully opposed both a national health service and national health insurance. The government plays a major role in the provision of services in selected areas such as infectious disease control, care of members of Congress and Native Americans, the armed forces (including former personnel through the Veterans Administration), and the mentally ill. (For a detailed account of health services in the United States see Jonas 1981; Roemer 1982; or Wilson and Neuhauser 1987.)

Instead, most medical care is delivered by self-employed physicians in private practice, with no administrative and little technical oversight. The estimated 30 to 40 million people with no or inadequate insurance cannot afford the fees charged by physicians for their services; often they have recourse to pharmacists, the emergency rooms of urban public hospitals, or a variety of unlicensed practitioners. The financial barrier to access has created two tiers of medical care in the United States, one for the rich and one for the poor. Medicare (providing assistance to the elderly) and Medicaid (providing aid to the poor) have allowed costs to rise by cushioning their impact, but they have not eliminated the effects of medical expenses on the elderly and the poor (Brown 1984).

Because it is in private hands, the U.S. health care industry is undemocratic; community participation is extremely limited and community control virtually nonexistent. The participation of impoverished residents in running neighborhood health center programs, which sought to provide comprehensive care in local facilities, was one goal of the 1965 War on Poverty. Despite "much success in delivering quality health care" (Davis and Schoen 1978, 170), this Office of Economic Opportunity program experienced changed directives and cutbacks which eventually transformed the centers so that they were no longer a source of political and economic power (Schoen 1977, 180). According to Hatch and Eng (1984), the isolated experiments in Mound Bayou, Mississippi; the Bronx; and the Lower East Side of New York—which were attempted in response to urban unrest and civil disorder—failed because health professionals, government officials, and local politicians were unwilling to relinquish power.

The only continuing popular contribution to health care policy in the United States is through consumer organizations that make demands; for example, the 28 million member American Association of Retired Persons was among the groups that successfully lobbied for the repeal of antisubstitution legislation that had blocked the sale of generic drugs, which are much cheaper than the same medications sold under brand names. On the other hand, the elderly have been no match for the multibillion-dollar nursing home industry, which delivers poor quality care in undesirable institutional conditions, despite years of criticism detailing negligence leading to death and injury, unsanitary conditions, poor nutrition, lack of fire protection, and overmedication (Harrington 1984).

Consumer groups have also been instrumental in obtaining legislation to protect the public's health by curbing private industry in the area broadly defined as product safety, which includes everything from unsafe cars to unsafe toys, adulterated food and dangerous drugs, flammable fabrics, and fradulent claims for "medical" devices. Upton Sinclair's novel *The Jungle*, which exposed the meat packing industry, provoked a public outcry that led to passage of the Pure Food and Drug Act in 1906. More than sixty years later, a revitalized consumer activist movement led by Ralph Nader, founding organizer of Public Citizen, helped obtain passage of the 1972 Consumer Protection Act. The obvious lesson is that demand-driven systems respond slowly and often inadequately to public health and safety, and the needs of voiceless or powerless groups are rarely addressed.

Another issue taken up by consumers is environmental health, which includes issues of household and industrial waste disposal as well as the impact of industrial and agricultural development on the ecology. Routine waste disposal is handled poorly by a mix of municipal and private agencies that are only loosely regulated by state and federal government (Anderson 1987). The result is a garbage crisis in the late 1980s: illegal dumping of consumer wastes by those who cannot afford the exorbitant fees of private collection companies and, more serious, illegal dumping by irresponsible medical and industrial concerns, which has longer-term and more far-reaching consequences for environmental health. Some companies try to dump their hazardous and toxic wastes in the Third World.

With the publication of *Silent Spring* in 1962, Rachel Carson sparked a movement for environmental protection that is now global in scope. The core of the movement opposes corporate control of natural resources and world energy markets; but, as James Ridgeway (1971) points out, industry has coopted consumers. The companies that create energy and cause pollution also take a leading role in the antipollution crusade and in the sale of antipollution technology. Corporate domination extends to legislation for clean air, clean water, and environmental protection, which was first passed in the mid-1950s. Although the U.S. Congress imposes stricter regulations every decade, industry sabotages their implementation by the Environmental Protection Agency.

Unlike other consumer initiatives, the environmental movement includes a broad array of politically diverse and sophisticated nongovernmental organizations (some with international links) interested in the conservation of nature, especially wilderness and wildlife, as well as the health effects of pollution. In a few instances they have lent the "Davids"— concerned citizens in small, powerless communities—support in their struggles with the "Goliaths"—multinational corporations such as Velsicol and Hooker chemical companies. But legal challenges have seldom been successful in the courts (Freudenberg 1984, 167).

More has been achieved by coalitions of trade unions, environmentalists, academics, and consumers willing to boycott company products over problems that involve occupational health and have ramifications for environmental and community health. These coalitions face corporate campaigns of "environmental job blackmail," a strategy that pits public desires for a cleaner environment against community fears of unemployment (Kazis and Grossman 1982). The Oil, Chemical, and Atomic Workers Union (OCAW) organized a successful nationwide strike against Shell Oil Company in 1973 to press demands for worker health and safety (Freudenberg 1984, 194–195). Guided by Tony Mazzocchi, a former vice president, the union was able to persuade environmental and public interest organizations and consumers that occupational health is a key to environmental health and that safety problems do not stop at the plant fence. More recently, the United Farmworkers Union, under the leadership of Cesar Chavez, organized a strike of grape pickers to press for safer pesticide practices; the union gained the support of a consumer boycott of table grapes with the argument that pesticide residues are harmful to health.

The legislative framework for occupational safety and health in the United States was created in the first decades of the twentieth century. Under the threat of growing social unrest, a coalition of radicals, reformers, labor leaders, consumers, and liberal business leaders (anxious to capture the movement) discussed workplace conditions. The coalition agitated for broad social concern about worker housing, sanitation, and general living as well as working conditions, but the government responded by passing limited state laws for workers' compensation covering accidents on the job (Rosner and Markowitz 1987, xiii–xiv). Corporate leaders successfully dominated the job safety movement for the next fifty years.

This bleak picture was relieved by an important piece of federal legislation in 1936. The Walsh-Healey Act, which required inspections and enforcement of work standards on public contracts, was passed amid severe labor unrest associated with the Great Depression and the organizing drives of industrial workers (Elling 1986, 393). Few further gains were made until 1969 when coal miners achieved federal protection, 100 years after the first mine ventilation act was adopted in a single Pennsylvania county (Corn 1987, 71). Despite a changeover from a Democratic administration under Lyndon Johnson to a Republican administration under Richard Nixon, the momentum for passage of the Coal Mine Health and Safety Act ensured rapid adoption of the Occupational Safety and Health Act in 1970, which had long been in the making (Coye, Smith, and Mazzocchi 1984, 83; Noble 1986, 90).

The Occupational Safety and Health Act gave workers a universal and substantive right to health and safety on the job, created a general employer duty to furnish employment free from recognized hazards, and established one agency (OSHA) to set and enforce workplace standards and another (NIOSH) to research hazards and develop standards; and it developed civil and criminal penalties for violations (Noble 1986, 95). Although the act obliged employers to maintain records on worker injuries and illnesses, it was silent on the need for independent medical services at the worksite or the need to integrate occupational health in medical care.[3] And whereas it provided for professional training, it did not require the presence of independent health and safety specialists even at large establishments, nor did it empower workers to fill this role. Many critics conclude that the act promised much, and in the late 1970s the Carter administration was able to introduce innovative concepts in standards; but it has not significantly protected workers from occupational hazards in the nearly twenty years of its existence (Coye, Smith, and Mazzocchi 1984; Elling 1986; Noble 1986).

To evaluate equity and access to the material conditions that promote health and to the means of production one must use a social indicator as a proxy—in this case mortality experience. The absence of data organized by economic class, which is the main determinant of access in the United States, complicates the review of mortality. One cannot measure here, as the Working Group on Inequalities in Health did in Great Britain (Townsend and Davidson 1982), whether the gaps in death rates between social classes I and V have closed. One can only substitute comparisons of African-American and White mortality, and even these are complicated by the dilution of African-American experience in the category "non-White," which includes Chinese- and Japanese-Americans whose death rates are much lower than rates for African-Americans.

Infant mortality rates, which are frequently used as an indicator of general social and economic conditions, have declined for all races. For Whites the rate fell from 26.8 per 1,000 live births in 1950 to 9.3 per 1,000 in 1985; the rate for African-American infants in 1950 was 43.9 or 1.6 times as high, and the rate in 1985 was 18.2 or nearly twice as high as the White infant mortality rate (U.S. Bureau of the Census 1987, 75). Maternal mortality rates—that is, deaths due to complications of pregnancy and childbirth—have dropped markedly since 1940, and the actual numbers are now quite low, but the current ratio of African-American to White deaths is almost four to one (ibid.). Until 1984, general mortality rates showed some improvement in the gap between the races: age-adjusted death rates declined for Whites from 10.2 per 1,000 population in 1940 to 5.3 per 1,000 in 1983 and for non-Whites from 16.3 in 1940 (1.6 times as high as Whites) to 7.0 in 1983 (1.3 times as high) (U.S. Department of Health and Human Services 1986, 24, 29, 34). But in 1985 and 1986, the decline reversed and mortality rates increased among African-American men and women (*New York Times,* 20 December 1988).

These time series give no clue to the different historical experience of African-American and White cohorts. In this sense the data are ahistorical and not comparable. Stark suggests (personal communication 1988) that in the post World War II period of economic expansion, African-Americans invested heavily in securing well-paid manufacturing jobs, often performing the hardest and dirtiest work, only to see this sector shrink; subsequent unemployment and family breakdown took their toll in mortality.

Centralized Planning: The USSR

The centralized planning model is best illustrated by the USSR. State health protection is the right of every citizen, proclaimed by the new constitution adopted in 1976, along with the right to work, rest, housing, and social security (Burenkov 1985). The Soviet Union, a country of 270 million people, 63 percent of whom live in urban centers, has a nationalized health sector, that is, there is no private health sector to speak of.[4] Public health, in the sense of free government health services, provides universal coverage. There was one doctor for every 270 persons in 1981; by comparison, in the United States there was one doctor for every 500 persons and in China one for every 1,730 (World Bank 1988).

The Soviet health system is highly centralized, highly stratified, hierarchically organized, and evenly distributed geographically. The Ministry of Health is responsible for overall direction, planning, supervision, and financing of all health and medical services and for establishing norms or standards for the provision of these services to the people. It is also responsible for coordinating medical research, determining the country's internal needs for medical supplies, deciding the amounts of supplies to be produced for export, and providing technical assistance to the health ministries of the fifteen union republics (Sidel and Sidel 1977).

The health ministry is responsible for executing central policy at the level of the republic, and for planning and operating health services within its own territory. Below the level of the republic's health ministry is the health department of a province or region. The regional or provincial health department plans and coordinates its areas (functions that it shares with higher levels of the structure), directly operates regional health facilities such as the regional hospital, and deals with the daily provision of special services. Attached to each of these departments are specialists (for example, in gynecology, pediatrics, obstetrics, and epidemic diseases) who are responsible for the quality of these services within their areas (Roemer 1976, 131–144).

Municipal and rural health departments, the most local level of health administration, directly finance and supervise the bulk of the health and medical services in the community. They hire and pay health and medical personnel, provide the equipment and facilities with which they work, and are responsible for the health protection and medical care of the people within the areas. In the rural areas, however, rural district hospitals have gradually taken over the functions of rural health departments and have actually replaced them (ibid.).

This unified system, in which all care—preventive and curative—is integrated, requires a small administrative bureaucracy. This is paradoxical when one thinks of the huge bureaucracy required in the United States to administer the plethora of private, voluntary, and government services. The Soviet Union, with its slightly larger population, employed some 6 million health workers in 1984 (WHO 1986c, 208); the U.S. health service industry employed 20.1 million people in the same year (U.S. Bureau of the Census 1987, 364, 804). Soviet physicians are salaried, as are all health personnel in the Soviet Union, and there is a distinct hierarchy with large differential increments in pay for length of service and for more specialized or higher administrative positions. In the hierarchy of personnel, specialists are more important than generalists, and physicians (both specialists and generalists) are more important than nurses and feldshers (who are like physicians' assistants).

There is little room in this model for popular participation in decision-making; on the other hand, according to Roemer (1976), there is significant delegation of responsibility peripherally and wide diversity is found in local practices. Responsibility for the operation of the health program is delegated to local committees made up principally of health service workers; these committees can influence how general policies are carried out.

Occupational health services, which provide preventive care and treatment to workers in a special network of health establishments located in large industrial enterprises, are organized separately for each industry (WHO 1980, 254). Varying in size, they are staffed by physicians and industrial feldshers and are administered and operated by the management of the industrial centers. Some, for example those at the major steel mill facilities, are large medical and hospital institutions with several hundred beds. According to one critic, the primary objective of these services, which were established in the 1930s and 1940s, was to reduce widespread absenteeism and disability due to illness (Navarro 1977, 43).

In addition to providing medical care, industrial physicians and feldshers also perform plantwide health surveys. Reports in the Soviet scientific literature of this public health approach to occupational hazards present a striking contrast to the individual case reports of single instances of illness common in the United States (Turshen 1982).

Soviet work rules are generally acknowledged to be stricter than U.S. occupational health and safety standards, especially in the areas of behavioral risks, electrical high voltage risks, and combined risks such as noise and vibration (Goldsmith 1980, 50). Standards are developed by the Institute for Industrial Hygiene and Occupational Disease of the Academy of Medical Sciences among others and set by the labor protection departments of each republic. The rules are enforced by some 20,000 broadly empowered federal inspectors based at local sanitary epidemiological stations (Sanipeds) and, more significantly, by about 5,500 inspectors from the labor movement based in large factories or in regions; inspectors have authority to close a dangerous plant or stop a threatening work process (ibid., 51). Penalties for failure to comply with the rules range from warnings and budget cuts to jail sentences and dismissal of plant managers.

The Soviets created their sanitary and epidemiological service (the Sanipeds) in the 1920s and 1930s to combat epidemics of infectious disease following the 1917 revolution and associated with the rapid pace of industrialization in the 1930s. The State Sanitary Inspectorate established in 1935 was responsible for inspection of construction in new towns and workers' settlements, water and sewage systems, as well as industrial and food hygiene (Lisitsin 1972, 92–94).

Many occupational health problems cannot be separated from environmental health problems, as the industrial accident at the Chernobyl nuclear power station brought home. The explosion and fire on 26 April 1986 resulted in acute radiation of over 200 workers and firefighters; some 30 deaths; the evacuation of 135,000 people (and tens of thousands of cattle) living within 30 kilometers of the plant; contamination of the ground, vegetation cover, buildings, bodies of water, milk, vegetables, and other foodstuffs in the Soviet Union as well as many other countries; and as yet unknown numbers of future deaths from cancer and genetic damage (International Nuclear Safety Advisory Group 1986). News stories on such disasters rarely report on the legislative framework for environmental protection adopted in the USSR. The following information is taken from a report by Elisabeth Koutaissoff (1986), which is based on papers presented at the Third World Congress for Soviet and East European Studies, held in Washington, D.C., in 1985.

The Soviet Union industrialized at accelerated rates but, until the 1960s, like most other countries it paid scant attention to the impact of economic development on the environment. Now it is suffering from common adverse effects such as pollution, deforestation, and loss of wldlife. Most natural resources are located in the harsh climate of the North, and their exploitation requires a powerful and often damaging human intervention—causing, for example, destruction of fragile tundra vegetation by the oil industry and loss of land and biota to huge reservoirs for hydropower stations.

Since the 1960s, especially since 1972, the USSR has adopted numerous laws; for example, there are decrees designed to protect the Caspian Sea from oil pollution (1968), the Volga and Ural Rivers from untreated sewage (1974), and the Black and Azov Seas from both pollution and overfishing (1974). A decree passed in 1976 prescribes the recultivation of lands ravaged by mining, peat extraction, and geological surveys. Other decrees reinforce earlier legislation for more rational exploitation of forests (1977), tighter regulations on air pollution (1980), protection of wildlife (1980), and better utilization of secondary or waste products of industry (1984). Since 1976 state five-year plans include environmental protection measures and numerous authorities have been set up to enforce this legislation. The USSR has joined many international environmental organizations, both intergovernmental, such as the United Nations Environmental Program, and nongovernmental, such as the International Union for the Conservation of Nature.

Implementation is harder to gauge. Koutaissoff (1986, 6) notes that funds allocated from the state budget amount to less than 2 percent of the total investment in industry and are often underspent for lack of adequate equipment and skilled personnel. However, Bahry and Nechemias (1981, 375) caution that central government spending may not reflect republic budgets for programs under republic subordination. Penalties are fixed by union republics and local authorities, undermining the impact of national legislation. Enterprises set aside sums for the payment of the small fines levied, which they consider less onerous than the interruption of production or the modernization of purification systems. The Soviets carry out detailed and sophisticated environmental impact studies on major construction projects such as the Baikal-Amur railway. Reportedly these analyses suggest remedial rather than preventive measures, and in the case of smaller projects are insufficiently thorough. Reports of ecological destruction to the Aral Sea, siphoned to irrigate the cottonfields of Uzbekistan and Turkmenia, suggest failure (*New York Times,* 20 December 1988).

To evaluate access and equity, the same measure of mortality used in the case of the United States is employed here. Because the most detailed data available are for deaths in the first year of life, only infant mortality—a sensitive indicator of a nation's health—is discussed. Rising trends in infant mortality in the USSR in the 1970s generated a heated debate over possible causes (Cooper and Schatzkin 1982; Davis and Feshbach 1980; Eberstadt 1981; Szymanski 1982). The numbers are very hard to pin down: Cooper and Schatzkin cite a low of 22.9 per 1,000 live births in 1971; current estimates in United Nations publications vary from 23 to 30 per 1,000 in 1986 (UNICEF 1988, 65; World Bank 1988, 287, respectively). Whichever figure is correct, at the very least the numbers indicate that infant mortality has not continued to decline.

The breakdown by region reveals that the rise occurred in the central Asian republics of Tadzhikistan, Turkmenistan, and Uzbekistan, an indication that equity and access might be judged by a comparison of infant mortality trends in the Slavic and central Asian republics. (It is ironic that Alma Ata, the capital city of Kazakhstan, which hosted the WHO/UNICEF International Conference on Primary Health Care in 1978, experienced a rise in infant mortality, suggesting a failure of the model system.) In the three Slavic republics (Russian Soviet Federated Socialist Republic, Ukraine, and Byelorussia), rates fell 77 percent from 33.9 per 1,000 live births in 1960 to 19.1 in 1974; in Tadzhikistan and Uzbekistan the figures rose 67 percent from an average 29.0 per 1,000 in 1960 to 48.6 in 1974 (1974 figures for capital cities only; Szymanski 1982, 486). Even if the earlier Asian figures were underreported and are too low, the disparities are great, rising from 1.2 times as much mortality in Asian as in Slavic republics in 1960 to 2.5 times as much in 1974.

As possible explanations Davis and Feshbach offer improved reporting of deaths, influenza epidemics, and rising birth rates. Eberstadt sees rising infant mortality as symptomatic of a crisis in Soviet society. Cooper and Schatzkin attribute the rise to the underdeveloped and dependent nature of the Asian republics. Symptoms include problems of child labor, overproduction of cotton, pesticide toxicity, and water shortages. Szymanski holds that the problem is minor, can be relatively easily corrected within the

Soviet system, and is mostly due to rapid urbanization, the employment of women, and the expansion of day-care facilities in this rich agricultural region. Bahry and Nechemias (1981, 371) warn that interregional comparison is tricky because different definitions of equality lead to different conclusions; "Studies that emphasize compensation fail to find much evidence of it, while those that look for equal funding or redistribution find that Moscow *has* subsidized less developed regions."

Some answers to these apparent contradictions may be found in Lubin's (1984) detailed analysis of Uzbekistan. Her investigation of the rapid modernization, urbanization, and industrialization that are occurring found ethnic Russians in most of the skilled industrial jobs and few Uzbek men (and even fewer women), despite Soviet-style "affirmative action" policies. Her explanation is cultural: Uzbeks prefer their rural way of life. (Perhaps this is true; certainly European colonists had to force Africans from their farms, which they preferred to slave wages.) Cotton exploitation results in diets short of milk and meat, poor sanitation due to the shortage of water, and extensive chemical pollution from pesticides. The *New York Times* (6 November 1988) reports a close correlation between heavy irrigation and high infant mortality rates. One is left to speculate on the health and health care of indigenous women in the modern farm economy and the relation of the declining quality of Uzbek life to rising infant mortality.

Decentralized Planning: China

The decentralized model is best illustrated by the People's Republic of China, a country of over one billion people, 21 percent of whom live in urban centers. Health services in China are not only nationalized, they are also socialized; they are not only owned by the people through their government, they are also run by the people through community agencies. The Chinese arrived at their unique system through the struggle for liberation during the Japanese invasion, which began in 1931, and the ensuing civil war. They describe their socialized, decentralized approach as the

Yenan Way, which, they say, emphasizes popular participation and community power and rejects domination by an administrative or technical elite operating through a centralized bureaucracy (Selden 1971).

Coordinating power is vested at the district level, and the township and village levels are the focus of government work in the rural areas; in urban areas the focus is the neighborhood and street levels. In order to bring about decentralization, the government found it necessary to curb the independent power of bureaucratic organs of government and to shift government work downward from regional and district offices. Not only was work shifted, but also workers were sent to the villages and set to labor in fields and factories. One purpose of decentralizing the government work force was to destroy barriers between an educated urban elite and deprived farm laborers in the countryside. Another purpose was to break down the distinction between mental and manual labor (ibid.).

With decentralization came possibilities of redefining community action by reconstructing village social and political leadership. After breaking the economic stranglehold of landlords by reducing rent and interest rates, it was possible to use traditional forms of mutual aid to reorganize the village economy. New economic approaches included support of the cooperative movement, and an organizational economy in which every organization and every leader participated in tasks ranging from the management of new industries to the collection of manure for the cooperative vegetable gardens of the local Communist party branches. Putting the leadership to work not only increased production and provided management experience, it also reduced taxes (because the party was self-sufficient and not dependent on tax revenues for support). Simultaneously, the popular education movement expanded the scope and modified the form and content of education, spread literacy, and introduced new ideas (ibid.).

The Yenan Way is described at length because the tendency in public health circles is to take out of their political and economic context certain innovations of the Chinese health care system, for example the "barefoot doctor" scheme, and to introduce them into a private ownership market economy, usually in the Third World. In China health care is one part of the reform of the political system, which implanted a new organization of the economy and engendered new social relations.

The Yenan Way translates into a health administrative structure in which the minister of health, at the center, is part of the Council of State. At the provincial level (there are twenty-one provinces), the health department is responsible to the minister of health. At the next lower level, the county (there are about 75 counties per province, or about 2,000 in all), the health bureau administers all hospitals and health centers within the county. Roemer (1976, 86–89) describes these responsibilities, both upward and downward on the organization chart, as not authoritarian but advisory and designed to be helpful in achieving local goals.

Each of the approximately two thousand counties has a 120-bed hospital, a sanitary and antiepidemic station, and a maternal and child health care center (WHO 1980, 324). Within the county are communes and municipalities (approximately 14 communes per county, about 50,000 communes in all). Each commune is typically served by a health center, which has ten or more short-term or transfer beds and is staffed with physicians. Within the commune are ten to twenty production brigades, which support barefoot doctors in small health stations; about 500,000 of these cooperative health centers are scattered through the rural areas. In cities the subdivisions are districts and within them neighborhoods; each neighborhood, which may house 40,000 to 70,000 people, is served by a general hospital. Neighborhoods are further subdivided into lanes, which are served by street doctors, the urban equivalent of the barefoot doctor (Roemer 1976, 86–89).

This administrative structure encourages democratic participation. Decision-making at each level—central, provincial, county, brigade, and production team in rural areas, and their urban equivalents—rests with revolutionary committees composed of representatives of three groups: political cadres, technically skilled workers (in this case health and medical workers), and the army. Care is taken to represent the young, the middle-aged, and the old in the distribution of membership. The responsible member or leader of a county health bureau would not necessarily be a physician with specialized training in public health; rather he or she would be the most politically reliable and respected member.

Likewise, the responsible member of the revolutionary committee of a hospital might be a veteran nurse or kitchen worker. In both examples, appropriately trained physicians would always be on the committee, and decisions are reached by majority vote (ibid.).

The policies that guide work in the health sector also encourage democratic participation; they are that health services should serve the workers, peasants, and soldiers (translated into the terms of the U.K. registrar general, health services should serve social classes IV and V); that prevention should come first, before curative measures; that classical Chinese medicine should unite with western medicine; that health services should combine with the mass movement (everyone in society is encouraged to play an organized role in the protection of his or her own health and that of neighbors); that health and medical work should emphasize the rural areas; that health care should promote local self-reliance; and that health workers should fight against bureaucracy (ibid.).

During a month-long trip to China in 1982 to participate in an exchange conference on occupational health sponsored by the Harvard School of Public Health and the Shanghai First Medical College School of Public Health, I had the opportunity to observe health services in and around Shanghai. I was struck by how little the western medical facilities were used, in contrast to the crowded hospital offering classical Chinese medical care. In my experience of Third World health services, the absence of patronage usually indicates a negative popular evaluation; as we say, people vote with their feet. Low attendance also generally indicates a lack of popular participation in the planning and running of services. With the exception of acupuncture anesthesia, I saw no integration of Chinese and western medicine; instead I noted the usual patronizing attitude toward traditional medicine on the part of physicians trained in biomedical science. And despite Chairman Mao's dictum, "Put the rural areas first," it is clear that urban workers are favored over rural peasants. These comments do not detract from the extraordinary accomplishments of the Chinese revolution in improving the people's health, but they question the success in implementing some of the policies that were to guide work in the health sector. A scientific account of health services in Shanghai County may be found in Hinman et al. (1982).

As in the Soviet Union, side by side with the network of national, provincial, and local facilities that service the whole population, is a network of industrial and other state enterprise hospitals and facilities that provide free services to workers in those enterprises. Available data indicate that in 1981 they provided about 25 percent of the medical care in China (Jamison 1985, 26). Enterprise facilities report to the health sections of various industrial departments, and they receive technical guidance from provincial and local health departments. Depending on the size of the enterprise, complicated cases are treated there or referred to the government hospital system; if a patient is referred to a district hospital, expenses are reimbursed entirely by labor insurance. Large enterprises handle almost all their own cases, and the Railway Ministry and Army, for example, even have their own medical colleges as well as hospitals (ibid.). Workers' compensation is extensive: any worker suffering from an occupational disease is given full pay as well as free medical treatment for life (Christiani 1984, 616).

Control of occupational hazards is accomplished by setting advisory standards (not enforceable by law); by fitting engineering controls in newly constructed factories and retrofitting older plants; by issuing personal protective equipment as an interim measure to workers in older plants as well as to agricultural workers exposed to pesticide poisoning; by training workers to recognize health hazards, early symptoms of disease, and proper work and hygiene practices; by early detection of occupational disease, administration of prompt treatment, or removal from further exposure; and by giving on-the-job training in occupational health to public health professionals (Christiani 1984, 612–615).

Environmental problems that are due to China's rapid industrial development include urban pollution caused by wrongly located factories, high consumption of raw materials and energy caused by low levels of technological development, failure to recover industrial wastes, and an ineffective penalty system. According to Qu Geping (1982, 31), deputy director of the Environmental Protection Office which was established in the State Council in

1973, these problems were corrected by a series of new regulations that closed serious polluters or relocated them to remote areas, chose no new factory sites upwind of urban areas or upstream of rivers, and protected residential and recreational areas, scenic spots, historical sites, and nature conservation areas. The gradual introduction of new and better technology reduced the level of pollution caused by the discharge of pollutants into the air and water; for example, many cement factories are adopting new technologies that reduce solid waste discharges by a million or more tons a year, and several iron and steel works are using energy more efficiently, which reduces pollution. More industrial wastes are recovered, and adoption of the principle, "the polluter pays," resulted in new initiatives to reduce pollution. My only comment is that, based on personal observation in 1982 of the area between Beijing and Shanghai, use of the past tense is not yet warranted.

Environmental problems that are due to the expansion of the agricultural sector (the least modern of the economy) include destruction of forests and grasslands in order to increase acreage for grain production; the misuse of land proved damaging to the ecological system, caused erosion and loss of top soil, and resulted in decreased fishing and pasturage. The state responded in 1979 by adjusting agricultural activity to suit nature, by protecting forests and establishing green belts—called Green Great Walls—and by substituting biogas for agricultural wastes so that residues can be returned to the soil and enhance fertility (Qu Geping 1982, 32).

The basic principles of environmental protection in China are full-scale planning, rational allocation of industrial, agricultural, urban and transport enterprises, mass mobilization, and environmental protection for the benefit of the people. The National People's Congress is developing environmental legislation. The first water law, drafted in 1987, addresses such problems as serious shortages of water in northern China, water pollution, overexploitation of underground water in urban areas, and irrational water supply schemes in domestic, industrial, and agricultural sectors (Management Committee 1987).

If in the United States equity and access are assessed by differences between African-Americans and Whites and in the Soviet

Union by differences between Slavic and central Asian regions, in China the major variation occurs between urban and rural populations. The nationwide decline in infant mortality is nothing short of spectacular—from 200 per 1,000 live births in 1949 to 34 per 1,000 in 1986 (Young and Prost 1985, 5; World Bank 1988, 286, respectively). There was a sharp increase in 1960, the period of the mismanaged Great Leap Forward, when major agricultural failure occurred in two successive years of bad weather. Infant mortality continued to decline during the years of the Cultural Revolution (1966–1976), when whole sectors of the economy (for example, light industry and agriculture) were neglected or damaged, and education, science, and technology suffered (Christiani 1984, 606). However, rural infant mortality rates are about twice as high as urban rates. And a two-year review (1974–1976) of twelve provinces and cities indicated that rural infant mortality may be four times greater than urban rates (Young and Prost 1985, 1).

This chapter redefined equity and access in terms of access to the means of production and to material conditions that promote health; it then examined public health practice in three different settings. In the United States, vocal or rebellious groups use the mechanism of consumer demand to overcome limited participation, equity, and access to some degree. In the Soviet Union, where goods, services, and access are more evenly distributed, residual regional differences may be redressed in much the same way; the outcome of current rebellions in the southern Caucasus will be indicative. The marked urban-rural differences in China reflect the priorities of a developing industrial worker state. Current policy pronouncements suggest that differentiation will increase within the agricultural sector; as in the past, farmworkers will have to pay for most improvements themselves.

Each of these systems constrains the role of public health workers. Wherever one is situated as a public health worker, at whatever level one works, or whichever institution one works for, one's ability to increase the equity of the health care system, to improve equality of access, and to encourage democratic participation will depend first, on the place of public health within the larger economic and political system, and second, on the articulation of levels and institutions within the public sector. No doubt planning helps to alleviate the maldistribution of health care that follows the uneven development of capitalist economies. But, despite seventy years of international experience in health planning, there is no instance of truly equitable distribution. Every service complains of the concentration of physicians in urban centers and the paucity of care in rural areas. Success in achieving equal access is necessarily tied to equitable distribution; high cost is not the only barrier to health care, availability of facilities and personnel is another. The democratization of health care appears to be the most difficult problem of all, with no country able to implement a successful nationwide solution as yet.

Chapter 5

WOMEN'S HEALTH

THIS CHAPTER SERVES several purposes. One is to illustrate how the new principles I have outlined result in a radically different approach to women's health from that taken by conventional public health programs or even by the women's health movement. A second purpose is to put women's health needs on the public health agenda, not in the narrow context of maternal and child health (which is usually about child health and not women's health anyway), nor in the restrictive sense of reproductive health (which is generally dominated by the medical concerns of obstetrics and gynecology), but in the broad context of what is commonly called women's status. Since status is a static word I prefer to refer to women's power. What I mean by women's power is not only the political participation of women in public life, but also the expression of women's status in legislation; not only the economic participation of women in the labor force, but also the payment of women for their work; and not only the ideology of women's roles, but also the amount and content of education to which they have access. These issues are explored in case studies of women's health in three African countries: Algeria, Burkina Faso, and Tanzania.

The relation of gender to health is often expressed in mortality differentials, that is, the differences in mortality patterns and death ratios between males and females. In advanced industrial countries, female life expectancy is longer than male life expectancy and female mortality rates are lower in each age group. In Africa, differences in life expectancy between the sexes are less pronounced than in advanced industrial countries, and in some

African countries female mortality is higher than male mortality in certain age-groups.

I shall explore the relation of gender to health by focusing on the social production of illness rather than on biological or environmental causes of disease. Explanations of mortality differentials range from the sociobiological to the sociocultural. Sociobiologists hold that women are biologically superior to men and endowed with greater stamina, which accounts for their greater longevity (Hammoud 1977; Lopez 1983; Montagu 1968). Sociocultural theorists hold that women indulge less than men in certain disease-producing behaviors (such as competing aggressively, smoking and drinking, and working in physically hazardous jobs) and therefore are less likely to suffer from the conditions associated with the principal causes of death (Waldron 1976). Sociocultural theory emphasizes the health consequences of discriminatory attitudes toward women in the Third World, citing the deleterious effects of frequent pregnancies (Bhatia 1983).

This chapter does not examine medical conditions specific to women's reproductive capacity or the clinical consequences of discrimination against women; instead it situates male/female mortality differentials within the theoretical framework of political economy and feminist work on the subordination of women (Young, Wolkowitz, and McCullagh 1981). The concept of women's subordination differs from that of discrimination in two important respects: first, subordination refers to relations of gender and to male dominance of those relations, not to any biologically determined roles or functions; second, subordination refers to relations deriving from the economic organization of society (Young 1979, 2). The concept is dynamic, not static, and historically specific. In this framework, women's health status reflects not only men's relative dominance of women but also changing economic relations—for example, new sexual divisions of labor, new forms of production, and changing conditions of reproduction.

The foremost determinant of people's health, irrespective of sex, is the economic formation that characterizes the society in which men and women live and work. To say that illness is socially produced is to say that the social relations of production and the forces of production determine disease patterns and health services, but it is important to separate the impact of the level of national development from the effect of the economic system. This chapter discusses the relation of private ownership and management of property to diseases of affluence among members of the dominant class, diseases of poverty among workers and proletarianized farmers, high urban concentrations of medical services catering to the ruling class, and limited access to health care by urban and rural wage workers. It also links the concept of highly socialized relations of production (meaning that workers are truly empowered and that government ownership is not merely a substitute for private ownership as in many nationalizations) to the more even distribution across classes of disease patterns and access to health services. Finally, it shows relationships between rising levels of development, the decreasing incidence and prevalence of diseases of poverty, and increasing numbers of health facilities and trained health personnel.

Women's health and health care are not necessarily the same as or equal to men's health status and services. Although conditioned by the limits and possibilities of the same economic formation, women's health and health care vary significantly according to the control women have of reproduction and of their labor, control that is a function of their economic, social, and political participation in society. Participation can be gauged by examining five areas of state policy suggested by Molyneux (1981): legislation, family policy, education and ideology, employment, and political representation. How women's interests are expressed in these five areas is predictive of whether women control definitions of health and illness, whether health care is adapted to their needs, and what access they have to health care.

These five areas of state policy are examined in Algeria, Burkina Faso, and Tanzania in order to describe the relation of gender to health in historically specific economic formations.[1] Algeria and Tanzania are representative of relatively developed and underdeveloped planned economies in which there is some socialization of capital but little of labor. Burkina Faso (Upper Volta before the coup d'état of August 1983) represents a relatively underdeveloped free market economy.

Burkina Faso

Burkina Faso was part of the French West African colonial empire from 1896 to 1960. From 1904 to 1919 it was administered together with Senegal and Niger. It was detached in 1920 but not considered economically viable; in 1932 the country was divided into three parts and apportioned to Niger, Mali (then the French Soudan), and the Ivory Coast (Songre 1973, 207). It was not reassembled as a nation until 1947. Lacking any mineral or other resources of commercial value to the French, this landlocked country to the north of Ghana and the Ivory Coast was exploited for its human resources (Cordell and Gregory 1982).

At the beginning of the colonial period, adult males were forced to work on roads, railways, ports, mines, and plantations, often at great distances from their homes. Although forced labor was eventually repealed,[2] men found it necessary to migrate (most often to Ghana and the Ivory Coast) in search of work to pay their taxes. The colonial power failed to provide alternative sources of local employment although family farms were overworked, yielding less each year and showing signs of severe soil erosion. The commercial cultivation of cotton, peanuts, and sesame for export was introduced, but this agriculture was never profitable enough to provide a livelihood and only curtailed food production. Migration appears to have quickened the destruction of soil fertility but not to have alleviated population pressure on the land of the central plateau.

There are two distinct modes of production in Burkina Faso. Pastoralism is predominant in the northern Sahelian region where the severe drought of the late 1960s/early 1970s decimated the cattle herds of the nomadic population (Franke and Chasin 1980, 17). Taylor (1981, 102) reports that desertification is progressing at an alarming rate. If drought recurs, he says, this mode of production may disappear.[3] In the southern region, rainfall while irregular is sufficient to support permanent agriculture. Most of the country's 8.1 million inhabitants (1986 estimate) are concentrated in the South on the central plateau.

Burkina Faso is among the ten poorest of fifty low-income countries in the world, one of the thirty least developed, and among the forty-five countries most seriously affected by adverse global economic conditions (Kurian 1978, 1509). Poverty is reflected in the principal health indicators: in 1986 the crude birthrate was 47 per 1,000 population, the crude death rate 19 per 1,000, infant mortality was around 140 per 1,000 live births, and life expectancy at birth was 47 years (World Bank 1988).

Burkina Faso is an open economy with a markedly uneven distribution of wealth, which was ten times greater in urban (9 percent of the population) than in rural areas by the mid-1970s (Taylor 1981, 104). The public sector is the major employer; the government controls marketing for export (mainly to France and the Ivory Coast), which amounts to nothing less than the bureaucracy skimming off a percentage of the profit from peasant production (Dumont 1981, 6; Reyna 1983, 218; Conti 1979, 81). There is practically no industry, and the paid labor force is small.[4] Since independence, Burkina Faso's dependency has been successfully maintained by the Ivory Coast which, backed by France, has blocked every breakaway initiative for regional economic cooperation (Bach 1982, 95–97). In August 1983 Thomas Sankara took power and initiated a remarkable period of innovative domestic policies, the establishment of self-help associations and cooperatives, and popular participation in political life, particularly by rural villagers (Harsch 1988). Unfortunately, he was killed and his popular regime overthrown in the October 1987 military putsch.

The scale of migration from Burkina Faso is staggering: close to one million people—17 percent of the population—were living in another West African country in 1975 (Zachariah and Condé 1981, 42). Most migrants are men and most go to the Ivory Coast (Songre 1973, 206). The migrants are paid substandard wages and the meager savings they send home are used to buy food, agricultural supplies, and equipment. These remittances are not a source of savings or investment for Burkina Faso and may even be a source of inflation (Songre 1973, 211–212). (See Gregory 1979 for an analysis of the impact of migration on development and independence in Burkina Faso.)

A study of the impact of migration on women was carried out by Ouédraogo and Ouédraogo for the United Nations Research Institute for Social Development in 1983. Three sites were chosen for the investigation, one a source of internal and international migrants, the second a region of spontaneous settlement of internal migrants, and the third a region of internal migrants settled by the Volta Valley Authority (*Aménagement des Vallées des Volta*, hereafter AVV), a government agency that depends wholly on West European capital.

In the first setting, represented in the study by the north central department, all energy is devoted to subsistence production of grain (millet and sorghum) on family plots, the harvest destined for family consumption. Because adult males are absent, women's agricultural tasks are increased, and productivity continues to fall, soils to lose their fertility, and the margin for survival in times of drought continues to narrow. More and more land is given over to food cultivation, including land that should be left fallow and the "personal" lands of women that normally produce surplus or reserves. Women can undertake fewer nonagricultural and complementary tasks (for example, handicrafts, food processing, and the cultivation of vegetables to supplement the staple cereal) that would add to the family's income, because they no longer have time for this work (Ouédraogo and Ouédraogo 1983, 9). In 1980–81, a drought year, the grain deficit in the north central department represented 55 percent of the population's consumption needs (ibid., 5).

Of the second setting, that of spontaneous internal migration, Dumont (1981, 11) says that these settlements have been more profitable than the government-sponsored (AVV) villages. In both cases, the land in the fertile valleys of the Volta River has been made accessible by the expensive, high-tech, internationally financed campaign to eradicate the black fly, carrier of onchocerciasis (river blindness), that infested the area; the reports of the campaign secretariat (which is composed of the sponsoring agencies) indicate that the AVV will eventually take over the spontaneous settlements (Joint Programme Committee 1980, 1981).

The situation of women varies markedly in the two settings, according to Ouédraogo and Ouédraogo. In the areas of spontaneous settlement, women's position is enhanced by the availability of fertile land, which guarantees food self-sufficiency, and by a favorable market structure, which permits women to attain some economic independence. On the other hand, their opportunities are limited by the lack of productive forces (for example, mechanized mills, water wells, wheelbarrows); by the failure of agricultural extension officers to train women because they do not produce cotton, the local cash crop grown by men; and by the distance they live from health and social services (Ouédraogo and Ouédraogo 1983, 16–17).

In contrast, women in the AVV settlements have no possibility of independent economic activity. The authority defines the labor unit on which land allocations are based as the nuclear family, and calculates its size by assigning a value of 100 to men between the ages of fifteen and fifty-five years, a value of 75 to women in that age-group, 50 to boys twelve to fifteen years old and old men fifty-five to sixty-five, and 25 to girls and old women (ibid., 22, 27). There is no room in this formula for the personal plots traditionally assigned to women that are a source of their economic independence. Nor, given the workload individual women bear without the assistance of cowives, is there time for commercial activity as an alternate source of income (Conti 1979, 88; Ouédraogo and Ouédraogo 1983, 26–27). The labor strategy adopted for the development of agriculture in Burkina Faso is to employ women in what Conti calls the capitalist organization of production through noncapitalist production relations. This strategy also reinforces the historical drive for men to migrate. The contrast to the Ivory Coast, where the labor strategy is to employ men (many of them migrants from Burkina Faso), is striking. (See Traoré 1981 for an analysis of how this labor strategy affects women in the Ivory Coast.)

Several authors (Conti 1979, 81; Ouédraogo and Ouédraogo 1983, 27; Reyna 1983, 215) note that the AVV system of making peasants responsible for growing their own food while maintaining control over the productive forces (land use, credit, fertilizer, machinery, and so on) entails the extreme exploitation of women and results in the production of very cheap cotton for the European textile industry.[5] Reyna (1983, 216) declares that AVV peasants are worse off than sharecroppers or wage laborers because the peasants bear a major portion of production costs and risks but have no control over land use decisions nor any way of insulating their incomes against failure.

Women have led a number of protests in the AVV settlements; many have insisted on leaving but their options are very limited.

In a study of divorce in the customary court of Bobo-Dioulasso, Bohmer (1980, 82) found that the divorce rate is rising; but, because the law discriminates against women, she does not infer that they are initiating proceedings more frequently. Before the new Family Code was proposed in 1986, divorcees could not hope for alimony or even a share of common property, and their children belonged to their husbands; they sometimes found their own families unwilling to take them back, while jobs that would support them were hard to find in the city.

The health of women in Burkina Faso is poor and in some areas appears to be deteriorating. Malaria is holoendemic, schistosomiasis and onchocerciasis are widespread, and leprosy is still an important disease (Merkle 1983, 195). Only 107 cases of AIDS were reported to WHO as of 10 February 1989, and if Burkina follows the pattern of other African countries, half of the AIDS patients are women (WHO 1989). In nine of sixteen five-year age-groups from birth to ninety years, women have higher death rates than men; the difference is particularly pronounced in the age-group twenty to twenty-nine years (Kabone n.d., 4). The rate of maternal deaths in government maternity wards was 330 per 100,000 deliveries in 1978, according to the World Bank (1982, 5, 51). As only 23 percent of deliveries take place in government wards, the Bank is cautious not to extrapolate this rate to the whole population. The countrywide rate is probably three times higher because "the number of deaths in women aged 15–44 exceeds by 4,500 the expected number if they had the same death rate as males in the same age group" (ibid., 5).

The World Bank reports that there is evidence of serious malnutrition among pregnant and lactating women; for example, data on birthweight reveal that over 20 percent of live-born infants weighed less than twenty-five hundred grams at birth, which suggests that "malnutrition in the mother is a significant factor in many infant deaths" (ibid., 7).

Health Services in Burkina Faso

Health services in Burkina Faso are public, and all western-trained medical personnel are employed by the government. Private practice does exist, although in theory it is restricted to medical officers who have devoted ten years to public service. In reality, most physicians see private patients in government facilities, and many nurses operate illegal clinics at home after business hours (World Bank 1982, 8). National health insurance covers only about 60,000 workers in the private sector and is limited to medical expenditures and disabilities caused by occupational injuries (ibid., 12).

There are forty rural health centers to serve the country's 7,000 villages. Regional differences in numbers and density of health facilities are pronounced, as are urban/rural discrepancies. On average only 45 percent of the population lives within ten kilometers of a health facility; in four of the eleven departments into which the country is divided, one facility serves 20,000 people. Sharp inequities in the allocation of health personnel follow this pattern. Whereas over 90 percent of the population live in rural areas, one-third of all health professionals practice in the two main towns of Ouagadougou and Bobo-Dioulasso. Two of the most populous departments, Koudougou and Kayu, and one of the poorest, Sahel, have the worst ratios of inhabitants to health personnel. The situation with regard to obstetrics is acute: 91 percent of midwives were reported at the end of 1981 to be working in and around Ouagadougou and Bobo-Dioulasso. In the countryside, maternal and child health services are available only in the administrative centers (World Bank 1982, 1, 9, 10). The World Bank estimates that only 10–15 percent of pregnant women and preschool children have access to any maternal and child health facilities (ibid., 9).

In this situation, given high rates of morbidity, it is clear that most people rely on traditional medicine for their health care.

Traditional Medicine

The average use of government health services is low—calculated at 0.47 visits per person per year—which suggests limited coverage of the population, that is, restricted access on a geographical basis. The figure may also imply rejection of the care offered at these centers. Merkle (1983, 195–196) reports a widely-spaced network of health posts staffed by paramedicals who, for lack of drugs and medical supplies, are often unable to treat patients; not surprisingly, villagers cease to attend the clinics, preferring to treat themselves or go to a traditional healer. Kabone (n.d., 6) believes that patients prefer traditional to western medicine—"They will not consult physicians unless they have had no success with witch doctors"—and ascribes this to "ignorance, the reluctance to expose one's body, and the lack of confidence in European medicine."

In Burkina Faso the traditional healer is the most important source of health care, providing complete coverage and a wide range of services, with an approach to diagnosis and therapy that we would call holistic (Merkle 1983, 196). The system is private but payment in kind is accepted, which increases accessibility.[6] Traditional midwives, in addition to their obstetrical work, perform excision—that is, clitoridectomy without infibulation. The practice is widespread in urban as well as rural areas, among Muslims (30 percent of the population), Christians (20 percent), and animists (50 percent). Under bad hygienic conditions, girls (the operation is usually performed between the ages of ten and twelve years) have been known to die of tetanus.[7] In 1975 the Federation of Women of Burkina Faso undertook a daily radio campaign against the practice; according to one of the organizers, the campaign "was short-lived and was discontinued on account of adverse reaction from many quarters . . . educated women, teachers, midwives and nurses were also amongst those who reacted against the campaign" (Triendregeogon 1982, 362).

The Situation of Women

The data on women's health in Burkina Faso show high levels of morbidity and mortality. Death and illness rates are related to the country's low level of development; that level also accounts in part for the poverty of resources including health resources. But while the developmental level may explain the population's poor health, it cannot account for the differences between male and female mortality rates. The concentration of health facilities and health service personnel in urban areas accounts for some male/

female mortality differentials because male migration leaves the countryside overwhelmingly female.

Let us turn then to an appraisal of women's position in Burkina Faso. In the brief four years of Thomas Sankara's government, a new Family Code was proposed to reconcile the conflicting Napoleonic Code and various customary laws related to religious traditions. Under the new code, monogamy is to be the rule, women are to have a say in making certain household decisions such as management of household income, divorced women will no longer automatically be deprived of their children, and widows will not be forced to marry one of their husband's relatives (Novicki 1986, 30). If implemented, the new policy should alleviate women's difficult situation and, in areas where men are absent for long periods, ameliorate the plight of women left behind.

Farm policy emphasizes the nuclear family in the new development areas and is creating new degrees of dependency for women on men. Often, women's work is not remunerated. In the AVV schemes it is literally discounted—judged to be worth half or three-quarters that of men's work. Ouédraogo notes that the trend in recent economic transformations is toward the loss of women's former economic autonomy (ibid., 28); enabling women to earn an income was a priority probably not accomplished by the Sankara government's Ministry of Family Affairs. The Sankara regime apparently did little to improve women's literacy rates, which are 2.4 percent in Burkina Faso (and only 6.7 percent among men) (Merkle 1983, 195). School enrollment is low for both sexes; nationwide 11 percent of children are in primary school, but the figure is 75 percent for Ouagadougou and between 1 and 4 percent in the countryside (Dumont 1981, 8).

The Sankara government created the Union of Burkinabe Women in 1985 to mobilize and organize women. The union started at the bottom by electing village delegates, then departmental and provincial delegates, before nominating women to the national bureau, in order to avoid the problems of many African women's organizations which are run by educated urban women who are out of touch with the needs of villagers (ibid., 29). The new union compares favorably with the former village women's groups, which with their low membership were hardly independent or the equal of government officials and merely provided an efficient channel for international aid (Taylor 1981, 106). The Sankara government included five women ministers in the cabinet, suggesting that women's interests were represented in government decision-making.

Women's subordinate position in Burkina Faso improved during the Sankara years, but the improvements may not be lasting and health data do not reflect the changes. Women's subordinate position correlates with their poor health, and a reorganization of economic relations is probably necessary before any positive change in gender relations can occur.

TANZANIA

Tanzania, an East African nation that attained independence from Great Britain in 1961, adopted a socialist policy in 1967 when it published the Arusha Declaration. A consistent objective of socialism in Tanzania is equity, to achieve a society in which all have a gradually increasing basic level of material welfare before any individual lives in luxury. Some progress has been made toward achieving that goal as measured by income distribution. A study by van Ginneken (1976, 41) showed little inequality in the distribution of household expenditure and only slightly more in the distribution of landholdings by farm size in rural areas. Not unexpectedly, the proportion of poor households was much larger in rural than in urban areas.

Since 1967, the importance of state participation in the economy has grown and the government has nationalized numerous sectors such as banking. Government corporations called parastatals, in which the government is sole or major shareholder, exist in almost every area of agriculture, commerce, and industry; they operate with commercial freedom and, like private companies, are expected to show a profit. There is a private sector, which operates under a number of government restrictions, but the public sector is dominant.

While there has been extensive socialization of capital, the same cannot be said of labor. Soon after independence the government restricted trade union activity: in 1962 it limited the right to strike, prevented civil servants from joining unions, and increased the Tanganyika Federation of Labour's control of its constituent unions; after 1964 it allowed only one trade union, NUTA (Coulson 1982, 139–140). The government established workers' councils in 1969 but management rapidly dominated them (ibid., 284). The *Mwongozo* of 1971 set forth new party guidelines for popular control (reprinted in Coulson 1979, 36–42). This policy was widely appropriated by workers in their struggles with management. Tanzania experienced a wave of strikes and workers' occupations in 1972–73; government suppression of most of them set the tone for years to come (Mihyo 1975). In Coulson's words (1982, 289) "Workers would not control their factories, and they would have little or no power over the Tanzanian state."

The colonial policies of successive German and British regimes blocked capitalist development, and since independence the level of development has remained low. Tanzania, which had a population of 23.3 million in 1986, is on the United Nations list of the world's twenty-five least developed countries. In 1980, 86 percent of the active labor force was employed in agriculture, which accounted for 60 percent of gross domestic product in 1986 (World Bank 1988); subsistence farming contributes about half of that amount. The country has few natural resources: diamonds, the most important mineral, are mined in a fifty-fifty venture between the government and Williamson Diamonds. There are coal and iron ore reserves for steel production, as well as chemical production based on gas from offshore wells, but none of these resources represents major deposits.

The industrial sector is small, employing a mere 90,000 workers in manufacturing in 1980; 136,000 workers were employed in mining, public utilities, construction, and transport; and 57,000 worked for wages in trade and finance (ILO 1982, 67). Levels of technology are correspondingly low, and the industrial sector displays characteristic dependence on imported technology. To illustrate this point, many new factories built under the import substitution program involved only the last stage of manufacture or assembly of imported materials (Coulson 1982, 192). There is no production of machines or motor vehicles in the country.

With productive forces so low, one expects to find high levels of poverty. In terms of food consumption, the recommended minimum calorie intake is 2,300 kilocalories, the Tanzanian daily supply in 1985 was 2,316. In terms of the minimum wage law, 65 percent of rural and 20 percent of urban households were living in poverty in 1969 (van Ginneken 1976, 32, 37). In 1981 the figures, calculated in a different way, were 14.7 percent of urban and 25–30 percent of rural households (ILO 1982, 88). These data are nowhere broken down by sex. Assuming that Tanzania follows the pattern of other countries, more women than men live below the poverty line, however defined.

Health and Health Services

The health picture reflects this high incidence of poverty. There is a paucity of morbidity data in Tanzania, where statistics are more often the by-product of administrative requirements. The lack is especially acute with regard to women because the few available data are not broken down by sex. Information from small-scale surveys and hospital records shows that diseases of poverty are rife. In the 1980s, malnutrition affects about 43 percent of the children under five years old with mild to moderate forms of protein-calorie deficiency and 7 percent of children with severe forms (UNICEF 1988, 66). Communicable and parasitic diseases account for a high percentage of all diagnoses made in hospitals, and malaria—Tanzania's foremost disease problem, which is on the rise—is the leading cause of hospital attendance and admission. Tanzania reported 4,158 cases of AIDS to WHO on 31 December 1988, the second highest number in Africa after Uganda (WHO 1989).

The government estimates that poverty-linked diseases account for about three-quarters of all deaths. According to official figures, one out of five children dies before age five, although there has been a decline in average infant mortality rates from 161 per 1,000 live births in 1967 to 108 per 1,000 in 1986, and a corresponding increase in average life expectancy, which is now about fifty-one years (World Bank 1988, 286). An analysis of the 1973 National Demographic Survey shows the class distribution of mortality: infant mortality is lowest among professionals—48 per 1,000—and highest among agricultural workers—91 per 1,000; life expectancy is correlated—sixty-four years among professionals and fifty-three years among agricultural workers (ILO 1982, 305). Given the much higher national average of infant mortality (and lower life expectancy), these figures do not give a true picture of class inequalities.

Life expectancy was fifty-five years for women and fifty-one years for men in 1986. Maternal mortality rates in hospitals in 1980 were 370 per 100,000 live births (World Bank 1988, 286). (In contrast, the rate in the United States in 1980 was 9 per 100,000.) The crude birthrate is estimated at 50 per 1,000 population in 1986 and total fertility at 7.0 live births per woman; both figures are higher now than ten years ago.

Much better information is available on health services and it indicates that after 1972 the government reoriented health programs to serve the rural masses. Tanzania established and operates a rural health service network, largely with foreign aid.[8] The pace of construction of rural health centers and rural dispensaries accelerated while the rate of increase in hospital beds slowed appreciably (ILO 1982, 93). Within the hospital sector, however, there was a perceptible shift toward high-technology medicine. Despite overall low levels of technology and resources in the country, the number of beds in hospitals staffed by highly trained specialists more than doubled. Over half of Tanzania's total health expenditure continues to finance urban-based, high-technology hospital services (Cornia, Jolly, and Stewart 1987, 175).

In terms of access to health care, Tanzania made important efforts to equalize the distribution of facilities. About 75 percent of Tanzanians live within one hour of a health facility (UNICEF 1988, 68). In 1984 there were 1,065 physicians, about 150 hospitals with 20,000 beds, 250 rural health centers, and 2,600 dispensaries (Omari 1987).

Most Tanzanians rely upon a combination of traditional medicine and western medicine for their health care (Feierman 1981). Western medicine is dispensed through a hierarchy of services. At the base is the village health service, which aims at providing simple medical and health care in villages. Run by part-time personnel known as village medical helpers, who are recruited from within the village on the recommendation of villagers, the system is consciously patterned after the Chinese commune health scheme staffed by "barefoot doctors." However, only one percent of the health budget is devoted to these "first aid boxes," and there is little incentive for the village medical helpers to use them (ILO 1982, 311).

Above the village health service is the dispensary, the primary unit for medical treatment under the British colonial regime, which remains the foundation of the health care delivery system. At the next level is the health center, which provides inpatient as well as outpatient curative treatment and midwifery services and, in principle, is responsible for such preventive work as maternal and child health care, immunization, health education, and environmental sanitation. Staffed by medical assistants, nurses, and health auxiliaries, these centers are perceived by health personnel as predominantly curative in function (van Etten 1976, 199). Next is the general hospital, which is usually located in the district capital and is staffed by a physician, who is often the district medical officer. As a result of this location and combination of duties, the district medical officer may neglect public health work in the face of the overwhelming clinical work load and the physician's personal preference for clinical care. Finally, there are regional and consultant hospitals, which provide specialist services and are not considered part of the basic health service structure. They were intended to serve large populations, but for the most part they draw patients from the urban centers in which they are located. Although the 1972 reorientation of health care pledged a halt to the construction of these expensive establishments which consume such a large part of the health budget in recurrent costs, two new consultant hospitals were constructed.

A new maternal and child health (MCH) program was initiated in 1974–1975 with a grant from USAID, the U.S. Agency for International Development, for the purpose of introducing family planning. The program trains MCH aides to work in dispensaries; reportedly there is a disparity between these aides' perception of health problems and that of the peasant women they serve. Other paramedicals staff rural health centers, which are equipped with a small six-bed maternity ward. Utilization rates are not reported, nor are figures broken down to show expenditures on maternal and child health. An average of 54 percent of all deliveries is said to take place outside health institutions; typically the figure is 70 percent in rural districts (ILO 1982, 312).

On balance, the government's record in providing health services and equalizing access to them has surpassed what might be expected of a poor country, one so little developed. To some degree this achievement reflects the socialization of capital; however, given the heavy dependence on foreign aid, important questions may be raised as to whether the government, let alone the people of Tanzania, is in control of this health care system. There appears to be little socialization of labor within the health sector, which mirrors the condition of workers generally.

Women's Participation

Women are conspicuously absent from nationalist histories of Tanzania. All the more reason, one would think, for paying attention to women after independence. The party program promised that socialist reorganization would improve conditions for women and children in the rural areas. The collective organization of production would assure an even distribution of labor. Although Nyerere (1967, 3) did not single out women as a group for whom collectivization would be especially advantageous, he was mindful of the need to improve their lot. He acknowledged that they were ill-treated and regarded as inferior in traditional society, which enforced their subservience even though they did, and still do, more than their fair share of the work in the fields and at home.

A report by Brain (1976) stated that women were signficantly worse off in a settlement than they had been in their traditional societies where they had held considerable rights in land: in the settlements all rights in land were vested in the husband and, as a corollary, all proceeds were handed over to him. If this report reflects conditions generally, then it would seem that the new villages adopted the more conservative customs of Tanzanian society and did not improve power and property relations between women and men. Cooperatives excluded women from membership in much the same way. When they designated men "head of household" for membership purposes, they excluded women from the societies, even though women were responsible for productive activities (Apthorpe 1977, 6). According to Bryceson and Mbilinyi (1978, 54), the marriage law of 1971 crystallized patrilineal organization, perpetuating the oppressed position of women as minors that was legislated by the colonial regime.

Koda maintains that there are no legal or official political obstacles to women's participation in any aspect of Tanzanian national life; only the traditional role of women in society constitutes a de facto barrier to their advancement (ILO 1982, 141). The mass adult education program of the mid-1970s largely eliminated discrimination against women in education; female literacy rose from 18 percent in 1970 to 88 percent in 1985 (UNICEF 1988, 70). After the government introduced universal primary education in 1977, the primary school enrollment ratio for girls rose from 18 percent in 1960 to 81 percent in 1983–1986, achieving parity with boys (about three-quarters of those enrolled actually finish primary school) (UNICEF 1988, 70). In secondary and university education, there is still an imbalance between male and female enrollments; the situation is even worse in vocational and technical schooling.

With respect to employment, women's labor force participation rates are estimated at 75 percent, if housework and subsistence farm work are included. Women's participation in the formal wage sector, however, was only 20 percent in 1980 (ILO 1982, 143). The majority are employed in medium skill jobs, such as teaching, nursing, and typing; their wages vary from just above minimum to three or four times that level (ibid.). In urban areas, there is growing participation of women in the informal sector where the sale of cooked food and home-brewed beer brings in a meager income. The position of women in this group is thought to have deteriorated considerably in the past few years. According to a survey of women workers in Dar es Salaam made by Swantz and Bryceson, women thrown out of work spend more time cultivating their small vegetable gardens and may turn to the casual sale of sexual services to supplement their incomes (Bryceson 1980).

Formal women's organizations existed before independence. Under the leadership of Bibi Titi Mohamed, African women developed a women's section of the male-dominated nationalist movement; their task was to mobilize rural women for political independence (Geiger 1982, 47). In 1962 the group was renamed *Umoja wa Wanawake wa Tanzania* (UWT), the United Women of Tanzania, and became an affiliate of TANU; thus from the beginning the party denied it the autonomy western feminists believe is an essential precondition for any successful women's struggle (Molyneux 1981, 180). The founding objectives of UWT were to bring together all the women of mainland Tanzania to think, speak, and act together; to promote the unity of the nation; to foster women's participation in economic, educational, political, cultural, and health activities; to cooperate with the government and the party on women's issues; and to uphold the rights and dignity of women (Kokuhirwa n.d.).

Membership in UWT is open to Tanzanian women sixteen years and over; groups of women as well as individuals can join. By 1979, reportedly there were 3,000 branches with 180,000 members on the mainland. Geiger (1982, 50) warns that membership figures are unreliable because it is difficult to keep track of women who fail to pay monthly dues. The administrative structure of the organization follows the pyramidal shape of government with elected and appointed leaders at the national level and paid workers in the regional and district offices. On the divisional level and below, the leaders are volunteers; most of them are retired teachers, nurses, mission workers—in principle women with a good level of literacy. In practice, UWT branches are understaffed at all levels, in part for lack of trained personnel (ibid., 51).

The provision of day care, which enables women to participate more fully in national development, has been an important activity; the UWT, in collaboration with the Ministry of Labour and Social Welfare, has succeeded in establishing day-care centers throughout the country. In 1980 nearly 3,000 centers were operated by a variety of agencies (ILO 1982, 145–146).

The UWT has its own institute for training women in leadership, home economics, needlework, child care, nutrition, hygiene, and agriculture. UWT projects include assisting women to produce clothing, training them to set up small businesses, and helping them to obtain credit from wholesalers, working capital from the Tanzanian Rural Development Bank, and machinery on the installment plan (UN Economic Commission for Africa 1976, 78–79). Other ventures set up with UWT's help to generate income were: small-scale industries, cooperative handicraft groups and shops, vegetable gardens and farms, poultry units, hotels, restaurants, and beer stores. Geiger (1982, 50, 59) points out that these projects do not challenge the conventional sexual division of labor; to do so, she argues, would provoke fierce resistance from village men. For her, the central question not addressed by UWT development projects is whether women control their own labor.

The UWT is credited with having provided women with a forum to air their grievances, to organize production, and to campaign against sexually discriminatory and exploitive laws and traditional practices. Critics say the organization is made up of big men's wives, has a predominantly urban rather than rural membership, and mirrors women's weaknesses and lack of unity instead of improving their position. One report from Moshi indicates both the great need for a protective society that would serve women's interests and the failure of UWT to play this role:

> There is no sign of a woman's movement designed to improve women's position at home and in society. Women do not know or cannot defend their most elementary legal rights (on rape, on maintenance of children, etc.), they work for half of the male wage (for the same work) on private estates, and tolerate oppression and neglect at home without ever considering any way of organizing to find a solution to any of these problems. If they do unite, it is usually to run a beer club, while every single one of them will complain about male alcoholism (von Freyhold, Sawaki, and Zalla 1973, 204–205).

Political representation could give women another power base from which to organize and solve their problems. Unfortunately, few women appear to be active in government or party ranks (Kjekshus 1975). In the 1975 general election, only nineteen female members of Parliament were elected or nominated; two female ministers were appointed and two others were elected to represent Tanzania at the East Africa Legislative Assembly. There was some better integration at higher levels of administration: one judge, six state attorneys, one first secretary, and two third secretaries were women (Reynolds 1975, 26). The Ministry of Health employed sixty women in professional positions and the Ministry of Education twenty-seven. Statistics are lacking on women's participation in the lowest ranks of the party; reports from the decade after independence gave the impression that few women were active (Proctor 1971).

An account of formal organization says nothing about informal mutual assistance among women. Like the contention that women are the real decision-makers in Mediterranean households, the assertion that women's true support groups are informal raises questions of how effective women can be if they are denied public power and restricted to informal, relatively private, levels of action. The answer lies in an analysis of the mode of production: in precapitalist modes of production where the family or clan held political power, women were empowered; in capitalist and socialist societies where power is in the public sphere, women are disempowered.

Women's economic, social, and political participation in Tanzania is not extensive enough for them to be able to influence the health care system and make it responsive to their needs or ensure that the health budget is adequate to guarantee them access to even the most basic level of care, let alone control definitions of health and illness. Although not commensurate with women's economic contribution, maternal and child health services are provided at clinics in rural health centers, indicating that women have earned some degree of recognition. It is in the lack of specific data about their health status and health needs—as described by them and not by the medical profession—that one sees a reflection of women's lack of power.

ALGERIA

Algeria won independence from France in 1962 after a bloody seven-year struggle that ended 130 years of colonial rule. The war for liberation inspired a progressive and antiimperialist perspective that combined the desire to recover national identity with a goal of economic development for the satisfaction of human needs. Because it was decided that this could be accomplished only under public auspices, state control of the economy has progressed rapidly. After 1965, the government nationalized successively banks, mines, oil and natural gas reserves, plus some land and housing, and it created national commercial societies to control critical industrial, service, and foreign trade sectors. In 1976 the Algerian people adopted the National Charter for Socialism in a nationwide referendum; it represents the ideological and institutional consolidation of the country's socioeconomic achievements, and it affirms the role of Islam as the state religion.

Algeria, with an estimated population of 22.4 million in 1986, is classified by the World Bank (1988, 223) as an upper middle-income country; national income in that year was $2,590 per person. The public sector dominates the economy; foreign investment is held within a fixed maximum percentage; and, to a great extent, capital is socialized. Fifty-seven percent of the population is rural; agriculture employed 31 percent of the labor force in 1980 and accounted for 12 percent of gross domestic product (ibid., 227, 283). There are three agricultural sectors, cooperative, socialist, and private; the socialist sector dominates wine, citrus, and cash crop production, and the private sector produces most of the vegetables, grain, and other fruit. Livestock and fishing are commercially exploited.

The country has abundant resources, which are the basis of an ambitious industrialization plan. Algeria is the sixteenth largest oil producer in the world and its gas reserves are the fourth largest (Gèze et al. 1987, 610). Oil and oil products account for 98 percent of export earnings. Development is concentrated in heavy industry, which produces petrochemicals, plastics, fertilizers, iron, and steel.

Algeria, like Tanzania, is a one-party state. Under the control of the *Front de Libération Nationale* (FLN) are the trade unions, the *Union Générale des Travailleurs Algériens* and its agrarian counterpart, the *Union Nationale des Paysans Algériens*. After independence, workers' self-management was established in the industrial, commercial, and agricultural enterprises abandoned by their French owners. In the socialist agricultural sector, workers' committees continue to manage production. Some western observers are critical of Algerian socialism and point to self-management as evidence of failure (Clegg 1971; Pfeifer 1981). Without passing judgment, one may note that labor is extensively organized, in the professions as well as in agriculture and industry.

Health and Health Care

The health picture in Algeria reflects the rapid pace of development: the pathology of industrialized societies coexists with that of underdeveloped countries. While the general death rate is declining, the crude birthrate is still very high (40 per 1,000 population), resulting in a high annual rate of population growth (World Bank 1988, 277). Infant mortality remains high—77 per 1,000 live births in 1986 (down from 165 in 1960), with gastroenteritis the leading cause of infant death (48 percent) and a major cause of child mortality (25 percent in the one-to-four-year age-group). Varying in inverse relation, life expectancy has risen from forty-seven years in 1960 to sixty-two years in 1986. Road accidents, work accidents, and occupational diseases are rising dramatically and are increasingly responsible for death, disability, and lost days at work. The government reported thirteen cases of AIDS to WHO on 26 March 1988 (WHO 1989).

Algeria has made progress in combating malnutrition, which was severe among 6 percent of children under six years old in 1964; in 1975 this figure fell to 2.6 percent, and by 1982 severe malnutrition was said to have all but disappeared (Kacha, Ouchfoun, and Yaker 1983, 9). Daily calorie supplies per person were 2,799 kilocalories in 1985. However, these figures tell us nothing about household distribution of food, either within families or across classes.

Class differences in infant mortality were indirectly measured (using education and occupation as indicators) in a survey undertaken in 1974–1975 by WHO and the Ministry of Public Health (WHO 1981). Infant mortality was 148 per 1,000 live births when the head of household (most often the father) was illiterate, fell to 131 per 1,000 when the head of household had attended primary school, and to 75 per 1,000 when he had undertaken secondary or higher studies. The rates were 161 per 1,000 when the head of household was an agricultural laborer, 134 per 1,000 when he was a skilled worker or craftsman, and 111 when he was an office worker.

Communicable diseases that can be controlled by immunization have declined, in some cases dramatically: diphtheria dropped from 3.52 per 100,000 in 1963 to 0.08 in 1982; tetanus fell from 0.53 per 100,000 in 1963 to 0.32 in 1982; whooping cough from 5.46 to 2.97 per 100,000; polio, after an initial decline, is actually on the rise (ibid., 3–4). On the other hand, the incidence of water-borne communicable diseases (typhoid fever, dysentery, cholera, and hepatitis)—few of which can be prevented by immunization—has soared in recent years. Evidently housing construction and water and sewage installations have not kept pace with urbanization and industrialization.

The incidence figures for communicable diseases are not broken down by sex. Death rates by age are, however, and they show that female mortality is higher between two months and four years (WHO 1981, 62) and in the age brackets fifteen to twenty-four years and thirty to thirty-nine years. The rate of maternal mortality was 129 per 1,000 live births in 1980 (World Bank 1988, 287). The percentage of births attended by qualified personnel rose from 25 in 1974 to 50 in 1984, but a lower percentage of pregnant women currently receive prenatal care. Algerian medical authorities attribute higher mortality in female adults to the increased risk of death in childbirth in the younger and older child-bearing groups (Kacha, Ouchfoun, and Yaker 1983, 8).

Taken together the figures on water-borne communicable diseases and general mortality rates suggest the low priority that Algerian national planners assign to women and to children under fifteen, even though they represent 70 percent of the population. Since women's participation in the waged labor force is barely 3 percent, most women in urban areas are at home caring for children, who often suffer from diarrheal diseases, in environmental conditions that are unsanitary and industrially polluted, where "at home" may be a shack in a shantytown or a two-room apartment that accommodates eight to ten people. These circumstances of greater exposure to infection may tell us as much about women's higher death rates as primagravidity (first pregnancy) and grand multiparity (women bearing more than six children).

Health services are well-developed in Algeria. They fall into three categories: the public sector (the state health system that is divided into 156 sanitary sectors [roughly *dairas* or counties], each with a hospital and its satellite centers—it covers the entire country and is responsible for training all personnel); the private sector; and social security (the parastatal sector).[9] In 1981 there were 8,590 persons for every doctor in the country and 2,630 for every nurse (World Bank 1988, 279). Health personnel are not evenly distributed: in the urbanized coastal province of Oran, there is one doctor for every 1,200 inhabitants; in the rural province of Jijel, there is one for every 9,000. One-third of the specialists are concentrated in the three major cities that have university teaching hospitals. In addition, the paramedical corps is heavily weighted toward curative, hospital-based medicine; a third of the paramedical personnel practice in the three urbanized provinces of Algiers, Constantine, and Oran. For the 4 million women of childbearing age there are only 806 maternal and child health centers and 850 midwives.

Les Algériennes

Women's participation in Algeria is the object of struggle. In 1976, fifteen years after independence, public debate was necessary to obtain the inclusion of a single paragraph on women in the National Charter for Socialism. That paragraph reads,

> The improvement of women's lot entails the transformation of a negative psychological and legal environment that is prejudicial to the exercise of the recognized rights of *wives and mothers* to material and emotional security. Thus there must be an end to exorbitant and ruinous dowries [brideprice], to the unscrupulous abandonment of defenceless mothers with children, to the snatching of children from their mothers, to groundless divorce with no provision for divorced women, to violence against women committed with impunity, and to the exploitation of women by antisocial elements (*République Algérienne* 1976, 71–71). [italics added]

The women's struggle erupted again in public debate in 1981 when the National Assembly attempted to pass a Family Code that was couched in discriminatory language and that would reduce women to the status of minors, dependent on husbands or fathers (Louis 1982). The brutality of the police when confronting the women's delegations and the refusal of the official organizations to deal with the objections of women from the university—even when they were backed by prestigious women who had fought in the war of liberation—angered women to a point at which they took to the streets to manifest their rejection of the bill.

The picture of women's position in education is a little brighter and continues to improve: in 1985, 104 percent of boys and 83 percent of girls were enrolled in primary school; 41 percent of boys and 50 percent of girls were in secondary schools (the figure for boys in primary schools is higher than 100 percent because it exceeds the usual age range [World Bank 1988, 281]).

Labor force participation rates for Algerian women are the lowest recorded in Africa; according to mid-1970s data from the ILO, the rate is over 50 percent in Burkina Faso, between 30 and 39 percent in Tanzania, and under 10 percent in Algeria (Tahon 1982, 45). Tahon studied women's employment in Algeria and found that women were increasingly excluded from the growing public sector and were shifting into marginal jobs in the tertiary sector. She concluded that "the concentration of women in socially unrecognized domestic employment is perpetuated by official policy in Algeria" (ibid., 43).

Finally, with respect to political participation, the *Union Nationale des Femmes Algériennes*, the women's organization, is dependent on the party (FLN) and, in the case of the debates on the family code, was not permitted to play an independent or truly representational role (Louis 1982, 168–169). Nor does the women's union dictate women's health policy: Annie Thébaud-Mony (1980, 415–416) examined the relation of the union to the definition of a health policy specifically oriented to women's health needs and concluded that physicians, not women, define those needs. The conclusion is clear and need not be belabored: Algerian women are not in control and the consequences of their subordination are to be seen in their poor health.

Health Consequences of Women's Subordination

To summarize, this chapter examined the specific situation of women in three countries, reporting what is known about their health in the context of gender relations and economic relations.

In Burkina Faso, changing economic relations are worsening women's material position and reinforcing male dominance. The dynamic of capitalist development and the process of imperialism in Burkina Faso spell an extremely exploitive and oppressive situation for women. The health consequences are seen in the appalling female mortality rates. As the government under the late president Thomas Sankara accepted the World Bank's conditions for loans, which include reductions in social spending, socialist rhetoric is unlikely to change the distribution of health services.

In Tanzania, changing relations of production affect women negatively, but positive changes in the distribution of goods and services offset somewhat the detrimental effect on their health. Paradoxically, Nyerere's policy of welfare statism has had a positive effect on the social relations of reproduction and a negative effect on production. Given the underdeveloped forces of production in Tanzania, that is, the very low level of resources and technology, one might have expected a health service hardly more developed than that of Burkina Faso. The policy of socialist redistribution, materially assisted by foreign donors, appears to have overcome this deficit partially by creating a dense network of rural health care posts. Women's key position in subsistence agriculture seems to aid their access to these services.

In Algeria, women do not appear to benefit commensurately from socialist relations of production nor from the country's real achievements in developing forces of production. Beyond the obvious advantages accruing to families from their control of women's labor, no explanation of the apparent importance of maintaining existing gender relations emerges from the data. Critics of an earlier version of this chapter pointed to the omission of any discussion of religious ideology, which might provide an explanation.

Western observers tend to oversimplify the contribution of Islamic religious values to Algerian women's subordination. Some

Arab women such as Nawal el Saadawi (1980) and Fatima Mernissi (1975) argue that to depict women's problems as stemming from Islam is tantamount to conceptualizing development as a process of cultural change, rather than as a battle for economic liberation from international capitalist domination of human and natural resources. Some North Africans such as the sociologist Abdelkebir Khatibi (1983) and the contemporary Algerian novelist Rachid Boudjedra recognize the need for a "double critique," that of their own societies as well as that of imperialist cultures.

That the existing social relations of gender operate to the extreme disadvantage of Algerian women is not in doubt, given the data presented on female infant and child mortality and maternal mortality. The question that remains unanswered is why the Algerian state uses the Muslim religious establishment to perpetuate existing gender relations at a time of rapid and radical changes in economic relations.

The propositions that emerge from this review of women's health may be expressed schematically as follows. Social relations of production and forces of production determine general levels of health and health services for men and women, but women's health is additionally affected by gender relations within the social relations of production as well as by the conditions of reproduction, which include the availability of maternal health services. In economies with similar economic formations, women's health tends to be better where women exercise control over reproduction. Where the ideology of those who control the state favors an equitable distribution of medical services, the conditions of reproduction may be improved. But improvements originating in state ideology cannot change health levels if gender relations and the social relations of production do not change fundamentally.

PART TWO

The Limits to Conventional Public Health

Chapter 6

CONTAINING DISEASE

ONE SURE AND COMPLETE way to protect the public's health is to ban the production and use of substances that endanger health. For example, we could ban the mining, manufacture, and use of asbestos or we could ban the production and proliferation of nuclear weapons and chemical and biological warfare. For the bans to be effective and enforceable, all nations would have to agree upon them. Unfortunately, legislators cannot banish all disease; so public health workers must select measures from among the three approaches available: cleansing the environment, eradicating disease, and containing disease. These approaches are the subject of the next three chapters.

When a hazardous agent has been disseminated in the environment, either by accident or carelessness or, possibly, ignorance, and public health authorities have determined that the population is endangered, the next step is to remove it—that is, to cleanse the environment of the offending agent, a costly and sometimes controversial procedure. Garbage collection and sewage systems are ways to cleanse the environment by removing wastes (which creates a new problem—how to dispose of the removed garbage and sludge). Another example is the removal of asbestos from schools and concert halls, a measure taken after parents and musicians' unions exerted pressure. In other examples such as nuclear waste, we do not know how to rid ourselves of the problem; the U.S. government proposes burial in salt mines as a temporary expedient.

A second, related, communitywide approach is disease eradication. In the case of smallpox, a global mass vaccination campaign achieved total eradication. To date no country has reported a case of smallpox since 1978. Although vaccination is a measure applied to protect individuals, the eradication of a disease requires planning and community organization; it is therefore a communitywide measure. In the case of malaria, a parasitic disease for which no vaccine is as yet in use, the practice has been to reduce the population of disease vectors—the anopheles mosquito, which transmits the disease—while suppressing symptoms with drugs such as chloroquine.

Another way to think of immunization is to regard it as a means of making individuals invincible so that they will not be affected by disease agents in the environment. Near invincibility can be achieved by the "space suit" approach, which is the encapsulation of a person in a clean environment that keeps out all contamination and stops contact with infectious and toxic agents. This approach is commonly used in industry, where workers are given protective clothing or devices to wear in hazardous environments.

The encapsulation of workers and the evacuation of threatened populations exemplify the principle of excluding disease agents from a clean area. Another example of keeping out hazards is the current attempt to create nuclear-free zones in cities and towns across the United States. Conversely, hazardous agents can also be contained in a limited area, as in the sealing of the nuclear reactor after the accident at Three Mile Island in 1979.

The French call the ring one throws around an area to keep out all infection a *cordon sanitaire*. This public health measure is related to the history of social stratification and the development of class society. When it was used to segregate towns, the *cordon-sanitaire* enabled the ruling classes to exercise control over colonial subjects and the working classes by concentrating them in ghettos. In minor epidemics, the *cordon sanitaire* separated the rich from the poor; in major outbreaks of disease, it entrapped the poor while the rich who had the resources fled to safety.

The three approaches—containment, eradication, and cleansing the environment—can be ranked in the same way as levels of public health action: the higher the level the more progressive the measure in that more people are protected. Of the three approaches, the most progressive is cleansing the environment, which removes disease habitats or several dangers simultaneously; the next most progressive is eradication, especially if it can be done by prohibiting the production and use of some offending agent; and the least progressive is the "space suit" approach because only the individual inside the space suit can be protected. But each approach, even when applied successfully, is limited. A public health program may help eradicate a particular problem (as mass vaccination helped eradicate smallpox) and still have little effect on overall mortality (the theory of nonspecific mortality) as well as not be applicable to other health problems (for example, malaria or malnutrition).

Containment occurs first historically, and it is the first to be examined in Part Two of this book. It was originally applied to diseases thought to be contagious. It is probably the oldest approach to public health work, predating scientific knowledge of disease causation. It is still in widespread use today and applies to hazardous materials such as dioxin as well as agents of infectious and chronic disease. The principle of containment underlies the cry of NIMBY—Not In My Backyard!

Four key concepts in containment are isolation, quarantine, notification, and surveillance. Isolation of the sick and their segregation from healthy people are the first measures taken when containment is implemented. By isolating the sick in a hospital or by placing a contaminated area under quarantine and prohibiting all traffic in or out of it, contact between the well and the ill is broken. For quarantine to function, public health workers must notify some governmental authority of outbreaks or of contamination: notification is another aspect of effective containment. Surveillance is the active monitoring of populations in delimited geographic areas to maintain control of the hazardous or infectious agent; it can also be undertaken as a preventive environmental measure. The success of containment depends upon police powers to halt flight or enforce orderly evacuation and removal of the sick from infected areas.

Two case studies—plague, from the history of epidemic diseases and dioxin from the annals of contemporary environmental disasters—illustrate the two aspects of containing disease within a defined area and of keeping it outside a clean space.

Case History of Plague

The social impact of epidemic disease is a favorite literary theme in which plague figures prominently. Probably the most famous example is the *Decameron* by Bocaccio, a series of narratives and conversations told in a villa near Florence during an epidemic of plague around 1348. Daniel Defoe's *A Journal of the Plague Year* (1970), first published in 1720, is not an authentic diary (the Great Plague swept London in 1665 when Defoe was only five years old) but a fictionalized account. Among twentieth-century French authors, Albert Camus described the plague in the Algerian port of Oran in 1942 (*La Peste*), and Antonin Artaud, the surrealist playwright and poet, wrote about plague as a social metaphor in an essay, "Theatre and the Plague." Artaud (1970, 18) compares theater to the plague because both act on large groups and disturb them in the same way. "Such a complete social disaster, such organic disorder overflowing with vice, this kind of wholesale exorcism constricting the soul, driving it to the limit, indicates the presence of a condition which is an extreme force and where all the powers of nature are newly rediscovered."

There are two kinds of plague, bubonic and pneumonic. The bubonic plague bacillus affects the lymphatic system and is insect-borne; the infected fleas are carried by rats. Bubonic plague is marked by fever, chills, prostration, and swelling of the lymph nodes in the groin, armpits, and elsewhere; hemorrhages occur, called buboes when they appear on the skin. When bubonic plague is established in populations, pneumonic plague, which affects the lungs and is air-borne, appears. Marked by difficult and hurried breathing and severe cough, pneumonic plague is more contagious and more fatal.

It is not clear whether all the deaths attributed to plague that occurred before the twentieth century were caused directly by the disease. Braudel (1967, 43–44) contends that diseases described in old texts are not readily identified by today's symptomatology. He thinks that famine, due in part to a general cooling of the climate in the fourteenth century, weakened resistance to disease, including plague. McNeill (1976) thinks famine prevented peasants from planting or harvesting crops; starvation rather than plague may have caused many deaths, and in their weakened, malnourished state, many more people could not resist other infectious diseases.

Historians have recorded four major outbreaks of plague. Little is known about the first pandemic (a pandemic is an epidemic of worldwide scale), which occurred in the fifth century B.C. in the area now known as Greece. The second pandemic occurred in 542 A.D. in the period of Justinian's reign in the Byzantine empire. The outbreak began in Egypt, affected all of western Europe but most especially southern France and Germany. It continued for 30, 60, or, in the case of England, 200 years before dying out (estimates vary in different sources). According to a contemporary account, deaths occurred in Istanbul at the rate of ten thousand per day. The historian Edward Gibbon thought that 100 million deaths had occurred by the end of the sixth century (Cloudsley-Thompson 1976, 60). On this scale, plague was impressive and it terrified people.

The third pandemic, which occurred in the middle of the fourteenth century, is the best known. Originating in China, it entered Europe between 1346 and 1348. Estimates of deaths are little better recorded than in the earlier pandemic: a total of 25 million people are thought to have died; some sources say 50 million. Mortality estimates are spectacular—75 percent of the population in southern France, 90 percent in parts of England. Some authorities think that Italy lost half of its population (McNeill 1976, 168).

According to some historians, the third pandemic of plague played a significant role in European demography by reducing the population dramatically and in ecology by reducing population pressure on land, pastures, and forests (Gottfried 1983). Plague also influenced European economic development by disrupting wage and price patterns sharply (wages rose as the number of workers declined and prices rose as food became scarce) and by exacerbating conflicts between social classes (McNeill 1976, 183). Sigerist (1943, 117) believes that the plague, along with famine (1315–1317 and 1340–1342), war (especially the Hundred Years' War), and social unrest (mass peasant uprisings), caused economic stagnation in the fourteenth century and the disintegration of the medieval economy. Kosminskii's (1971) interpretation differs in that he deemphasizes the contribution of plague; he does not find sufficient evidence of economic decline to justify the conclusion that epidemics caused stagnation, and he characterizes the discussion of population decline as Malthusian. Kosminskii sees an economic crisis in the way feudalism hindered the expansion of productive forces and dates the weakening of feudalism from the end of the fourteenth century when peasants balked at paying rents, sabotaged the system of forced labor (*corvée*), and finally rose up against their seigneurs. His interpretation is borne out by the English historian A. L. Morton (1974, 114–120), who examines the rise of competing commercial and industrial classes in the towns.

The clear antagonism between commercial interests and public health authorities is an interesting aspect of the history of the containment of plague. Chambers of commerce that want to protect trade or tourism do not advertise that plague or any other contagious disease is in the area because visitors and traders would avoid the city. The nobility and upper-class Venetians concerned about their health wanted to invoke a quarantine, which traders and the poor resisted; but on March 20, 1348, a year or two after plague entered Europe, the city of Venice appointed a sanitary council to place infected ships, goods, and people under quarantine. They did this at state expense, even though Italy did not exist as a unified nation then; Venice was a city-state and the highest civil authority to which one could appeal.

The sanitary council imposed a quarantine, literally forty days of isolation. The city ordered ships moored in the lagoon outside Venice and did not allow them to dock or unload. Infected sailors and travelers were sent to the island of Lazaro (the stem of the word *lazaretto,* which was the name of medieval hospitals for people with infectious diseases and later became identified with leprosy). The forty-day quarantine was largely ineffective; for the next five centuries epidemics repeatedly occurred in European cities, towns, and the countryside and caused a disproportionate number of deaths among the poor.

By 1485, 140 years after the first epidemic, the sanitary council had become a full-blown Council of Health that fixed the regulations adopted throughout the Mediterranean in all ports and harbors. The measures were: isolation and treatment of plague victims, who were generally the poor; purification of their personal effects; and segregation of all persons coming from infected countries. Initially authorities applied these regulations only to plague, but later they extended them to leprosy, yellow fever, and Asiatic cholera. With respect to cholera, the regulations appear to have helped little and, as plague declined, their failure to contain cholera gave rise to extensive questioning and eventual rethinking of the whole proposition of quarantine. By the mid-nineteenth century the British were the major maritime power, and they felt that quarantine impeded their commerce, especially as corruption had crept into the administration of the system (Howard-Jones 1975).

The system of quarantine was developed and substantially revised before the germ theory of disease was known. In the mid-nineteenth century people did not know what caused plague or cholera. There were two schools of thought: the miasmatists and the contagionists. The miasmatists believed that disease had external origins; they thought that a miasma (something in the air) was the cause of illness. Possibly malaria (which means bad air) was their archetypal disease, for they thought that the sources of disease were swamps, general filth, and decomposing corpses, which putrefied the air. In contrast, contagionists thought that disease had internal origins, that it arose within the body of the sick person and then spread from person to person (Sigerist 1943, 173).

Both theories lent support to the imposition of quarantine, but the contagionists preferred to use the *cordon sanitaire* in order to break contact between the person in whom the disease first arose and others to whom he or she might pass it on. They reasoned that if one could keep infected people out of a clean area, the healthy population would be safe. Quarantine was frequently used in the British colonial empire: in each of the capitals and major towns, a *cordon sanitaire* was set up to segregate residential areas for Whites only, with the so-called natives residing outside of them, which reinforced the colonists' prejudices about subject populations (Stock 1988). Colonists ignored the fact that the Whites-only areas had sanitary services, including garbage collection and night-soil removal, safe water supplies, housing codes and housing inspection, while the filthy "native" quarters had no such services and in general were overcrowded, with dilapidated housing.

The fourth pandemic is fairly recent; plague erupted in 1894 in China and traveled to all the important seaports of the world (McNeill 1976, 153). The barriers erected to contain the epidemic were breached at Indian ports, and the disease reached the interior where it killed some 6 million people in ten years (1898–1908). In most other countries containment was effective; epidemiologists identified the source and diffusion of the disease, and authorities followed with prophylactic measures.

With the changing nature of epidemics, the eradication of smallpox, and the development of effective antibiotics for the treatment of many contagious diseases including plague, public health authorities resort less often to the *cordon sanitaire* to contain epidemics of infectious disease; however, the threat of an AIDS epidemic has raised questions about the isolation of people with the syndrome. Communities protesting the location of new toxic waste sites or incinerators frequently invoke the principle of *cordon sanitaire*. Governments still use the principle of containment when they isolate the mentally ill and criminal populations (and, some would charge, the elderly) in institutions. And industry practices containment when it buries hazardous and toxic wastes that cannot be neutralized. The limitations of this strategy are made clear in the case study of dioxin.

Case History of Dioxin

If the *cordon sanitaire* represents a clean circle inside of a generally dirty area, the approach to the containment of dioxin illustrates the opposite: it tries to keep all of the hazardous material within a circumscribed area. Dioxin is the most toxic substance ever synthesized and probably the most powerful carcinogen known to science. It is a group of seventy-four chemicals; the ones most frequently of concern are a group called TCDD.[1] Dioxin does not fit the germ theory of disease because it is associated with a variety of conditions and illnesses: cancers, birth defects, spontaneous abortions, liver and kidney complaints, chloracne (a severe skin condition), and central nervous system disorders.

Dioxin does not break down in the human body, and there is no known antidote.

The history of dioxin is brief but well documented; scientists have studied few chemicals so extensively. In 1899, industry was using chlorinated aromatic compounds, and chemists knew they were powerful skin irritants causing chloracne, as the medical literature from that date indicates. In the 1930s, Dow Chemical Company introduced chlorophenyls and reported cases of chloracne in the medical journals. In 1936 the Dow plant in Michigan that manufactured chlorophenyls experienced an accident; it affected twenty-one workers, but the company did not follow the medical history of these workers or carry out any other medical studies. In 1949, an explosion occurred at a Monsanto plant in Nitro, West Virginia, a plant that produced 2,4,5-T, a herbicide made with a chemical that produces TCDD as a by-product.[2] This accident affected 228 workers and seriously injured 122. From that date the rhythm of accidents accelerates.

In 1953 a BASF plant in West Germany had a serious accident; in 1961 a second accident occurred at the Dow plant in Midland, Michigan; in 1963 there was an accident at the Phillips plant in the Netherlands; in 1968 the Coalite products plant in England experienced a serious problem; and on July 10, 1976 a severe explosion occurred at the *Industrie Chimiche Meda Societa Anonima* (ICMESA) plant in Seveso, Italy.

As this history indicates, there is little mystery about dioxin; knowledge of its toxic properties dates back to the 1930s, and the record contains extensive occupational experience with the chemical. Yet the environmental effects were unknown and unstudied before the accident at Seveso. Interestingly, the information needed to solve environmental problems is frequently to be found on the other side of the plant fence, within occupational health records. Despite this direct link, occupational and environmental conditions are often studied separately and handled differently, even by different government agencies. In the United States the Occupational Safety and Health Administration (OSHA) is in charge of occupational health, and the Environmental Protection Agency (EPA) has responsibility for environmental health. Occupational health problems can be kept from public scrutiny, whereas the environmental impact cannot be hidden (although periodically there are cover-ups, for instance of the effects of fallout from aboveground nuclear tests in Utah and Nevada in the 1950s). Sometimes occupational health problems are solved only after they are disseminated in the general environment and come to public attention—for example, lead and mercury poisoning and low-level ionizing radiation.

The ICMESA plant is located thirteen miles from Milan in the Lombardy region of northern Italy. Like the Monsanto plant in Nitro, West Virginia, it produced the herbicide 2,4,5-T. ICMESA is a subsidiary of Givaudan, a multinational company that has branches in five U.S. locations; Givaudan is owned by another multinational corporation, Hoffmann-La Roche, the giant Swiss pharmaceutical firm. Like the 1984 MIC chemical explosion in Bhopal, India, the accident in Seveso occurred over a weekend when few employees were at the plant. An automatic device controlled the temperature of the acid vats; when it climbed to over 662°F, the safety valves opened as foreseen, protecting the plant but releasing a dense red cloud over the neighborhood (Cerruti 1977, 12). Few workers died; in all, about thirty-six people were hospitalized.

Outside the plant, the material that shot into the air had an immediate effect on plant and animal life: within two days it defoliated most of the vegetation and killed hundreds of rabbits, thousands of chickens, and an unknown number of mice and rats. Eventually 50,000 animals were slaughtered (Fuller 1977, 41). The company failed to inform anyone of the presence of dioxin, allegedly to avoid panic, and government authorities (probably correctly) attributed these deaths to poisoning with 2,4,5-T (Gough 1986, 150). People who were out of doors when the explosion occurred and were underneath the trajectory of the plume of material carried by air currents away from the plant experienced nausea, severe skin lesions, headaches, dizziness, and diarrhea (Whiteside 1979, 33). Later, between 200 and 400 cases of chloracne developed, mainly in children (Fuller 1977, 78; Gough 1986, 152). Doctors performed abortions on an estimated 150 women who feared giving birth to deformed infants (Whiteside 1979, 41); Gough (1986, 105–120 and 153) maintains that the records do not show an increase in dioxin-related birth defects. We know of at least one death of an elderly woman from cancer of the pancreas, but the authorities refused to certify that it was related to dioxin (Fuller 1977, 79–80).

The Seveso area produced two commodities: vegetables and furniture. Because of the commercial gardening, government authorities announced immediately after the explosion that people should not eat local produce. Government officials knew that the accident released 2,4,5-T but not until five days later did the company tell them about the dioxin contamination, which condemned the whole area surrounding the plant. According to the organizational sociologist Charles Perrow (1984, 295), who has analyzed many industrial accidents, Hoffmann-La Roche was well aware of the danger of dioxin contamination, and he calls the accident a "calculated risk." It took two weeks for the authorities to act. Initially they evacuated 750 people from an area of 265 acres. Sometime later they became even more concerned, realized that a much larger area was contaminated, and evacuated another 5,000 people from an additional 665 acres. In all, about 1,000 acres were contaminated and almost 6,000 people were evacuated (Fuller 1977, 46; Whiteside 1979, 37).

The authorities housed people in hotels, told them to leave behind all of their possessions, and in particular to bring no food with them. The police sealed off the area, and only workers wearing space suits were allowed to go in. Some people, desperate to rescue some of their possessions from would-be looters, tried to sneak back but were arrested and dragged away. People repeatedly and openly displayed their disregard for safety rules; they reoccupied their homes in symbolic demonstrations and pulled down the fence surrounding the zone (Pomata 1979, 74–75). This apparently irrational behavior was a hostile reaction to the ineffective way in which public authorities were handling the situation.

Meanwhile, scientists tried to figure out how to decontaminate the area. They divided it into three zones—A, B, and a buffer zone—supposedly according to how much contamination had occurred; the second area, zone B, was further away from the plant and less exposed, while no dioxin could be detected in the buffer zone. The people's experience contradicted the partition: animals went on dying in zone B, and the spatial distribution of chloracne did not correspond at all to the distribution of dioxin plotted on the map (Pomata 1979, 73). The distinction between zones was false because no amount of dioxin is safe; the map had chiefly political and psychological meaning.

Laura Conti, a medical doctor and Communist party representative in the regional government of Lombardy, had firsthand experience of the Seveso accident. As a scientist she knew there was no safe threshold, but as a local government authority she knew the people would experience as persecution a mass evacuation of the 30,000 residents potentially affected. She writes,

> Since there is neither a way to detect the presence of dioxin in the human body nor a way to measure the level of exposure to dioxin in people, and since the pathogenic effects of dioxin are nonspecific, we could not announce a new disease, we could only forecast an increase in mortality, too abstract to be perceived by the people as a concrete danger, worth fleeing from. We could only say that 'one day' (and we did not known when) 'somebody' (and we did not know who) would have fallen sick (and we did not know of what). For the people it was as if we knew nothing at all (quoted in Pomata 1979, 72).

It was relatively easy to decontaminate the second area; workers raked off some topsoil, turned over other soil, and allowed it to be aerated and exposed to the sun. Scientists believed these measures were sufficient, and they allowed people to move back into zone B. But the first area, zone A, presented much greater difficulties. Contaminated soil in zone A reached a depth of twelve inches; someone calculated it would take thirty months to bulldoze the area, and then the question arose as to what to do with the contaminated soil, houses, and so on. One suggestion was to incinerate the materials, but that raised the problem of flyash; people became hysterical at the idea that they might be exposed a second time, and the government dropped this plan. Authorities then decided to truck the topsoil out and incinerate it in some uninhabited place, but everyone living along the routes that the trucks would travel objected. The plan that was finally adopted reads like an old family recipe: spray the area with olive oil and hope that, with sunlight, the oil would help to break down the contamination. Zone A remains a ghost town; authorities never allowed the people to move back in.

With the evacuation of Zone A, dozens of small factories shut down permanently, and many in Zone B closed for lack of orders. The entire economy of the area collapsed because, in addition to the official ban on fruits and vegetables, an unofficial boycott of the furniture produced in Seveso occurred spontaneously (Whiteside 1979, 78ff.). We think of Italy as a highly developed country, but industries introduced assembly lines only in the 1950s and many skilled workers, disliking Ford's system, preferred to work at home by subcontracting to larger firms in a scheme reminiscent of nineteenth-century cottage industry. Around Seveso, side-by-side with the modern ICMESA factory, furniture parts were made in home workshops by highly skilled craft workers. They produced not knockdown unpainted pine bookcases but elegant furniture. After the accident, people throughout Italy refused to buy this furniture because they were terrified of contamination.

The government haggled with the company, both ICMESA and its parent, Hoffmann-La Roche, to get a cash settlement for the victims. The people of Seveso directed their pressure against the government because they recognized that efforts directed against Givaudan or La Roche would have been less effective (Pomata 1979, 77). The Communist party, which supported the regional authorities, was rebuffed in its attempt to mobilize the people in an environmental cleanup campaign. Eventually the corporation paid some money. Whether the amount was sufficient to repay people for the loss of their livelihoods or the stress of living in hotels for almost two years is not known. Hoffmann-La Roche purchased and destroyed the houses in the most contaminated area (Gough 1986, 151).

The long-term result of the accident at Seveso was a reform of environmental laws in Italy with much stricter controls imposed on companies operating there. (Italy is a peculiar case in the industrial development of Europe; it had always allowed much more latitude to companies to come and produce there. Italy did not regulate companies as closely as France or Great Britain or even Germany [Whiteside 1979, 48–49].)

As public health strategies, containment and the use of the *cordon sanitaire* were partially effective before the twentieth century; they limited the spread of contagious diseases such as plague and protected some people (usually the wealthy) at the expense of others (usually the poor). In the case of dioxin at Seveso, containment led to the creation of a ghost town and the permanent uprooting of working people from their homes—not what one would call a successful strategy. In general, containment can be described as a strategy of last resort because its measures—quarantine and isolation—blame the victims and leave many problems unresolved. Nevertheless, public health authorities continue to apply containment frequently in the United States, as they discover dioxin contamination in more and more areas; with each new discovery—Love Canal (Niagara Falls, New York), Times Beach (Missouri), and Ironbound (Newark, New Jersey)—they rope off, seal, and abandon more areas. Communities resist containment strategies and refuse to allow landfills, incinerators, or burial sites in their neighborhoods. So, containment, a very old approach to public health is still in use today although it is not a satisfactory solution.

Chapter 7

CLEANSING THE ENVIRONMENT

IN CLEANSING the environment of communicable diseases, public health workers have two choices: the first is to remove the disease agent or vector, and the second is to remove the habitat in which the vectors breed. For an example of the first—removing the disease agent or vector—consider the public health campaign undertaken in China in 1951, just after the revolution. The Chinese population waged war against four pests: flies, bedbugs, mosquitoes, and rats. They mobilized to exterminate all of these vectors in order to eliminate them from the environment (Sidel and Sidel 1977, 201). An example of the second approach to vector removal is the nineteenth-century British sanitary reform movement which instituted municipal systems of garbage and night soil removal to deprive vectors of their habitat.

This chapter offers a new perspective on the sanitary reform movement, considered to be the archetype of public health work. The new perspective shows how the movement encoded changing beliefs about the nature of poverty, linking it theoretically and practically with environmental degradation as well as population growth. The conceptual link between poverty and the environment is equally direct but less familiar than the connection between poverty and population (especially population growth as described in the adage, "the rich get richer and the poor get children"). Ecologists relate poverty to environmental degradation more often in Third World countries than in industrial countries, and in Third World countries more often in rural settings than in urban environments.

Poverty and the Environment

News stories name environmental degradation—deforestation and desertification (the encroachment of the desert), for example—as the cause of recurrent drought and famine in Africa. Reporters quote ecologists as saying that deforestation and desertification are occurring because Africans mismanage their farms and herds and because Africans are poor and backward and do not know how to preserve their environment (Grainger 1982). In a typical report, a March 2, 1985, *New York Times* article on Mauritania (a poor West African country that borders on the Sahara Desert) said that desertification and drought had turned the world of nomadic cattle and camel herders upside down. In the 1950s the nomads increased their herds during a period of high rainfall, which resulted in overgrazed land, the destruction of grass cover, and desertification. Now that the rainfall has ceased, they are suffering the consequences of their mismanangement. Both the naturalization of drought and the victim blaming of nomads are wrong.

Mauritanians know their environment is fragile; they know about cycles of high and low rainfall and used to be able to plan for them. The expansion of herds and the end of traditional grazing restrictions and long-distance transhumance, which stressed the environment, were the results of French colonial programs to improve water supplies and vaccinate herds. If the other sectors of the Mauritanian economy (mining, fishing, and agriculture) were profitable, herders would be able to buy food and fodder in the dry years and wait for the rains. But Mauritania has no control over the fluctuating prices of copper and iron ore, and production is in the hands of foreign companies (Amin 1973). At the time of the drought, iron ores prices were depressed and the government could not afford to import food and fodder (Gèze et al. 1984, 291). Mauritanian herders said something similar to what American farmers have been saying: if international buyers paid us a reasonable price for our products and if interest rates weren't so high, we could pay our debts. Poverty-stricken farmers around the world are pointing to the structure of agribusiness as the source of their hardships, while their critics in government are pointing the finger back at them and saying they have only themselves to blame.

In 1985 the Reagan administration was taking the victim-blaming approach toward American family farmers who were accused of creating their bankruptcies in several ways: by mismanaging their farms, by overextending their holdings (the equivalent of nomads having too many cattle in their herds), and by overborrowing to accomplish this. American farmers expanded during what one might call the "wet years" of low interest rates when bankers drove along farm roads begging people to borrow money for expansion. When interest rates rose, farmers could not roll over their debts and suffered the consequences of their "mismanagement."

In both instances—Mauritania and the United States—ecologists and governmental officials blame environmental degradation on its victims. Stock (1988) found that colonial authorities in Nigeria adopted the same victim-blaming approach in sanitation programs and labeled "natives" as the primary threat to the health of the British. Significantly, Stock finds the attitude persisting in contemporary Nigerian environmental sanitation campaigns, which emphasize individual "indiscipline" as the fundamental cause of Nigeria's public health problems. The Nigerian example is particularly interesting because it describes the link between poverty and environmental degradation in a Third World urban setting. At the time of colonial occupation, northern Nigeria had several substantial cities on which European settlements were grafted. The environmental problems addressed by the nineteenth-century sanitary reform movement were also urban.

At first glance current environmental problems in the United States seem to relate to affluence rather than poverty; they seem to be very different from those of nineteenth-century England—cleaning up a chemical spill is quite unlike the sanitation problems of London's slums—and yet there are structural similarities in the two situations. For the sanitary reformers to create a public health service, which the public health act of 1848 did, was to fly in the face of the prevailing economic philosophy, that of laissez-faire industrialism, with its principle of noninterference in the market, a principle that guided the Reagan administration in the 1980s and was the basis of the administration's opposition to government regulation of occupational and environmental health services. Public health is predicated upon state intervention, an observation as true of fourteenth-century Venetian quarantine laws and nineteenth century British sanitary reforms as of present-day environmental and occupational health regulations.

The Sanitary Reform Movement

The association of poverty with environmental degradation emerged in the nineteenth century. The government leaders who reformed the poor laws in 1834 later led the sanitary reform movement. When Edwin Chadwick, who was the architect of the 1848 public health act, talked about environmental problems in nineteenth-century England, he indicted the filthy environment in which the poor lived and in which disease and social unrest bred. Chadwick wrote before the germ theory of disease was known; in his day there were two contending theories of disease: one was the miasma or pythogenic theory, the other was contagion. Chadwick was a miasmatist who did not believe that contagion spread from person to person but rather that disease arose from filthy conditions, which were the result of poor sanitary arrangements and poor housing design. In contrast, Engels believed that deprivation created an unhealthy environment in which working-class families rapidly perished (Hobsbawm 1969). Engels understood that the causes of mortality were not medical (contagion) or environmental (miasma) but industrial (cyclical overproduction that led periodically to unemployment, and the concentration of industry that led to dense and overcrowded slums). As Stark (1982, 65) notes, "Engels builds his epidemiology from a dialectical tension between *political theory* (capitalist development, class struggle, the revolutionary potential of the proletariat) and *intimate experience* (Chadwick's data, the sort of direct observation that shocked Virchow during his famous typhus inquiry in Silesia)."

The antecedents of the nineteenth-century sanitary reform movement are firmly rooted in the political economy of the industrial revolution and in the emergence of capitalism as the dominant mode of production. Locating the reform in this context does not deny the contribution of humanitarians and of liberals who understood that change was necessary in order to maintain the political status quo. But the force motivating Chadwick and his colleagues, despite disclaimers by public health historians such as George Rosen (1958), was the necessity of reform to economic expansion. They undertook sanitary reform for the benefit of the industrial revolution in England, not for the poor and working classes. They were opposed by individual industrialists because the reforms drove up their costs.

The industrial revolution was preceded and made possible by an agricultural revolution that was based, not on any new scientific discoveries comparable to the green revolution (it did not apply new scientific knowledge to grow food or industrial crops or to increase yields, although some new technology was involved at a later stage when new labor-saving mechanical harvesters and reapers were used) but on social reorganization; the agricultural revolution was primarily a social revolution. The important social transformation involved the consolidation of landholdings and the enclosure movement, which dispossessed English peasants and deprived them of access to 6 million acres of common fields and common lands from 1760, and withdrew the forest rights that entitled them to gather dead wood for fuel and to bag small game for food, privileges the peasantry had enjoyed from medieval times (Hobsbawm 1962, 185). Together with the ruined operators of cottage industries such as weaving, this dispossessed peasantry (consisting of small farmers, tenant farmers, and day laborers) became the working class of the industrial revolution.[1]

When English peasants and artisans came to the centers of the industrial revolution, they left a rural way of life. In their new urban life, the first challenge was to secure food and shelter. The process by which they obtained food changed from that of subsistence farming, in which they produced it for themselves, to that of buying it from someone else, either in a market or as prepared food, with no guarantee as to quality and no safeguard from adulteration. In the era before refrigerators, freezers, microwave ovens, canning factories, frozen foods, supermarkets, and the U.S. Food and Drug Aministration, workers had to shop every day in open-air farmers' markets set up inside towns. Modern urbanites romanticize the fresh fruit and vegetable markets they use to supplement their supermarket purchases, but for nineteenth-century workers putting in twelve- and fourteen-hour days at the factory, they held little charm. Urban life entailed a radical change in the diet of the working classes, with white bread substituted for whole grains, cheese for vegetables and occasional meat, cooked fat for butter, and tea for milk, cider, or home brewed beer (Thompson 1968, 347–351).[2] Fruit, which peasants had eaten in summer when available, became a rare commodity. The new diet was far less healthy than the old one.

The need for shelter near the new factories drove workers to rent not cottages as in the countryside but unheated, unventilated, single rooms, sometimes in wet basements with an outdoor privy and no indoor water, toilet, or bath. The unmet demand for cheap housing led to overcrowding, with several families sharing one room or even a single bed. Poor housing and the lack of drains and sewerage promoted the rapid spread of communicable diseases in the malnourished and debilitated population.

Urbanization was a necessary concomitant to industrialization because the processes of early industrialism were not labor saving but labor intensive and required a large work force within walking distance. The advent of high technology following World War II brought a shift of industry out of cities, but in the nineteenth century factories had to locate near water supplies, which provided water to power mills and (later) hydroelectric power. Also, before there were railways, rivers and canals provided routes of transportation and links to ports. Communication with the outside world allowed raw materials to be shipped in and finished products to be shipped out. This conjunction of laborers, factories, and communications created new cities and spurred enormous growth in urbanization. In the late eighteenth century there were fifteen cities in England with a population of more than 20,000. By the mid-nineteenth century there were sixty-three such cities. The urban population rose from 1.5 million to 6.25 million. At the beginning of the nineteenth century, 26 percent of the population of England and Wales lived in cities; by the end of the century, 68 percent did (Encyclopaedia Britannica 1984, 1076).

High death rates accompanied urbanization and industrialization in the early part of the nineteenth century, threatening the ability of the working class to reproduce itself and provide the next generation of laborers (Thompson 1968, 356–366). The cities had outgrown medieval arrangements for water supply, waste disposal, and burials, which now were a source of disease, choked the cities, and prevented industrial expansion (Turshen 1977). Typically the wealthy lived in the west end of the city and the poor were concentrated in the east end; epidemics spread from east to west. The Benthamites and their disciples, Edwin Chadwick foremost among them, argued on utilitarian and pragmatic grounds for sanitary reform and the importance of engineering. Several attempts to pass bills were unsuccessful because many of the regulations entailed considerable financial losses for industrialists and others with vested interests. Eventually, Parliament passed the first public health act in 1848, which was subsequently amended in 1866, again in 1872, a third time in 1875, and so on. By 1875, there was a flourishing public health service in Britain. Its heyday was very short, however. By the end of the century not only did it lack funds, but as an approach to disease eradication it had been superseded by the emergence of clinical medicine in the bacteriological era.

The fact that industrial expansion required reform does not explain the legal or administrative shape that reform took. To explain why the poor law reform of 1834 (Checkland and Checkland 1973) and the sanitary reform movement of the 1840s and 1850s (Flinn 1965) were the answer, we need to look at the role of these reforms in the discipline of the new industrial labor force.

The Redefinition of Poverty

In 1770 Samuel Johnson wrote: "A decent provision for the poor is a true test of civilization" (quoted in Himmelfarb 1985, 3). Britain was the first country to institute a national system to care for the poor. The Elizabethan poor laws, which date from 1597 and 1601, established the principle of a legal, compulsory, secular, national system of relief. Prior to that time, care of the poor was a religious duty; it had never before been a concern of secular government. During the preindustrial period in Europe, the poor had a high moral and social status; their status declined dramatically after the industrial revolution.

The poor laws made it the duty of every parish to provide for anyone who was destitute, including workers who did not earn enough to survive. This provision—the so-called "poor rates," not unlike present-day property taxes—was raised by assessing the gentry of the area. These rates rose rapidly, from 2 million pounds in 1784 to 7 million pounds by 1821, and they continued to increase until 1834 (Checkland and Checkland 1973, 19; Himmelfarb 1985, 134; Morton 1974, 396). The new poor laws reorganized the way in which relief was granted. No longer based on local parishes, relief was centralized; three appointed commissioners administered the laws and imposed a uniform policy throughout the country. Able-bodied workers were no longer eligible for the outdoor relief that would have permitted the poor to continue living in their own homes. The law mandated that impotent (bedridden sick and elderly) and able-bodied alike were to live in workhouses. Applicants now determined their own qualification for relief because none but the utterly destitute and homeless would willingly submit to confinement and loss of liberty. Limited medical relief continued out of doors (Himmelfarb 1985, 163–168). In the words of E. P. Thompson, "The impractical policy of systematic starvation was displaced by the policy of psychological deterrence: 'labour, discipline and restraint' " (1968, 295).

Workhouses were not a creation of the 1834 poor law reforms, but they took on a new significance with the abolition of parish relief. Readers of *Oliver Twist* will remember Charles Dickens's description of conditions in the workhouses.

> For the next eight or ten months [after his birth], Oliver was the victim of a systematic course of treachery and deception. . . . The hungry and destitute situation of the infant orphan was duly reported by the workhouse authorities to the parish authorities . . . [who] resolved that Oliver should be 'farmed' . . . to a branch workhouse . . . where twenty or thirty other juvenile offenders against the poor-laws, rolled about the floor all day, without the inconvenience of too much food or too much clothing, under the parental superintendence of an elderly female . . . [who] appropriated the greater part of the weekly stipend to her own use, and consigned the rising parochial generation to even a shorter allowance than was originally provided for them.

Dickens had personal experience of the workhouse in childhood when his father was imprisoned for bankruptcy, which motivated him to write the novel. He was a very active sanitary reformer, worked closely with Edwin Chadwick, and was responsible for many of the social changes that were made[3] (Himmelfarb 1985, 184).

The redefinition of poverty was based on faith in the capitalist system to provide jobs for anyone willing and able to work. The able-bodied man or woman without a job for any length of time must either be unwilling to work or of bad character: an idler, inefficient laborer, or a blacklisted trade unionist. Chadwick believed that workhouse discipline would reform his or her character and spare the honest laborer the demoralizing spectacle of the idle eating bread and meat (Lewis 1952, 25). The new definition played a legitimizing role in the shift of blame for environmental degradation from the capitalist system and its new industrialists to the lowest wage earners and those disabled and enfeebled by the process of industrialization, sometimes referred to as the "depraved classes" (Donzelot 1979, 32).

Poverty and Population Growth

One cannot understand the poor laws without reference to the Reverend Thomas Malthus. At the end of the eighteenth century, Malthus published an essay on the principle of population in which he argued that population increases in geometric ratio while subsistence increases only in arithmetic ratio: unless checked, population always outruns subsistence (Flew 1970). Positive checks on population, which raise mortality rates, are starvation, sickness, war, and infanticide. Preventive checks, which slow the birthrate, are marriage at a later age for women to restrict the number of years of childbearing, and sexual restraint within marriage to limit the number of pregnancies. Malthus held that state intervention in the operation of these checks, as in state dispensation of relief, would only increase what he described as the improvidence and promiscuity of the poor, their "misery and vice." By promoting population growth, relief would accelerate the day when the limits to subsistence would be reached.

This discourse, as Donzelot (1979, 54) points out, addressed the problem of pauperism and indigence in the context of labor discipline and the new free market economy; "The face-to-face encounter of a bourgeois minority and a barbarian populace that haunted the cities more than it inhabited them raised the specter of their destruction." All who debated the issues of private (church-run) versus public charity agreed on the need to restore "the ties of obedience that had once united the rich and the poor" (ibid., 62). Malthus advocated abolition of the Elizabethan poor law, not its reform: in this he was defeated because social economists saw welfare as a way to negotiate with the poor. But his attitudes, which indicted the victims of the industrial revolution for their own poverty and degraded the poor from their early Christian high moral and social status, prevailed. New distinctions between the deserving and the undeserving poor, between the independent poor who were working, and the dependent poor who needed relief to survive, informed the 1834 poor laws.

Although Malthus's ideas were not incorporated directly into the new poor law, the spirit of his philosophy survived as the Malthusian legacy and is enshrined in European and American welfare legislation as well as in attitudes toward the Third World. The legacy would have us believe that poverty is inevitable (as in the adage "the poor will always be with us") and that it is somehow a natural state for one group of people to be poor. The laboring poor were persuaded to accept their lot because anything would be better than to fall into the class of paupers—the undeserving poor. The horrors of life in the workhouse and the degradation and shame attached to being paupers were to be avoided at all costs, including the costs of sacrificing one's health at work or living in conditions that were substandard. Malthus's ideas are still current today: Paddock and Paddock (1967) and Paul Ehrlich (1968) who write about the population "time bomb" and the population "explosion" are disciples of Malthus.

The Proletarianization of the Poor

By focusing on the labor force and on the importance of making the laboring poor resigned to their work and working conditions, one can understand the meaning of the poor law reforms and of the later sanitary reforms. The Elizabethan poor law had restricted labor mobility by limiting eligibility to the parish in which the applicant was born. The residential condition on relief had the effect of keeping the poor in depressed rural areas even as the new industries were creating jobs in the cities. Industrialists intended the reformed poor law to create a "free" labor market by removing the last feudal restraints and enabling workers to move where the jobs were.

Rosen (1958, 194) asserts correctly that care of the poor became a great burden in the nineteenth century, but he locates pressure for reform in the landed gentry who paid the rapidly rising tax rates and in the middle classes whose liberal members were aware of widespread destitution and the need to care for increasing numbers of poor. These two sections of the ruling class were engaged in a savage struggle; the industrialists pressed for cheaper food, which would allow them to pay lower wages, and the landowners (in revenge) campaigned against long hours and oppressive conditions in the factories (Morton 1974, 376). Neither had the interests of the poor at heart.

Rosen does not consider that pressure to redress the evils of industrialism came from the laboring poor and unemployed themselves. Yet the historical record of popular uprisings in the period is well documented. Illpaid workers, artisans dislocated by mechanization, and dispossessed peasants voiced their demands in riots and strikes, in the Chartist Movement of Robert Owen, in the socialism of William Godwin, and in the Luddite Movement, which smashed the new machines that put artisans out of work. Although the government outlawed trade unions in 1799, workers organized in the early 1800s and strikes were common (and tenacious). From 1824 (when the antiunion combination laws were repealed) there was an unprecedented outburst of organizing activity and strikes: all through 1826 almost continuous strikes gripped Lancashire (the center of the textile industry), with wholesale destruction of looms and frequent clashes between strikers and soldiers (Morton 1974, 426). The threat of revolt, of civil disorder, and the specter of revolution haunted all continental monarchs in the period between 1789 and 1848 and forced the British government to reform the poor laws.

The judgment that pressure for relief comes from the unemployed themselves is reached in a study of public welfare in the United States by two contemporary U.S. sociologists, Frances Fox Piven and Richard Cloward (1971). In their book, *Regulating the Poor*, the authors show how welfare, the American equivalent of the British poor laws, is initiated or expanded during outbreaks of civil disorder, which it is designed to mute. They argue convincingly in a case study of the 1930s depression that relief rolls expand to deal with dislocations in the work system that lead to mass disorder and they contract as soon as it is politically expedient to cut them back; relief is then retained in an altered form to enforce work norms.

This analysis goes some way toward answering the question of why reforms take the shape they do and not some other. The demands people make are for a political voice and better living and working conditions, not for relief or legal reform of relief. Their demands are transformed by the state into a very different set of responses. In nineteenth-century Great Britain, workers agitated for universal suffrage, a secret ballot, annual parliaments, shorter work days, higher wages, better factory conditions, and the abolition of child labor. The responses were parliamentary reform in 1832, which enlarged the electorate only slightly; the 1833 factory act, which regulated but did not abolish the employment of children; the callous poor law reform of 1834; a mines act, passed in 1842, which prohibited the underground employment of girls and women and of boys under ten; the ten-hours act, which limited the working day to ten hours, passed in 1847 after three decades of agitation; and finally, in 1848, the first public health act. These acts not only fell far short of workers' demands, they were written so as to benefit the rising class of bourgeois industrialists at the expense of landed gentry and the established church.

To this picture of poverty—redefined, codified, and institutionalized in workhouses and low-wage work—of population growth explained so as to heap additional blame on the poor for their poverty, and of environmental degradation ascribed by Marxists to the capitalist system, came the germ theory of disease. Industrialists welcomed the germ theory because it gave clinical medicine the scientific foundation needed to treat individual patients successfully and to take over the work of ensuring the reproduction of the labor force from public health. Meanwhile, working class reforms (mainly limiting the workday and week) without substantially lowering wages led industrialists to intensify work and refocus their attention from periodically driving workers below subsistence level (in order to maintain profitability) to persuading them to tolerate speedups and other forms of intensification. By the 1870s when wages finally did rise, workers were eating better, their health was improving, and mortality rates were once again falling.

Marx was positively impressed with the ability of capitalism to create conditions going beyond subsistence to substantially reduce hardship and work. Capitalism also created a new historical actor, the industrial worker, whose primary interest was in change to overcome the existing state of things. It was this combination of working-class struggles and a bountiful mode of production that was responsible for healthier conditions; the sanitary reform movement may have contributed to the improvements but was not solely responsible for them, as some public health historians claim.

The Decline of Public Health

By the end of the nineteenth century, public health practitioners in Great Britain had been upstaged by their clinical medical colleagues, and their status in the government community had declined drastically. The usual explanations for the decline of the prestige of public health are that public health deals with collectivities rather than individuals, that public health practitioners do not have intimate relationships with their patients as personal physicians do, and that public health improvements are not as dramatic or noticeable as curative techniques such as surgery.

More fundamental reasons for the decline of public health can be advanced. The main beneficiaries were urban workers and the unemployed, the urban poor who were made destitute when they were too ill to work or when there was no work to be had. Public health services helped the poor and powerless, the group least able to confer status and prestige or offer rewards for the aid they received. While the sanitary reform movement advanced the industrial revolution as a whole, it hurt many middle-class individuals. Public health workers attacked people who had wealth and power, namely the slum landlords, the bourgeois factory owners, and the proprietors of burial grounds, sewage disposal rights, water supply companies, and so on. Those with vested interests in property affected by the sanitary reformers were not about to confer prestige and status on the profession that attacked them, put them out of business, or reduced their profits.

In their different ways, Chadwick and Engels exposed the tainted sources of many respectable fortunes: Chadwick by naming slumlords and water companies, Engels by exposing factory owners and the capitalist system. The contemporary environmental movement is doing much the same thing: in their confrontations with corporations, environmentalists and political ecologists face many of the same problems as the nineteenth-century sanitary reformers.

The nineteenth-century organization of industry that "created" the poor also "created" the unsanitary environment of the factory towns. It degraded the environment by dumping stinking industrial refuse on land and in rivers; it created poverty by viewing people as units of labor, rather than as social beings, a view inherent in the profit motive that drives the capitalist system. Preindustrial societies organized themselves and their relation to the environment differently; for example, the American Indian approach to the environment is to mesh humankind with nature, a view that continues to clash with the industrial approach, which is to dominate the natural world (Johansen and Maestas 1979, 25).

A recent study by the United Church of Christ Commission on Racial Justice shows that toxic waste generation sites and treatment facilities are located in the residential neighborhoods of minorities (*New York Times,* 16 April 1987). It is no coincidence that toxic waste dumps are located in poor communities lacking the political power to oppose corporations successfully. Freudenburg (1984, 36–41) documents the way industry operates in the United States and how corporations determine where and when to build or move factories and to dump toxic waste, as well as which technology to select; he explains why the public, which is excluded from corporate decision-making processes, collides with industry when trying to clean up the environmental contamination that results. Victim blaming is only one of the strategies employed by industry to control communities; the political manipulation of science is another, and a third is to influence government, which might otherwise defend the people.

Freudenberg's answer is to redefine democracy so that people participate in making the decisions that affect their neighborhoods and workplaces. The problem with this solution is that it pits one community against another because it leads to NIMBY, the Not In My Backyard syndrome, and struggles over what Frank Popper (1985) calls "LULUs," locally unwanted land uses. As communities successfully block the allocation of land for uses they oppose, approved waste sites become a scarce commodity, the cost of toxic waste disposal rises, and illegal operations such as midnight dumping spring up. There can be no individual, only collective, solutions to environmental management.

To change the economic and political relationships that govern the industries which generate environmental pollution requires structural reorganization. Capitalism dictates an approach in which people and the environment are sources of profit for industry. The system is the source of contemporary environmental problems in industrial and Third World countries. In this analysis, structural reorganization and not sanitary reform is the essence of public health work and the basic principle of cleansing the environment.

Chapter 8

DISEASE ERADICATION

THIS CHAPTER looks beyond the control of disease to examine the eradication of disease, and it goes beyond state control to consider international disease eradication campaigns. It is the third in the sequence of chapters that moves from an examination of measures taken by local and municipal authorities using police powers—the use of the *cordon sanitaire* to confine or keep out disease—through state assumption of public functions greater than regulation, namely the provision of services for cleansing the environment, to world programs. Public health action has progressed from the role of the city-state in fourteenth-century Venice, through the rise of the nation-state and the nineteenth-century sanitary reform movement in England, to the role of a supranational body in twentieth-century global eradication campaigns.

The development of the field of public health has depended upon the political evolution of the state and the beginnings of international government. The first movement for collective international action resulted in the nineteenth-century cholera conferences (Howard-Jones 1975) and came to fruition in 1907 with the foundation, in Paris, of the International Office of Public Health, which was the forerunner of the Health Section of the League of Nations (Goodman 1971, 326). The League was followed by the creation of the United Nations after World War II and the establishment of WHO in 1948.

WHO is central to both of the case histories of disease eradication considered in this chapter: one a success and the other a failure. The first is a study of the successful global smallpox eradication campaign, launched in 1967; the second is of the failed malaria eradication campaign undertaken in 1957 and abandoned in 1973. The good news is that smallpox has been eradicated from the world. The bad news is that malaria is resurgent.

The Successful Eradication of Smallpox

Smallpox and not cholera was probably the model for the germ theory of disease. Smallpox fits the model perfectly. It is a systemic viral disease of sudden onset; it is extremely acute; it starts with symptoms of rash and fever and can lead to death within five to seven days. Unlike the course of most communicable diseases, the outcome of smallpox does not depend upon the nutritional status of the victim. Case fatality rates among the unvaccinated are high; even in populations with some exposure to smallpox, fatality rates (for variola major) run 20 to 40 percent or more. Death rates are highest among pregnant women. Survivors of epidemics do not catch smallpox a second time; it is not a recurrent disease. It is transmitted through close contact with respiratory discharges, suppurating skin lesions, or contaminated materials. Smallpox is an ancient disease identified in Egyptian mummies. Death statistics give some sense of its epidemic nature and why it was such a feared disease: 60 million Europeans are thought to have died of smallpox in the eighteenth century. In 1967, at the start of the intensified eradication campaign, smallpox still killed between 1–2 million people annually and disfigured or disabled another 10–14 million (Fenner et al. 1988, 1363).

Smallpox has a curious political history. The fact that mortality rates were highest among previously unexposed populations was widely known and observed, particularly by conquering peoples. Colonists used this fact in the conquest of the Americas: smallpox-infected blankets were distributed to American Indians in an effort to start epidemics and eliminate populations without having to fight them (Wain 1970, 182).[1] This may have been the first instance of germ warfare. The last major smallpox epidemic in the United States occurred in 1949 in the Rio Grande valley of Texas.

The English physician Edward Jenner developed the smallpox

vaccine at the end of the eighteenth century, quite early in the history of modern medicine. He observed that a mild case of cowpox conferred immunity to smallpox, a belief commonly held among milkmaids. Jenner used that observation to create a smallpox vaccine based on the cowpox virus (Wain 1970, 189).

But vaccination was not the only preventive measure known or practiced in the eighteenth century. Traditional healers used a technique called variolation or inoculation, in which a bit of the infected material from a smallpox victim was put into a scratch to give a mild case of the disease to a healthy person (Langer 1976). Healers practiced variolation throughout Africa and in parts of the Middle East and Asia (Wain 1970, 173). Variolation seems to have held smallpox in check before the colonial conquests. In effect, people found ways to control the ancient disease of smallpox long before they were able to identify it scientifically. There is still no cure for smallpox, but, remarkably, we eradicated the disease before we learned how to cure it.

In 1967, WHO launched an intensified global smallpox eradication campaign, financed by the United States, Sweden, and the USSR (among others), and by WHO's regular budget (Fenner et al. 1988, 464). The campaign reached its goal in December 1979 when WHO declared that smallpox had been eradicated from the world. A $1,000 reward is still posted for anyone who finds a new case. The last endemic foci of the disease were India, Bangladesh, and Ethiopia. In India and Bangladesh, population densities made the organization of the campaign extremely difficult; in Ethiopia the obstacles were the paucity of health services, the mountainous terrain, and the lack of roads or other means of reaching rural people isolated in mountain fastholds.

This success was achieved by using the basic public health techniques I have discussed, primarily quarantine and vaccination, and by coordinating the campaign at the international level. Let us look more specifically at the techniques employed in this mass campaign. First, by definition a mass campaign is designed to reach everyone, 100 percent of the population, adults and children alike. Health authorities in the United States assume that primary vaccination is routine, that most children will be born in hospitals or will be taken to clinics quite soon after birth, and that they will be vaccinated according to a standard schedule of childhood immunizations. This assumption is wrong for poor and minority children, but the government does not carry out mass campaigns until confronted with a serious outbreak of contagious disease. If an epidemic is anticipated, a campaign may be mounted to immunize the population at risk. But generally health services are assumed to be sufficiently dense to provide routine primary vaccination. In the Third World no such assumption can be made, and a special campaign for smallpox vaccination had to be mounted.

The 1967 campaign against smallpox differed from mass vaccination in that it employed reporting and surveillance techniques to target groups for primary vaccination carried out through a vertical campaign. Vertical programs address one problem only; smallpox was the only health problem addressed by this campaign and by all of the health workers involved in it. The simplified, single-purpose training course, which initially consisted of teaching people to recognize smallpox and to use a jet injector vaccination gun and later a simpler bifurcated needle, facilitated the rapid mounting of the campaign (Henderson 1976). Program leaders trained large numbers of field workers quickly and paid them at very low levels. Revaccination every three to five years followed the initial mass vaccination campaign for a number of reasons: the vaccine confers protection for a limit of five years, no previous campaign reached 100 percent of the population (when coverage attains 80 percent, public health authorities consider a campaign extremely successful), and the second round reached children born after the first campaign.

The second public health technique employed was surveillance, which is more than case reporting. Smallpox surveillance comprised data collection, analysis, and dissemination, the initiation of field studies, epidemic control, and the modification of campaign procedures (WHO 1967). For years health inspectors carried out routine surveillance at airports, harbors, and border crossings. Public health authorities supplemented these controls by a reporting system; every traveler was supposed to carry a yellow booklet issued by WHO in which the date of vaccination was stamped. At the port of entry, health inspectors distributed notification cards and told travelers to report certain symptoms to a physician. Local health departments required physicians to report cases of smallpox; these notification reports eventually reached WHO. (National reporting of such quarantinable diseases as smallpox to WHO is an obligation of membership in the organization.) WHO publishes a weekly epidemiological monitor, which carried the reports around the world and enabled health inspectors to pay special attention to travelers from infected areas.

The third public health technique employed was isolation of infected patients to break the transmission of the disease. (Isolation applies to infected individuals, whereas quarantine applies to restrictions placed on healthy contacts of an infected person.) To ensure that transmission had not already occurred, officials also isolated contacts, especially in families with many children. The fourth technique was disinfection of all materials in contact with the sick person—clothing, bedding, even interiors of homes, especially when walls were not tiled but made of straw and mud. The fifth technique was vaccination of whole communities in the event of an epidemic or, in the case of small isolated outbreaks (when the campaign had been running for a number of years), vaccination of all contacts. Sixth, there was case finding—the active seeking out of new cases. Here again the campaign was aided by the fact that smallpox is easily identified; programs can train workers very quickly to recognize the disease and can employ low levels of auxiliary personnel in the case-finding process.

What did all this cost? Although it was a huge undertaking involving the rapid mobilization of an army of field workers, the campaign was not terribly expensive: $98 million for the period 1967 to 1979 (Fenner et al. 1988, 459). In contrast $2.5 billion were spent from 1957–1975 on the unsuccessful malaria eradication campaign (ibid., 383). In 1968 the United States spent $150 million in direct and indirect costs associated with vaccination, surveillance, and loss of productivity (ibid., 1365). Economy was one of the arguments the U.S. Centers for Disease Control used to persuade Congress to appropriate funds for the program. The Centers for Disease Control released a number of staff members to work with WHO at its Geneva headquarters and regional and national offices; WHO field staff helped to carry out the program.

Why was WHO successful in eradicating smallpox, and how does the organization account for its success? Henderson (1976), the U.S. director of the campaign, ascribes success to efficient management and dedicated workers. My analysis suggests that the campaign was successful because it required absolutely no change in the economic or political structures of any of the countries involved, not in the United States, not in any of the Third World countries that cooperated. It did not even require a change in the structure of the health service system. It was a separate entity, a program introduced from the outside, it had its own budget, trained its own personnel, and it did not touch anything in place.

Low levels of technology also favored the campaign. Because a freeze-dried vaccine was used, the campaign did not require a "cold chain" (a string of refrigeration facilities between the place the vaccine is manufactured and the place of vaccination), which is one of the obstacles to eradicating measles; measles vaccine must be maintained at a constant, low temperature. In Third World countries, where the climate is often tropical and where rural electrification programs rarely exist, refrigeration is provided by a small, private generator or a gas-powered stove, an erratic source of energy that is frequently interrupted. With no need for refrigeration, smallpox field workers could carry a vial of freeze-dried vaccine in their shirt pocket, trek through the jungle, reconstitute the vaccine on the spot, and vaccinate isolated homesteaders. The only other apparatus needed was the bifurcated needle.

The success of the smallpox eradication campaign is hard to interpret. It alleviated a specific form of suffering and eliminated a particular way of death, but one cannot claim that it improved world health. It was a triumph of organization, but of the sort described in ancient dramas as deus ex machina. Dropped in from on high, the campaign gave people no greater control of their lives, which is one of the goals of primary health care. The smallpox campaign cannot be duplicated, so it set no precedent for other public health work, perhaps of higher priority to the country. All the old problems that cause poverty and ill health were left untouched, and the health services functioned no better afterward. The latter is key to the failure of malaria eradication.

The Failure to Eradicate Malaria

Malaria is a more complicated disease than smallpox; it does not fit the germ theory of disease quite so nicely. Unlike smallpox, which is an acute, self-limiting disease, malaria is recurrent and chronic. Whereas smallpox is independent of nutritional status, a bout of malaria can precipitate malnutrition, especially in children under five years old (DeMaeyer 1976, 29). A warm and humid climate is favorable to malaria, but a cold climate is not a deterrent; and the disease reached epidemic and endemic proportions in southern Canada and New England during the seventeenth century (Ackerknecht 1945, 54). Four diseases constitute the human malarias; the most serious—falciparum or malignant tertian malaria—is life-threatening (Benenson 1985, 225). The current total number of people infected with malaria worldwide is about 240 million (WHO 1986, 179). There is no cure.

Germ theorists identify a parasite as the cause of malaria, but medical historians confirm the fundamentally social character of the disease (Ackerknecht 1945, 130). Invading armies, colonizers, and migrants are all highly effective in propagating malaria. The malaria parasite has a complex cycle of development, including a spell in an intermediate host, the anopheles mosquito, which transmits the parasite by biting human beings. The transmitted parasites enter the bloodstream and lodge in the human liver where they multiply (asexually) and then migrate back to the bloodstream where they undergo another phase of development. When the mosquitoes next bite a person and ingest blood, they also swallow the parasites, which reproduce (sexually) in the stomach of the mosquito, before being discharged with saliva when the mosquitoes bite again, thus completing the cycle of transmission (Cloudsley-Thompson 1976, 76–78).

Common symptoms of malaria are chills alternating with fever and bouts of nausea and headache, followed by profuse sweating. High mortality is associated with falciparum malaria, especially in infants who have not yet acquired immunity or who are weakened by concurrent infections or malnutrition (Benenson 1985, 226). One-tenth of all infant mortality in Africa, where rates are typically 150 deaths per 1,000 live births, is due to malaria. The long-term effects of this chronic illness are crippling; recurrent bouts of fever cause prostration and leave the victim debilitated and anemic because of the action of the parasite on the red blood cells. Malarial bouts are exhausting, and on a Tanzanian agricultural collective where a malaria epidemic prevented villagers from bringing in the sugarcane harvest, I saw people prostrate and unable to go out into the fields to cut cane, even though the village's survival depended on the harvest. Health economists oversimplify inferences from the inverse correlation between the incidence of malaria and agricultural productivity.

Because the disease vector is the mosquito, there are several points of intervention at which to break the cycle of transmission. The sanitary measures used before the development of DDT were effective (more so in urban than in rural areas), but they were also expensive and labor intensive; in effect, they amounted to environmental cleansing. They included public health engineering (filling in ditches, draining marshes, covering pools of stagnant water, and so on) to prevent breeding; fumigation of adult mosquitoes with incense; biological control of larvae by stocking bodies of water with certain species of fish; and larviciding, in which oil was sprayed on water surfaces to kill the mosquito in its larval stage.

Chemoprophylaxis and chemotherapy are other techniques used to control malaria: quinine (a traditional Peruvian remedy based on the bark of the cinchona tree) and, more recently, synthetic chemical analogs are used to suppress symptoms. Researchers are inventing new drugs as parasites develop resistance to old ones—artemisinine (based on a traditional Chinese herbal remedy) is at an advanced stage of development, and halofantrine is ready for clinical trials (UNDP/World Bank/WHO 1985). But resistance develops almost as quickly as new drugs can be marketed: resistance to mefloquine, a new drug in 1983–1984, is already reported in the Philippines, Thailand, and Tanzania (WHO 1986b, 179).

Researchers are also working to develop sophisticated biological controls—for example, organisms (such as the *bacillus sphaericus*) are replacing chemical larvicides. Current research on a vaccine against malaria is at an advanced stage of development and, periodically, successes are announced in the news (*New York Times,* 17 May 1985; 27 May 1986; 10 March 1988), but no vaccine is routinely used as yet (Martinez 1988, 5). Scientists have carried out much of this research under the auspices of, or in collaboration with, WHO, the World Bank, and the United Nations Development Program, which have mounted a tropical diseases research program that features malaria as one of six diseases receiving priority attention. The research program is a joint venture with the commercial pharmaceutical industry.

Other long-standing preventive measures are window screens and mosquito bednetting, which represent attempts at containment. Wearing long-sleeved shirts and long trousers and staying indoors after sundown in areas where mosquitoes bite at night can be helpful. Isolation and quarantine are not used in malaria programs, but the disinfection of aircraft, ships, and vehicles traveling from malarious to malaria-free areas has helped control international transmission. Sanitary improvements were particularly effective in controlling malaria in urban areas, but the most effective eradication measure of all was economic development.

Malaria disappeared from England, France, Germany, Denmark, the Netherlands, and other countries long before the advent of DDT. By 1900 it had disappeared from the Upper Mississippi Valley (roughly the states of Minnesota, Wisconsin, Iowa, Illinois, and Missouri), where it had been highly endemic at the end of the eighteenth century.[2] Ackerknecht (1945, 129) attributes the disappearance foremost to prosperity—increased wealth, better agricultural methods, improved housing, education, cattle breeding (the relation to malaria is called, cryptically, animal diversion because when given their druthers, mosquitoes prefer ox blood to ours), and a decline in the intense immigration the area experienced between 1830 and 1860, coupled with the shift of population inland from watercourses. He assigns little or no importance to organized drainage enterprises, the screening of doors and windows, and the use of quinine, which merely interrupts an acute malarial attack (however, it enabled workers to return to their jobs and to build immunity to the disease).

The debate on how to approach malaria control goes back to nineteenth-century England. Malaria was seen as an impediment to colonial expansion in Africa, and the debate about control techniques turned into a power struggle between Patrick Manson (1844–1922), a parasitologist and founder of the London School of Hygiene who pursued an approach similar to the one later taken by WHO, and Ronald Ross (1857–1932), a Nobel prize-winning physician at the Liverpool School of Hygiene who called for large-scale environmental transformation. Manson won. At the end of the nineteenth century, Joseph Chamberlain (1836–1914), the imperialist British statesman, decided to fund Manson at the London School rather than Ross at Liverpool.

The decision against environmental transformation was taken, not only on grounds of cost (the British government was unwilling to make such large capital investments in the colonies), but also because it did not conform to the ideology of the era, which called for a technological fix, if not a magic bullet. Needed was a specific, not a general, remedy that could be applied where, when, and to whom the ruling classes decided. Germ theory provided a disease paradigm better suited than environmentalism to that policy.

With the development of DDT[3] in World War II it became possible to kill adult mosquitoes cheaply and effectively, and WHO based the international malaria eradication campaign it mounted in military style in 1956 on the use of DDT combined with mass distribution of chloroquine. Teams of sprayers, with five gallon drums of insecticide strapped to their backs, descended on villages to spray every surface on which mosquitoes rested; they sprayed the walls, ceilings, and eaves of huts, the undersurface of furniture, the undersurface of the roofs of sheds, and the undersurface of granaries. Some villagers resisted the campaign. Public health officials depoliticized their complaints, noting dislike of the side effects of DDT and objections to displacement during the spraying. Wessen (1986) chided the teams for their insensitivity to village custom and sentiment.

Initially the global malaria eradication campaign undertaken by WHO and its member states met with great success. Public health workers eradicated malaria from countries having an aggregate population of one billion people. But by 1962 it was already evident that a decade would not suffice to achieve the goal of worldwide eradication (WHO 1962). By the end of the 1960s, scientists recognized the pernicious effect of DDT on the environment, adding to the problem of mosquito resistance to the insecticide, and officials phased out the use of DDT as a pesticide in a number of industrial countries (Graham 1970, 193, 238). Parasite resistance to chloroquine, the inexpensive drug of choice, compounded the difficulties.

Some critics of the campaign concentrated on failures of organization and management, rather than technology and engineering. One argument turned on whether WHO was mistaken in advocating the integration of "vertical" malaria programs in the "horizontal" health service structure, given how few underdeveloped countries had adequate health services. Those who argued for integration reasoned that malaria eradication required a dense network of health services; it could not be run as a vertical campaign the way smallpox was. Ongoing surveillance of populations involved more sophisticated medical training of personnel than disease recognition or vaccination. Malaria work required trained laboratory technicians who could use microscopes to examine blood smears for parasites; it required medical auxiliaries who could administer chemoprophylaxis and chemotherapy. The establishment of a dense network of clinics with laboratory facilities implied radical structural changes in health service organization, which most countries were not willing to undertake.

M. A. Farid, a former WHO staff member, has reflected with some bitterness on his experience; he feels that WHO took all the wrong decisions at the critical turning point in the 1960s. Instead of extending the use of conventional antilarval, engineering, or biological methods, the organizers continued to rely on DDT: "confidence in DDT spraying blinded everybody to the need to promote research" (1980, 15). Farid believes the leaders should have recognized and corrected their technical errors; they should have coped with the problems of insecticide and drug resistance that were developing. Farid felt that these technical problems should have been confronted directly, but instead the goal of the campaign was revised.

WHO abandoned the international aspect of the program and from 1965 called it simply the "Malaria Control Campaign"; malaria was to be a national responsibility. One result was the breakdown of safeguards on international frontiers; and malaria, which is no respecter of national boundaries, was quickly transmitted by migrants who had established their patterns of travel long before colonial administrations set up artificial national barriers. Malaria traveled with the migrants from areas that were not yet free of malaria to those where malaria had recently been eradicated (Prothero 1965). National governments, feeling that their budgets were overburdened, discontinued monitoring procedures such as the routine examination of blood samples for parasites; countries that did not put malaria high on the list of priority diseases dismantled their eradication programs. At least that was the explanation current in WHO as to why the campaign failed and why malaria was on the rise again.

A serious resurgence of malaria in many parts of the Third World followed the failure of the original campaign. There are several controversial explanations of what happened. Harry Cleaver (1977), an economist, interprets this failure not as caused by limited medical knowledge or technical know-how, which is what Farid is implying, but as the result of deliberate economic policy on the part of the advanced industrialized nations. Cleaver believes the developed countries want to keep certain parts of the Third World underdeveloped and conspire to do so; he sees disease as a weapon of social repression. He thinks that colonists, and now neocolonialists, used poverty and illness to weaken and control the work force by draining the energies of the working class which would otherwise be available for struggle to end poverty.

In a sharp rebuttal, Gish (1978) argues that Cleaver fails to show that malaria eradication is a key measure of government commitment to health or that declining support for malaria eradication is related to a general decline in support for all health programs; therefore Cleaver is wrong to single out the malaria program as some sort of imperialist conspiracy against the poor. Gish takes the position that governments were right to end the vertical campaign and to integrate malaria control in basic health programs.

Chapin and Wasserstrom (1981) explain the campaign's failure differently. They interpret the resurgence of malaria as a consequence of the commercialization and intensification of agriculture in the Third World by the multinational corporations referred to collectively as "agribusiness." Drawing their evidence from case studies of India and several Central American countries, they look specifically at increased cash crop production, the intensive use of pesticides, and at the conflict between pesticide-resistant strains of mosquitoes and the increased use of pesticides generally, not just

DDT and malathion, which were used in malaria eradication campaigns. They also ask who is promoting increased production of cash crops, which are often industrial crops and not food crops, and why there is increased use of pesticides on these crops. On the basis of patterns of commercial production familiar in large-scale farming in the United States, Chapin and Wasserstrom conclude that the areas of pesticide-intensive cash cropping are the ones where malaria is resurgent and where new epidemics of the disease are being created. Their analysis is disputed by a recent study of the Indian case: Sharma and Mehrotra (1986) argue, unconvincingly, that the resurgence of malaria preceded the problem of insecticide resistance, that it occurred in towns where control measures did not rely on insecticides and in regions not affected by resistance, that it occurred before the introduction of the green revolution and did not correlate with production of cotton or rice or with intensive agriculture.

In a comparison between the success of smallpox eradication and the failure of the malaria campaign, bear in mind that the social and biological effects of the diseases are different: the high death rates and the stigma of survivors disfigured by smallpox probably motivated popular acceptance of the eradication campaign, whereas the slow course of the less fatal malarias sapped energies, especially in the consolidation and maintenance phases. The strategy of the smallpox eradication campaign was to use a technological fix (freeze-dried vaccine and bifurcated needle), in this case what I would call a "happy" technology well adapted to the circumstances. The strategy for malaria eradication was to break a complicated cycle of disease transmission by killing mosquitoes with insecticides and suppressing symptoms with chemotherapy. This technology was less happy and it could not be applied rapidly enough to forestall mutations of pesticide-resistant vectors and drug-resistant parasites.

The alternative and potentially successful antimalarial strategy—environmental transformation—would have come into conflict with overriding political and economic considerations, namely the opposition of urban elites to rural improvements and of agribusiness to any restraints, such as restrictions on the use of DDT, which would affect the profitable green revolution. Pharmaceutical firms, which owned seed companies that sold the new high-yielding varieties and which were often subsidiaries of chemical companies (themselves subsidiaries of oil trusts—and oil was the basis of the new agricultural technology [Payer 1982, 186–188]), pressed for the two-pronged approach based on DDT and drugs. The chemical corporations that produced insecticides rejected the evidence of Rachel Carson (1965) and those who followed her, which showed that DDT was the source of many environmental and health problems (Graham 1970; van den Bosch 1978). International public health experts, in alliance with agribusiness, said that Third World countries could not afford the luxury of taking DDT off the market and continued to use it.

Finally, unlike smallpox, malaria eradication required fundamental changes in health service organization. Admittedly, the smallpox strategy required a complicated organizational and administrative setup, centralized at WHO headquarters where the global sequence of the operation was plotted. But the administrative structures established for smallpox eradication could be external and temporary; malaria eradication required permanent national health services in place.

PART THREE

Non-Medical Approaches in Public Health

Chapter 9

PREVENTIVE MEDICINE

PART THREE OF THIS BOOK is concerned with health issues that are conventionally conceptualized and treated as medical problems, even when they form part of public health concerns and programs. My purpose in examining preventive medicine, nutrition, mental health, and AIDS in the next four chapters is to use the concepts outlined in Part One to show that public health can offer a broader, more comprehensive, non-medical approach at the community level to each of these issues.

Preventive medicine is a public health measure that illustrates the interacting roles of science and politics in public health work. For this chapter two traditional activities, immunization and screening for the early detection of disease, are selected to represent preventive medical care. These activities are described in two case studies: a swine flu vaccination campaign undertaken in 1976 and industrial programs of genetic screening. Both case studies exemplify the misapplication of preventive health measures and the confused equation of prevention and preventive medicine. In these examples it seems that public health workers were caught between bad science and self-interested politics. By analyzing how public health workers got into that squeeze, we may come to a better understanding of the decision-making process in governmental health services.

Immunization is an important public health tool and is central to preventive medical practice but it is not ultimately the best way to improve health on a communitywide basis. (On an individual basis, it is part of the routine practice of family medicine.) Immunization is only as good as the vaccine and the science behind the use of the vaccine, including epidemiological studies; mass immunization campaigns are only as good as the analysis of the political situation in which they are mounted. Of the two, science and politics, the political analysis of the decision to mount a vaccination campaign is the less understood and in this sense the more important to public health workers.

The Swine Flu Immunization Campaign

The National Influenza Immunization Program, an unprecedented attempt to inoculate every American against swine flu in a brief period of nine months, was announced by the U.S. government in March 1976 following the isolation of the strain in a soldier who died of it. Congress allotted $135 million to combat the threatened epidemic, and state health departments conducted the program. After a late start in October, the campaign was suspended in December and terminated in March 1977. In that brief time, the inability of public health to deliver services and the power of the pharmaceutical and insurance industries were exposed. The swine flu epidemic never materialized, but the vaccine produced a serious side effect—Guillain-Barré syndrome, a neurological disorder characterized by an ascending paralysis.

Influenza, which resembles a number of other infections, differs from smallpox, which is a clearly defined, easily recognized disease. Also, the severity and outcome of influenza are conditioned by nutrition, a fact that suggests other approaches to the prevention of death from the flu virus, especially in the elderly, whereas smallpox is one of a very small number of diseases that are not affected by the nutritional state of the host. The flu vaccine is unlike the smallpox vaccine, which is a very good one with 200 years of experience behind it. A good flu vaccine is difficult to develop because influenza is made "slippery" by the mutations of its virus and changes in its antigenic character (antigens are proteins that stimulate the production of antibodies). The strategy is to isolate the virus as soon as an outbreak appears and to prepare vaccine based on the new antigenic variant. In the past, the potential effectiveness of flu vaccine ranged from 20 to 75 percent, far lower than for nonflu vaccines (Berliner and Salmon 1976). Two vaccines were developed for this campaign, one specifically against swine flu and a second bivalent combination against swine flu and A/Victoria flu, which considerably complicated matters (Neustadt and Fineberg 1978, iii).

The federal government decided on a universal vaccination campaign instead of vaccinating the high-risk groups (populations at high risk of dying from influenza are the elderly and people with a serious chronic disease such as emphysema, asthma, heart disease, and diabetes—a total of about 40 million people or one-fifth of the U.S. population in 1976). The reasons given for this decision were that a universal campaign would protect many elderly people who would not normally be reached against two potentially fatal flu strains and that it would calm widespread public fear of a global pandemic such as the one that followed World War I. In that epidemic 20 million people died, 500,000 of them in the United States (Berliner and Salmon 1976); the highest case fatality rate was among young adults (Benenson 1985, 193). Press reports intimating the possibility of a killer swine flu epidemic generated fear at a very early stage. The story appeared on the front page of the *New York Times* on February 20, 1976. Reporters played up the similarities between the 1918–1919 pandemic and the current swine flu. People were frightened by the specter of a recurrence. Given the increase in international travel since 1919, infectious disease can spread more quickly and easily today than fifty or sixty years ago.

The medical basis of this fear of an epidemic was the death of a soldier on February 4, 1976, at Fort Dix, New Jersey; this new recruit refused hospitalization despite flu symptoms, went on an overnight hike in especially cold weather, and died (Neustadt and Fineberg 1978, 5). Camp doctors diagnosed thirteen other cases of swine flu at the fort. By February 19, the Centers for Disease Control had made the decision to mount a national campaign and vaccinate the entire population of the United States. In the month following the death, a survey carried out at the army base revealed that 500 contacts had caught the disease and resisted it; they had no overt symptoms. (The recruits were a captive population, easily studied and followed up.) There were no further cases at Fort Dix, no further cases at any other bases in New Jersey, or among civilians in the area around Fort Dix, or anywhere in the United States or abroad.

Two hundred and twenty-three deaths occurred during the next two years, allegedly as a direct result of the vaccine rather than of the disease itself. In addition to these deaths, about 2,500 people claimed personal injury as a result of the vaccine. In March 1977, Joseph Califano, then Secretary of Health, Education, and Welfare, faced with mounting scientific skepticism and widespread public opposition, announced that the moratorium declared in December would be continued indefinitely, in effect killing the program.

Public health officers faced with decisions on the allocation of resources considered various alternatives. One group said "Wait and see, don't rush into action now, there's no reason to mount a total campaign, let's just hold off." A second group of people said "Maybe we should stockpile some vaccine in order to have it ready. If an epidemic breaks out it will be relatively easy to apply as needed; people will cooperate because they will understand the danger." In the second scenario, it was thought that the epidemic could probably be kept under control if the most vulnerable population, those 40 million people at high risk, were vaccinated first. Yet another group said that swine flu vaccine should be provided as part of the regular health service, the way any other flu vaccine or any other kind of immunization is offered. They were answered by the panicky, "There isn't sufficient time." But there was another reason: the United States does not have regular, affordable, accessible, primary health care services for every American, and our routine preventive care does not include regular immunization for all age-groups. If we had primary health care provided by the government in this country, there would have been no need for a mass campaign.

The cost of the vaccination campaign, which actually reached 40 million people before it was stopped, was $135 million. Of that sum, $100 million went to the four pharmaceutical firms that manufacture vaccines—Richardson-Merrell, Merck, Wyeth, and Parke-Davis—more than WHO spent over ten years to eradicate smallpox. In addition, damage claims against the government for deaths and injuries amounted to $2.64 billion at last count. If one takes into consideration what an unpopular, indeed unnecessary, campaign this was (some punsters even said it was a manufactured campaign), it was an expensive fiasco.

There were some unofficial reasons advanced for mounting a total campaign to vaccinate everyone in the United States. First, 1976 was an election year. Gerald Ford, who was filling out Richard Nixon's term of office, was running for election against Jimmy Carter. According to Berliner and Salmon (1976), Ford thought it would be to his credit if he mounted this massive public health effort. Second, the Centers for Disease Control acted to protect itself against any accusations of unpreparedness that might be made in the event of an epidemic. Third, the pharmaceutical industry saw quick profits with guaranteed sales of 200 million doses of vaccine, with the government paying the insurance premiums and the liability bill.

From the beginning, there were questions raised about lagging immunization rates for childhood diseases, which would be slowed further by the deflection of personnel and resources to a swine flu campaign. The public health services simply could not handle both. For example, the state of Massachusetts was faced with a choice between a prior commitment to administer measles and polio vaccines to school children and the new federal demand for mass flu vaccination. Lacking the funds and personnel to carry out both programs, the state opted against flu vaccination and decided to store swine flu vaccine instead (Kass 1979). There are problems of inadequate production of all types of vaccine in the United States, and in 1976 the pharmaceutical industry was unable to meet the need for massive amounts of flu vaccine at short notice. In addition, vaccine manufacturers said that liability claims were driving them out of business, and the insurance industry was unwilling to cooperate in the swine flu campaign without government guarantees.

The conclusion drawn in chapter eight is that a global vaccination campaign against smallpox was acceptable and applicable because it could be mounted without changing the status quo of the health services or the political organization and alignment within a country. In the case of swine flu (albeit an illness with different characteristics), the potential epidemic showed the need to change the organization of health care delivery in the United States and challenged the political forces committed to the maintenance of the medical status quo. The vaccination campaign clearly revealed the ineffectiveness of the U.S. public health services in a critical situation.

A number of conclusions can be drawn from the swine flu affair. First, with hindsight it is clear that the announcement of a total campaign two weeks after the first death was reported and one week after the virus was typed was premature. The data were insufficient for a sweeping decision to vaccinate the entire population of America, and there was no time for a calm assessment of the epidemiologic situation. Two months after the decision to launch the campaign, government scientists realized their mistake, changed their minds, and advised the president to stop. But by then, events were moving too quickly to be reversed easily. Second, it was foolhardy to launch a national vaccination campaign without first carrying out a small pilot project. The data on toxicity and efficacy of the proposed vaccines were inadequate, and even excellent laboratory data are not transferable to epidemiologic settings (Kass 1979). Third, the government acted irresponsibly in releasing a vaccine that had not been tested for side effects. The pharmaceutical companies were smarter; anticipating lawsuits, they insisted that the federal government underwrite liability coverage. The experience raises the question of whether the government should produce vaccines in its own laboratories, removing the profit motive from vaccine production.

Fourth, publicity for the campaign reinforced belief in the germ theory of disease and in a technological approach to prevention and cure. A good vaccine may be a quick fix, but it does not meet long-term needs for ongoing routine health care. Fifth, the campaign illustrated that public health in the United States is designed primarily for marginalized subgroups. It also obscured the political significance of the economic and emotional plight of the elderly in our society by reducing people over sixty-five to a biological category, the "high-risk" group. The chronically ill were similarly reduced to a medical category, and the social nature of their conditions was ignored. Sixth, the campaign created the illusion that public health services can reach everyone and work for all Americans; clearly it does neither.

Screening for the Early Detection of Disease

We turn now to another aspect of preventive medicine, screening for the early detection and treatment of disease, in order to illustrate the limits of preventive medical strategies in public health and the influence of politics on allegedly technical decisions. This section begins with a description of the general principles of screening and then turns to the uses of genetics and finally to the specific case of genetic screening.

First, we should distinguish between the periodic physical examination (the annual checkup) and screening for a specific condition (for example, mammography for breast cancer). The confusion arises between screening and checkups because multiphasic screening is used in annual checkups by some large health maintenance organizations (such as Kaiser Permanente). Public health workers use screening to find cases of single diseases, more often these days in the Third World than in industrial countries: the best known examples are screening for tuberculosis and venereal disease. Multiphasic screening, which was developed in the 1950s, combines tests for many different conditions, in particular incipient chronic conditions as opposed to the earlier search for single communicable diseases. Screening for a specific condition such as glaucoma (raised pressure in the eye) appears to be more acceptable to the public than periodic general examinations. A few years ago the American Medical Association revised its schedules for periodic checkups, reducing the number and frequency from what they had previously recommended.

Screening is not intended to be diagnostic. It is capable of wide application. It is relatively inexpensive, especially when compared to an annual physical, in part because it requires little physician time. Nursing and auxiliary personnel can administer many screening procedures, and the physician can interpret the data rather than administer the procedures directly.

There are problems in connection with mass screening. First, it may raise demands for care that cannot be met. In the United States, the elderly are repeatedly screened for problems such as high blood pressure about which nothing may be done subsequently. In poor Third World countries it may make no sense to screen all children for eye problems or hearing problems when corrective lenses or hearing aids cannot be provided for those with impaired vision or hearing. Second, screening can create anxieties about false positives or marginally pathological findings. Or the contrary can happen: screening can create a hollow sense of security when there are false negatives. Third, screening may create social problems: there are stigma attached to the diagnosis of conditions such as PKU (phenylketonuria, which results in mental subnormality) and sickle-cell anemia (which lowers the blood's capacity to transport oxygen). Fourth, screening may be used by employers to discriminate against or exert social control over workers, as in screening for AIDS or illegal drug use.

Screening procedures can invade the privacy of healthy people, and technically complicated tests may convey more information to the agency doing the screening than to the person being screened. Hubbard and Henifin (1985, 231) suggest that preventive screening readily lends itself to coercion, especially when the physician doing the screening is a member of a more privileged race, class, and sex than the patient. Mass screening raises economic questions for public health workers: Is this screening procedure the best use of resources? There are five specific criteria for the decision to screen for a disease, which are in common use in widely different settings; for example, they can be used in recommendations for pap smears to find cervical cancer or for prenatal diagnostic tests such as amniocentesis to screen for such congenital disabilities as hemophilia (in which the blood fails to clot properly).

The first criterion is the importance of the disease for which public health workers are screening. The usual measure of importance is the prevalence of a condition or disease. One might question whether that is the best measure or whether severity or pain might be better. Some public health officials justify screening for antibodies to the human immunodeficiency virus (HIV) linked to AIDS, which is still relatively rare, on the grounds that AIDS is a fatal communicable disease; although there is no effective treatment and the period of infectiousness is ill-defined, identifying carriers of the virus may help stop the spread of the disease.

Second, is there a test for this disease that is simple, accurate, reliable, and acceptable? Tests like the Wassermann for syphilis meet this criterion. Third, is it a disease that is easily recognized in its early stages, and does it progress in an even and known way through other stages? Thus, can one make a differential diagnosis? Fourth, is there efficacious treatment available? (One can define efficacity as relieving pain, prolonging life, or as curing disease.) Fifth, do the benefits of screening outweigh the costs? Some of these issues are now being discussed in relation to proposed universal testing for AIDS.

Before turning to the use of genetic screening in industrial hygiene, it is necessary to discuss briefly the theoretical basis of genetics in relation to the diagnosis of disease and the prediction of human behavior.

Theories of Human Genetics

Genetics is the systematic description of hereditary mechanisms. Based on the rediscovery at the turn of this century of the experiments done by Gregor Mendel (1822–1884) in the 1860s, genetics has been successful in clarifying many aspects of the heredity of physical characteristics in plants, animals, and human beings. But some geneticists and biologists make a much larger claim for the field and hold that human behavior is determined by genes, a claim that Ruth Hubbard (1982), a professor of biology at Harvard University, describes as based on genetic reductionism (see also Gould 1981; Lewontin, Rose, and Kamin 1984).

Hubbard's point is that nothing in the concept of a gene implies a causal line to human character or behavioral traits, as a close reading of the works of Mendel confirms. To draw causal implications from genes is to commit a fallacy, and Hubbard compares the fallacy of hereditarianism to that of the germ theory of disease. To say that bacteria cause disease is the same sort of reductionism as saying that single genes or groups of genes cause character traits. In both cases, the generative power of the particles is overemphasized, while the contribution of everything with which they interact is undervalued or ignored. In a complex system of reactions, such as protein synthesis, which requires many components and conditions that interact in nonadditive ways and that are often interdependent, it is wrong to single out any one substance or event as causal over any other.

Hubbard argues that, to a large extent, genetics is the reading into nature of the twin ideologies of hereditarianism and individualism. These ideologies were dominant during the period of the invention and proliferation of genetics, from the late nineteenth century to the 1950s when Francis Crick and James Watson discovered the mechanism of DNA. The ideologies of hereditarianism and individualism have been the impulse behind many genetic experiments in the mistaken belief that genetics can be useful for purposes of genetic and social engineering. Hubbard calls this illusory and says that genetic engineering cannot fulfill its promise to solve genuine scientific or social problems. Genes and DNA, as they are often conceptualized, are the reductionist self-fulfillment of hereditarianism.

Barry Commoner (1968; quoted in Hubbard 1982) reviews this same issue, which he explains in the following way: if the specificity transmitted in inheritance is determined by a multimolecular system vastly more complex than a single DNA molecule, any promise to control inheritance by chemical manipulations of DNA is likely to be illusory. Hubbard contends that most traits or types or phenotypes that geneticists work with are far more complex than a protein molecule such as hemoglobin and involve composite anatomical structures, physiological functions, and even behavior. For these kinds of traits, reductionist postulates about master molecules are simply inappropriate.

From this basic misinterpretation of how genes function come false ideas of genetic programming and genetic control. Some scientists such as E. O. Wilson (1975, 1978) evoke genes as the originators of specific traits as well as of major structures and functions of organisms. They call upon genes to explain orderly transformations of development and aging, and they say genes decide long-term evolutionary change and speciation (the formation of new biological species). According to Hubbard much of this rests on assertions that have no basis in observation. Appropriate experiments cannot even be envisaged, let alone designed. This critique is also the basis of her objection to sociobiological arguments for women's inferior nature, which she claims are really constructed on the Victorian stereotype of the active male and the passive female (Hubbard 1979, 21–26).

How corporate executives and their medical advisers use these genetic hypotheses in industrial screening programs is the subject of the next section. The issue of genetic screening is selected for the case study because it is becoming a prominent concern, not only to geneticists giving advice in family planning clinics on hereditary diseases, but also to public health workers and trade unionists increasingly aware of reproductive hazards associated with occupational and environmental exposures to radiation and mutagenic chemicals (Hubbard and Henifin 1985; Mazzocchi 1984).

Genetic Screening

Turning to applied human genetics—genetic counseling, genetic screening, and genetic engineering—we can use Hubbard's critique of the field as a context for a realistic appraisal of its practical scope. Jeremy Green (1983), in an article that examines how genetic screening was developed, who developed it, the scientific bases for its development, and how it has been applied, discusses the misuse of the concept of genes in industrial hygiene. Green is particularly critical of a research group that worked with H. E. Stokinger at the National Institute of Occupational Safety and Health (NIOSH) between 1962 and 1973. This group argued that a small minority of workers have genetic abnormalities that make them hypersusceptible to toxic exposures (Stokinger and Scheel 1973). At levels of exposure that are considered safe for so-called normal workers, these workers would contract disease. Thus environmental controls, this group argued, are not sufficient to ensure a completely safe workplace. It is also necessary to screen the work force, preferably at a prehiring medical examination, for their genetic abnormalities.

Stokinger's group selected five genetic abnormalities using the criteria I have given to select diseases for screening. They chose glucose-6-phosphate dehydrogenase or G-6-PD deficiency (the enzyme G-6-PD maintains the integrity of red blood cell walls); SAT deficiency, which stands for serum-alpha-1-antitrypsin (a lack of SAT reduces the body's ability to cope with lung irritants); sickle-cell trait (which causes red blood cells to become crescent or sickle shaped);[1] and hypersensitivity to certain chemicals—organic isocyanates and carbon disulfide.

Interestingly, the first three abnormalities affect very small populations easily distinguished on racial and religious grounds. Twelve percent of African-Americans and 60 percent of Sephardic Jews have G-6-PD deficiency, which is also found in Sardinia and among some other Mediterranean peoples. Thirty-seven industrial chemicals can precipitate hemolytic anemia in people who have this deficiency, but there is no recorded case of this having occurred; there is nothing in the literature to substantiate Stokinger's assumption. An investigation of a single case of an Iraqi Jew in Israel revealed that the disease was precipitated in a different way. There are some well-known precipitating agents such as fava beans, an ingredient in falafel, a popular Middle Eastern dish.

Sickle-cell trait, associated with African-Americans who are eighty-three times more likely than Whites to be carriers, has very little medical significance. Nonetheless, the Air Force Academy screened for the trait from 1971 to 1981 and used positive test results to turn down African-American applicants for flight training and for the officers' program (Hubbard and Henifin 1985, 244). Workers at NIOSH thought that extreme physical exertion combined with exposure to lead, benzene, cadmium, and other metals that produce anemia could precipitate a severe attack in people with the sickle-cell trait. Again, this hypothesis was never demonstrated. The fourth and fifth hypotheses about hypersensitivity to isocyanates and carbon disulfide are similarly unsubstantiated.

Obviously, there is wide scope for abuse in such a procedure. When this research scheme was first proposed in the 1970s, many critics felt that industry would use it as a cheap way to avoid toxic injury and as an easy way to evade cleaning up the workplace. These critics were concerned because of the specificity of the racial and religious groups affected by this particular set of deficiencies, and they saw it as an opportunity for industry to institute discriminatory employment practices.

Although Green thought that few companies were employing genetic screening, a survey conducted by the National Opinion Research Center for the U.S. House of Representatives Committee on Science and Technology found that between 1970 and 1982 at least eighteen of the country's largest companies and private utilities used one or more of these tests (Hunt 1986, 55). As of 1982, fifty-nine intended to, or thought they might, within the next five years; these included Du Pont, Dow Chemical, and Johns-Manville. The real figures were probably higher, because one-third of 561 organizations surveyed did not reply.

In the January 1984 issue of *Occupational Health and Safety*, Alexander Strasser, clinical assistant professor of preventive medicine, family rehabilitation, and occupational medicine at the University of Rochester School of Medicine and Dentistry, reported that six companies were using one or more genetic screening tests as one-time attempts to determine whether an individual had a particular trait that might dispose him or her to disease or harm from a specific substance. They were also using genetic monitoring, an ongoing process of testing workers to determine if genetic damage has occurred over time. Strasser dismisses the opponents of genetic engineering and genetic screening, saying that no industry would introduce genetic screening to avoid cleaning up the workplace, nor would any industry use it as a way to discriminate against certain workers. He believes that occupational physicians must recommend the use of genetic screening and that government officials should become more realistic in the interpretation of legal statutes; if there are statutes against discrimination or for occupational safety and health that require a clean workplace, they should be interpreted more flexibly to allow for the use of genetic screening.

This brief review suggests a number of conclusions about genetic screening. First, invasive individual procedures should not be used lightly, and in industry workers should participate in the process by which this decision is taken. Second, with so much at stake in terms of equal opportunity, privacy, and autonomy, industry needs the results of further scientific research on the reliability and efficacy of such tests before adopting these procedures. Public health workers who have to make these decisions should be in close touch with scientists, labor unions, and ethicists. Green searched the literature for critiques of Stokinger's work. Of the sixty-one articles he was able to cull on the subject, only two were critical and both of those accepted Stokinger's basic premises, questioning only some of the details. Before public health workers recommend such procedures, they need to be in touch with critics of science such as Hubbard and Green and to be aware of controversies and debates surrounding the science.

Third, when doing cost-benefit analyses, public health workers should ask: "Whose costs? Whose benefits?" In countries such as the United States where the expense of training personnel, especially health and medical personnel, and the price of insurance with third party insurance systems are often hidden and not obvious, the costs may be hard to reckon. Similarly, it is necessary to weigh whether a procedure is to the worker's benefit or to the employer's benefit. In the context of a system in which people do not have free access to routine medical care, one must ask whether the money would be better spent on establishing regular medical care, rather than on mounting mass screening programs.

In these cases of the swine flu affair and genetic damage caused by exposure to toxic chemicals, U.S. public health workers are being asked to make up for a deficient medical care system and for the failure of regulatory agencies and procedures. Maybe some problems such as epidemics of communicable disease that can be effectively prevented are better handled on a routine basis by medical services rather than dealt with as public health crises, and perhaps public health workers would not be blamed for campaign failures if they were not called in at the last minute to handle these crises. Problems of exposure to environmental hazards are better prevented by non-medical measures. If ongoing monitoring were in place, if ongoing government inspection were functioning, then public health workers might not become targets of public frustration and anger. Instead, to move companies it seems to take a crisis the size of the industrial accident at Bhopal in which an estimated 2,000 persons died (and then they act in response to liability issues rather than public concern).

The value of prevention is proverbial, but just as health cannot be equated with health services, prevention and preventive medicine are not one and the same. The limits to preventive medicine are not only technical and economic but also social and political (Holtzman 1979). Given these limits, the extension of preventive medicine may not produce the results desired by its supporters. The answer is not to return to curative medicine but to design non-medical approaches to prevention.

Chapter 10

NUTRITION AND AGRIBUSINESS

We all know that good nutrition is essential to good health and that poor nutrition is associated with illness and disease. Nutrition is therefore a critical part of preventive public health, but until recently it was the object of uninspired planning and unimpressive programs that emphasized habits of consumption—the last link in a long food chain that begins with land policies. This chapter challenges conventional public health wisdom about food, agriculture, and nutrition. It begins by contradicting a series of sayings, then examines the food system and its implications for global public policy, and finally discusses entitlements as a focus of nonmedical public health policies to improve nutrition.

First, it is commonly said that the problems of nutrition in developed and underdeveloped countries are fundamentally different, that overnutrition and undernutrition have different causes and different consequences. I would argue the opposite—that they are one and the same; that malnutrition in Africa can no longer be separated from the high fat, high sugar diet implicated in so much ill health in the United States; that both are traceable to the same single cause, namely, the food industry, also known as agribusiness, which is a collection of multinational companies familiar to us under such trade names as Dole and Delmonte.[1] In both cases the consequences are nutrition-related diseases: diabetes and heart disease linked to overnutrition; kwashiorkor and marasmus linked to undernutrition.

Second, it is commonly said that obesity in developed countries is a product of the quantity of food consumed—that is, we eat too much—and that the problems of undernutrition in underdeveloped countries are mainly poor quality and secondarily inadequate quantity. I would argue the opposite: the problem in developed countries is qualitative, and the problem in underdeveloped countries is quantitative. The food industry has lowered the quality of the food we eat in the developed countries by the use of chemicals in production and processing, by overrefining our foods, and by the use of seed varieties selected for advantages in picking, transport, and packaging, not for nutrition. We consume too many empty calories.

The same food industry has reduced the amount of food available to people in underdeveloped countries in the following ways: (1) by using good arable land to produce nonedible crops such as cotton, jute, or sisal, crops that have no food value at all;[2] (2) by devoting much valuable acreage to crops that are considered food but have no nutritive value, for example, beverage plants like tea and coffee; (3) by converting food into feed, as in the cultivation of crops such as corn and soy that can be eaten but are destined mainly for animal consumption, the meat and hides to be exported; and (4) by transforming food into exportable cash crops, as in the production of peanuts and sesame, and even certain varieties of rice, which might be consumed locally, adding nutritive and caloric value to the diet, but which instead are exported for their value as oil seeds, in exchange for foreign currency.

The corollary of Third World exports of primary commodities is the growing need to import food. In the period 1974–1986, sub-Saharan Africa increased cereal imports by 122 percent and food aid rose by 302 percent (World Bank 1988, 235).[3] Food imports consume scarce foreign exchange, which is no longer available to purchase needed machinery and which forces industries to close. The price of imported grains is higher than locally grown produce and beyond the means of the neediest peasants.

Traditional diets in most Third World countries stand up well to the scrutiny of modern food chemists who find them nutritious and well-balanced (Béhar 1976). The original diet of people in underdeveloped countries is adequate; the primary problem is that the poor in the Third World do not get enough of their own foods to eat, either because they are not able to grow sufficient food crops anymore, for lack of land and labor power, or because they cannot afford to buy available food.

The situation in northeast Brazil is illustrative. The small parcels of land that each *campesino* (peasant) was given to grow rice and black beans, dietary staples of the peasantry, are being repossessed by the big sugar estates (Da Conceição 1981; Linhart 1980). Every scrap of land is more valuable since it was discovered that the methane gases of decaying cane could be converted into gasohol. The discovery created a boom in the sugar industry, which is rushing to meet the energy needs of a country deficient in oil, gas, and coal. Consequently, Brazil imports black beans at highly inflated prices that are beyond the reach of *campesinos* (Berthelot and de Ravignan 1980, 72–75; Turshen and Thébaud 1981, 44).

Third, it is commonly said that modern agricultural technology has vastly increased food production and therefore the amount of food available to feed the world's hungry people (*New York Times*, 9 September 1986). I would argue not exactly the opposite because one cannot refute production statistics but that the outcome of increased production has been opposite to what was intended. Instead of more food being available to hungry people, the poor eat less today and they eat less well. Increased production does not directly affect consumption, nor are lowered levels of food availability necessarily associated with either chronic malnutrition or famine, as is popularly supposed. Rather, how deprived people obtain sufficient food to survive is a question of entitlements.

The pattern of entitlements is affected by different ways of producing food. Large, highly capitalized farms may increase food production but rarely at competitive prices (and even more rarely are any savings passed along to consumers); meanwhile these farms reduce the land available to peasants, and the capital-intensive technology they employ reduces opportunities for wage labor (Raikes 1986, 161).

Fourth, it is commonly said that starvation is a function of food availability. Amartya Sen (1982) finally discredited this notion; in his book *Poverty and Famines*, he shows that the major famines of this century (he analyzes four of them, beginning with the great Bengal famine of 1943 in which 3 million people perished) were due not to crises of food production but to the inability of certain groups of people to obtain available food. The people who starved were not entitled to food because the harvests did not belong to them and they could not afford to buy rice or pulses.

Sen documents what happened in Bengal in 1943. He shows that the food supply was practically unchanged that year; production was perhaps 5 percent less than it had been on average in the preceding five years. In 1941 production had dropped by a much greater 14 percent, but no famine ensued. He concludes that a decline in food availability was not the cause of the Bengal famine. Nor was a decline in food availability the cause of the famines of the 1970s in Ethiopia or in the Sahel, the region on the southern border of the Sahara desert. What did change in all three situations, and changed radically, was people's purchasing power, either because their wages fell, or in the African case because the value of livestock fell, which amounted to the same thing.

Sen pinpoints the groups of people who were hardest hit by the Bengal famine. He explains why these groups were unable to purchase food by showing how they lost out in the radical economic and political changes of World War II in an embattled India still under British colonial rule. An interesting appendix on the epidemics of disease that hit Bengal in 1943–1944 shows that the peak of deaths from starvation in the initial period of the famine was followed by a much higher peak of deaths from disease. Starvation was the secondary cause of death and disease was the primary cause, which pushed the final toll over 3 million.

The entitlement approach sheds light on the recent cycle of drought that began in 1980 and affected most of the African continent. Mass starvation and extensive death were recorded in Ethiopia, Mozambique, Chad, and Sudan; in these countries, agriculture was disrupted by civil war, which was about peasant entitlements, and the situation was aggravated by drought. In drought-stricken regions of South Africa, hunger and malnutrition were patently due to policies that deprive the Black population of fair shares of the country's wealth and to the Bantustan system that guaranteed faulty distribution (Turshen 1986).

Fifth, it is commonly said that people in developed countries are overweight while people in underdeveloped countries are undernourished. I would argue that this characterization is inaccurate because there is obesity in underdeveloped countries and there is malnourishment in developed countries. Obesity among poor women, especially during pregnancy, is often a function of diet rather than a question of abundance or scarcity, as they seek to fill their stomachs with cheap carbohydrates. In the United States, according to a recent study by the Physician Task Force on Hunger in America (1985), 20 million people go hungry several days each month.[4] There is also a small group of hungry teen-age girls and young women in the developed countries who are anorexic, victims of the food and fashion industries.

This characterization of the fat First World and the thin Third World is misleading because it turns our attention away from the central role of the food industry and focuses either on individual eating behavior—what I call the "hand in the cookie jar" syndrome, which spawns huge industries such as Weight Watchers—or on the so-called ignorance of the poor, leading us to believe that the malnourished eat the wrong foods because they do not know any better. Ryan (1976) calls this attitude the "blame the victim" syndrome because it blames the poor for the consequences of their poverty. Victim blamers assume that the high price of food is no barrier to the educated consumer, and periodically we are treated to news stories of high government officials proving that a family of four can eat well on a welfare check (Sidel 1986, 151). Hidden from sight is the responsibility of the food industry for inflated food prices.

Accusing farmers of being backward because they refuse to adopt the technological innovations of the green revolution is another way to blame Third World people for their own hunger. Sympathetic studies of peasant resistance often reveal the solid economic logic behind this refusal—the additional cash outlay the peasants must make to adopt the new technology, the additional labor time they must expend, the added risk of indebtedness if the harvest fails or falls short of expectations, and the likelihood that profits will be siphoned off by government bureaucrats rather than be returned to the peasants (Berthelot and de Ravignan 1980).

In summary, agribusiness—which is a group of multinational corporations that grow food with too many chemicals and overstock our supermarkets with overrefined, oversweetened, oversalted, and overprocessed foods—has transformed Third World economies from self-sufficient food producers to starving cash-crop exporters with serious consequences for the environment as well as for human nutrition North and South.

Food Systems

To understand the problem of malnutrition, we need to conceive of it in both developed and underdeveloped countries as the outcome of a faulty system that includes issues of land tenure (that is, ownership or tenancy arrangements such as sharecropping); arrangements for access to soil, water, seed, fertilizer, pesticides, credit, and machinery; the sexual division of labor; harvesting, processing, preservation, and storage (processing and preservation are major issues in tropical underdeveloped countries that lack refrigeration; storage is a problem because rats consume large proportions [perhaps 25 to 40 percent] of each harvest); distribution, marketing, food preparation, and finally consumption.

Obesity, wrongly regarded merely as the result of overconsumption, is as much an outcome of this faulty system as is starvation, wrongly regarded simply as the result of underconsumption. Only by defining the problem in terms of a faulty system can we account for the 400 to 500 million people still hungry in a world of food surpluses. Yet almost all of what public health workers do about nutrition emphasizes consumption, the tail-end of this issue, and it is rare to find a nutrition program that takes into consideration the entire food system.

What constructive role can public health workers play in the issue of nutrition? To display the range of possible activities I have superimposed suggested measures along a line marked off by health at one end, death at the other, and the onset of illness in the middle (see figure 3; also see figure 1 in chapter one). The activities are divided into public health intervention on the health side of the scale and clinical intervention on the illness side. Public health intervention is subdivided into communitywide and individual measures. Reading from the left, we begin with the reorganization of the food system, which is the most progressive (in the

Figure 3. *Roles for Public Health Workers in Nutrition*

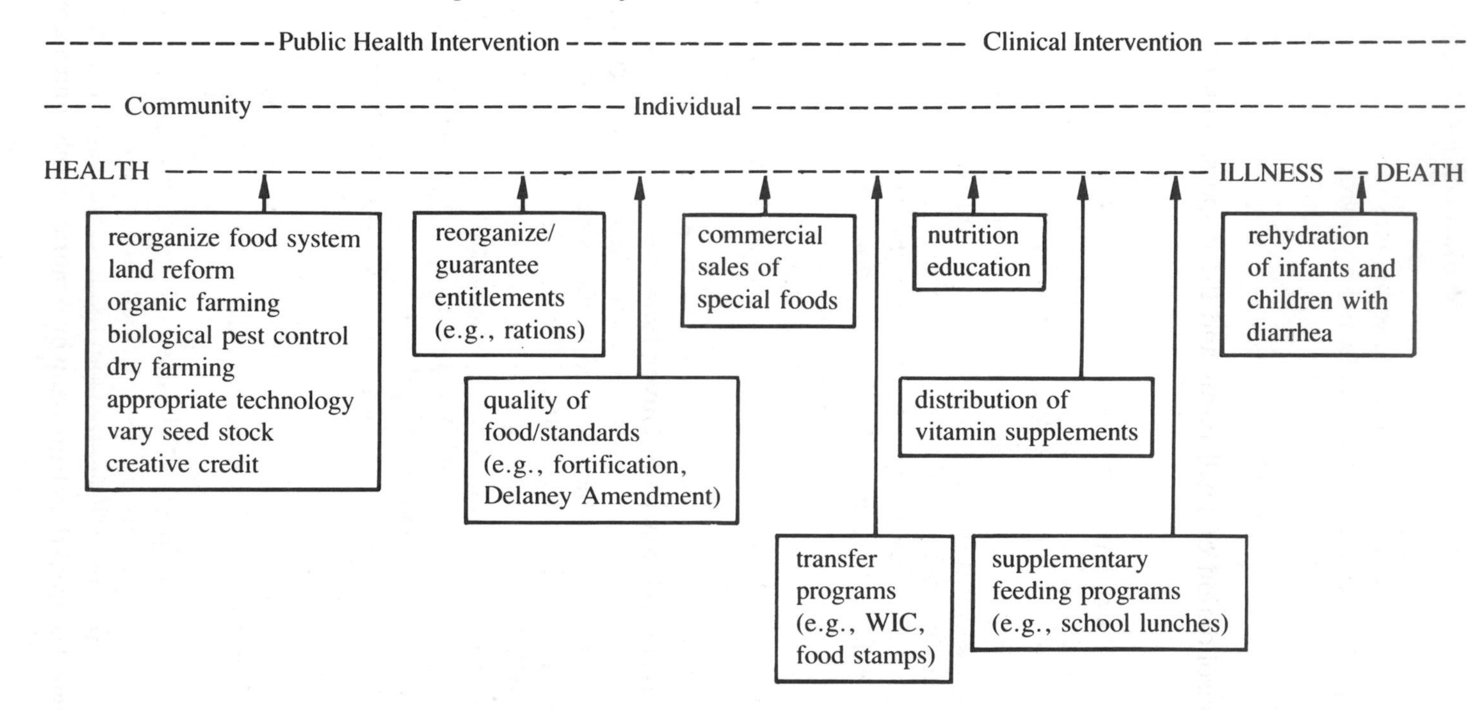

sense of the most people reached) measure public health workers could take. It also consists exclusively of non-medical activities.

The first issue, and the most political one, is land reform (Wolf 1973). At the moment land reform is as much an issue in the United States as it is in parts of the Third World because of the consolidation of small farms and the dispossession of the family farmer. In the United States, farm size is increasing steadily, the number of farms is decreasing, the number of people living on farms is declining, and ownership is concentrated in fewer hands (Belden 1986). It is virtually impossible for an individual who has not inherited a farm to enter American agriculture because the estimated start-up cost of $750,000 for land, machinery, stock, and seed is prohibitive. In Asia and Latin America, land concentration is still the critical obstacle to food self-sufficiency (ILO 1977; Stavenhagen 1970). Schuyler (1980) describes the situation in Venezuela, long a land of abundant, oil-fed wealth that fails to feed its hungry and must rely on food imports. Land redistribution is not the central issue of hunger in Africa, which has no tradition of *latifundia* (great landed estates) outside of areas such as the Highlands of Kenya or the commercial farms of Zimbabwe colonized by White settlers, but women's unequal access to land is an issue (Afonja 1986; Guyer 1984).

The second and third issues—organic farming and biological pest control—involve the chemical industry, which promotes extensive use of chemical fertilizers and pesticides in farming, and the pharmaceutical industry, which promotes the use of antibiotics and hormones in livestock production. (The package of farming technology comprising fertilizers, pesticides, high yielding varieties of seed, and irrigation is the substance of the green revolution.) Chemical companies circulate "detail men" to sell their products, and as a result Third World farmers tend to apply five times more fertilizer and pesticides than First World farmers. These practices are destructive of the environment, dangerous to farm workers, and detrimental to consumers (Bull 1982; Weir and Schapiro 1981).

The ill-effects of chemical and drug use in farming are felt in both the United States and the Third World, but Third World environments are often more fragile (in the geographical and geological senses) than European or American soils, and marginalized societies are more threatened by failure than established ones. For the sake of the land as well as consumers, more research is needed on organic fertilizers, recycling human wastes, and use of natural composts, as well as on biological methods of pest control. We also need research on methods of food preservation that do not require chemicals.

The next problem is water. Chemical fertilizers and pesticides are polluting water supplies. In addition, the demand for water, which is increased by the irrigated farming techniques of the green revolution, is outstripping supplies (Sheridan 1981). According to a study in the United States by Marc Rejsner (1986), irrigated farming has severely depleted the nonrenewable Ogallala Aquifer, which supplies seven states from Texas to South Dakota. In other areas of the United States, the accumulation of toxic salts in the soil has killed off farmland; and in the Kesterson Reservoir of California, it has caused a drainage crisis that has poisoned wildlife. We need, at the very least, to publicize the failures in American farm technology (so dramatic on the Great Plains) and to send the message to the Third World. Beyond that, we need more research on dry farming—how to farm in conditions of low natural rainfall—and on how to grow crops that are drought resistant.

The ecology of water is intimately tied to forests and to fuel. Wood is the primary source of energy in the Third World, and government policies to arrest deforestation have succeeded only where alternative sources of energy are available, as in Algeria where cheap supplies of natural gas are abundant. Water and fuel are also women's issues because it is a woman's task to provide both for cooking and other domestic uses (Sen and Grown 1987).

Appropriate technology, the fifth issue, provides farming techniques that are not dependent on economies of scale to justify such capital-intensive technology as irrigation, high yielding seed varieties, pesticides, and fertilizers. Initially, the appropriate technology movement emphasized the adaptation of machinery to Third World realities by scaling it down for use on farms of few acres (Dumont and Cohen 1980). More recently, soil and water conservation technicians have adapted their techniques to conditions of Third World farming—that is, to communal, sharecropping, and squatter tenure systems (Millington and Mutiso 1986).

Third World agricultural extension workers often make technology accessible to men only, even where women are the primary farm laborers. Because women are rarely registered as farm owners, they are often an invisible labor force (Benería 1981). The sexual division of labor in agriculture was one of the first issues of feminist investigation in the Third World (Boserup 1970). Women do not work in the fields in all societies, and some upper-class women can pay others to do their labor. But in most of Africa, the unequal division of agricultural labor imposes serious burdens on women, affecting their health and nutrition and the well-being of their children (Henn 1984; Guyer 1984).

The next issue is the need to preserve seed variety. Pharmaceutical corporations, both U.S. and other multinational firms, acquired the companies that supply seed to farmers at a time when they were developing genetically engineered seed (Kenney 1986, 223). The firms restricted the types of seed offered, in part by lobbying successfully for changes in patent law to protect new seeds (Yoxen 1983, 145). For hardier indigenous seed types, the companies have substituted a reduced number of hybrid varieties that require pesticides and fertilizers to produce higher yields (Weir and Schapiro 1981, 43–46). The germ plasm of most crops originates in the Third World, but most plant breeding is done in developed countries; ironically, Third World farmers are paying royalties for varieties of their own plants. Wild seed types are fast disappearing, despite the development of seed banks to preserve indigenous species, and with them valuable genetic traits such as drought resistance and tolerance to toxic soil salts (Feldman and Sears 1981).

The disappearance of wild varietals is illustrated by the history of the apple. U.S. supermarkets carry half a dozen varieties: red and golden delicious, MacIntosh, Granny Smith, Rome, Stayman. But the annals of colonial American history describe hundreds of varieties grown in this country. Most of them have disappeared.

The last issue in reorganizing the food system is creative credit. The provision of government subsidies and the establishment of credit arrangements provide very effective means of economic, political, and social control (Yoxen 1983, 144). In the Third World, peasant cooperatives often supervise credit and attach stringent conditions to loans, which are given in the form of fertilizer, machinery, and seeds rather than cash; the lending agencies prescribe farming technology and guarantee repayment by requiring that harvests be delivered to the government purchasing agency (Payer 1982, 231–232). In these circumstances, farmers bear most of the costs and risks but have no control over land use decisions and no way to insulate their incomes against failure. New ways to finance farming are needed—in the United States because there is a credit banking crisis going on right now, and in the Third World where women, particularly, need access to credit (Ceesay-Marenah 1982; Egger 1986). Women were often denied membership in credit societies in the colonial period even when they were de facto heads of rural households.

Entitlements

The second non-medical measure for public health workers to consider is the issue of reorganizing and guaranteeing entitlements (the ways in which people can obtain food) raised by Sen (1982). Two percent of Americans obtain food by growing it; they are entitled to what they raise because they own their farms. The remaining 98 percent rely on cash purchases; most of them are entitled to buy food by exchanging the wages they earn through the sale of their labor power. For the 15 percent of Americans below the poverty line, various government transfer programs such as the one for food stamps entitle the deserving poor to food. When those programs are insufficient, as they were under the Reagan administration, charitable arrangements such as soup kitchens feed the "undeserving" poor. Those whom even charity does not reach go hungry in America.

Given the fundamental necessity of adequate nutrition to disease prevention, a radical change in the system of entitlements is needed as a first step to ensure public health. Norway adopted an effective national nutrition and food policy that establishes professionally determined acceptable levels of nutrition and plans the food supply accordingly (Ringen 1979). Sweden operates an extensive system of transfer payments (Sidel 1986). The United States has experimented successfully with guaranteed incomes as a substitute for welfare payments (Kershaw 1972); Britain adopted a winning variant in 1948, an institution popularly known as the "dole" (Titmuss 1968, 188–199). Several Third World socialist countries have systems of rationing to ensure that scarce resources are equitably distributed; the most successful of these programs operates in the People's Republic of China (Croll 1982). Nicaragua planned an excellent national nutrition policy—including credit and technical assistance, land reform, and the organization of cooperatives and training in managing them—but the experiment is failing because of U.S. interference (Barraclough 1982). Seventy years of experience worldwide, beginning with the Soviet experiments in 1917, surely provide a sufficient basis for reorganizing the system of entitlements in wealthy countries such as the United States so as to guarantee everyone enough to eat.

One major issue is eligibility: Should entitlements be universal (such as Medicare, the U.S. health insurance program for everyone over sixty-five) or restricted to selected populations (such as Medicaid for the indigent)? Selectivity is cheaper in the short term but more costly because of its insidious debasement of society (Medicaid mills, two-tiered systems of health care). Piven and Cloward (1971) point out that selective programs have a political purpose: they discipline the working poor in order to enforce low-wage work during periods of stability. Universality lifts all social stigma from such programs and guarantees their political life. Universal programs are popular with the middle classes because their redistributive effect is not from the upper and upper-middle classes downward but within the wage- and salary-earning class (Gough 1979, 114).

With a bill sponsored by Senator Daniel Patrick Moynihan, the United States succeeded in 1988 in replacing Aid to Families with Dependent Children (a misnomer for assistance to female-headed households which is the main part of the highly selective U.S. welfare program) with a combination of workfare, enforced child support payments, and government cash benefits to one- and two-parent families (*New York Times,* 2 October 1988). Contrary to popular perception, single mothers do not account for most of the poverty and hunger in this country; White families in which husband and wife are present are numerically the largest category of families living below the poverty level (Children's Defense Fund 1985, 49). High unemployment and falling wages are the factors most responsible for the new poverty since 1980 according to voluntary groups that operate New York City's 500 soup kitchens (up from 30 in 1980) (*New York Times,* 25 June 1987). The issue is precisely one of child care and jobs; not the public jobs that Moynihan's bill proposes for welfare mothers, but full-time, year-round employment at wages above the legal minimum and comparable to those paid to male workers.

Next is the issue of standards for food quality. In the past year, five authoritative reports published by the General Accounting Office, the Centers for Disease Control, and the National Academy of Sciences have provided more convincing evidence than ever before that modern food production, and the inability of federal agencies to inspect food adequately and to detect toxic substances, may be jeopardizing the health of Americans (*New York Times,* 22 June 1987). Impure foods, contaminated by pesticides and antibiotics used in production, put 1.5 million Americans at risk of cancer and cause 500,000 cases of salmonella poisoning annually. Congress is considering new bills to improve the purity and safety of food, but it is unlikely that they will address the logic of capitalist farming, which necessitates the use of chemicals.

Another issue is subsidization of commercial sales of particular foods, a policy that is not peculiar to underdeveloped countries. In the European Economic Community, dairy exports are heavily subsidized; the internal price is roughly twice the world level (Raikes 1986, 166). Many Third World governments subsidize the price of certain basic foods in order to keep staples such as bread cheap enough for the urban working class to survive on low wages (Andrae and Beckman 1985). The World Bank recommends the withdrawal of these subsidies on the grounds that higher prices would provide an incentive to producers, but where the bank's advice was followed and prices rose, food riots broke out (Seddon 1986).

There is a particular group of foods often subsidized in the Third World, sometimes called infant formula, baby foods, or weaning foods, which target the population of infants and small children. When purchased by poor, illiterate women, who dilute the powder to stretch quantities and prepare the foods under unhygienic conditions, the result is not nourishment but malnutrition and diarrhea. Corporations promote and sell commercial infant foods as safe substitutes for breast milk in deceptive ways, for example by dressing saleswomen as nurses and sending them into maternity wards with free samples. This and other scandalous practices in the Third World are the object of boycotts, lawsuits, and international legislation (Chetley 1979; *New York Times,* 1 January 1989).

The next category, moving over toward the individual scale, is the distribution of vitamin and mineral supplements. This form of compensation for dietary deficits was common in the United States thirty or forty years ago but was replaced by the general supplementation of processed foods with chemical additives. Vitamin distribution is still common in Third World countries, sometimes pushed by pharmaceutical companies for sale to hungry villagers (Muller 1982).

Similarly, supplementary feeding programs were once common in the United States but are now restricted to special groups such as impoverished children. While the Reagan administration repeatedly tried to cut back the school lunch program, the government began contributing to soup kitchens run by charities. The U.S. Department of Agriculture periodically distributes surplus cheese or butter, but more often surpluses are sent abroad (George 1976; Lappé and Collins 1978). Many Third World countries still operate supplementary feeding programs, some supplied by foreign aid (Bessis 1979; Solagral 1984). One of the rare evaluations of the efficacy of such programs was carried out by Solimano and Hakim (1979); they studied school feeding programs and milk distribution in Chile, which began in 1924, were expanded in 1970 under the Allende government, and then cut back severely in 1973 by the Pinochet regime. They concluded that the measures improved nutritional standards somewhat but that persistent malnutrition reflected patterns of production, distribution, and consumption, which were reinforced by the country's economic development strategies.

Nutrition education is last on this list of public health measures. It is least important because most basic diets are good. The problem is not that people eat the wrong foods out of ignorance but that in the United States unhealthy fast food is cheap, widely advertised, and readily available, and in the Third World people are not eating enough of their traditional diets. The impact that the correction of these two problems would have on nutrition and health far outweighs what education can accomplish. Nutrition education too often shows people how to adjust to intolerable situations; in an extreme example, South African nutrition education programs teach Blacks how not to starve on starvation wages.

On the other side of the scale is clinical intervention. Of the many measures that could be mentioned, rehydration is singled out because it is an individual, clinical intervention promoted by the U.S. government, WHO, and UNICEF as a public health program that could save the lives of millions of children in the Third World. Rehydration of malnourished children suffering from diarrheal diseases was a procedure performed only in hospitals before the technology was simplified. Now village primary health care workers can teach oral rehydration with a sterile sugar and salt solution to illiterate parents (WHO 1976). The investment of scarce public health rupees, pesos, and shillings in this remedial effort makes senses only if it is part of a combined preventive and curative program that includes non-medical measures. Otherwise the children return to the same sickening environment and fall ill again.

Is the reform of food systems and entitlements all pie-in-the-sky or something that can be realized in our lifetimes? We are in a period of reconceptualizing solutions to many problems: indicative are the push of social responsibilities into the private sector (for example, privately run prisons in the United States), the reduction of government programs and government intervention, and the cutbacks in social services demanded by the International Monetary Fund, which result in fewer resources available for public health programs.

What should be the response to the new private solutions, which pose a special dilemma for public health workers? We may feel that hospitals offering only curative services are not good, that they are not public health institutions, but we may also feel obliged to fight back when a hospital closing is threatened, especially if it is a public hospital that serves the poor. Do we defend programs such as school lunches, even when critics say that they are not the most efficient way to provide food for poor people, or do we accept the death of these programs, shrug our shoulders and say, "Well, they weren't very good anyway"?

Or do we do something very different: use this transitional period to push the struggle for public health to another level, reconceptualize public health policies, and rethink what nutrition programs should entail, not only in this country but worldwide? These are not rhetorical questions. They reflect controversy over strategy. There is an ongoing debate about whether incrementalism is the best way to achieve change (national health insurance first, national health service later), or whether the time is right for radical proposals.

I would argue that, given the crises in U.S. agriculture and Third World nutrition, the time is right for radical proposals. The new thinking on nutrition presented in this chapter—food systems, a phrase first coined by the United Nations Research Institute for Social Development, and entitlements, an approach developed by Amartya Sen—makes a difference to the way we understand hunger. The new ideas enable us to design radically different nonmedical approaches to national nutrition problems.

Chapter 11

MENTAL HEALTH

THE PURPOSE of this chapter is to describe the limits of classic, individualistic mental health care and to suggest alternative, non-medical and community approaches to the prevention of mental illness. Although the concept of community health is usually applied to physical illness, there is some experience with it in the mental health field. A few governments have had limited success in applying community approaches to restore mental health, for example in Belgium (Muth 1961, 38–41), and recently there has been a conscious attempt to organize communities for the prevention of mental illness. For example, the U.S. Centers for Disease Control issued guidelines to help communities prevent clusters of suicides, especially among teenagers (*New York Times,* 30 August 1988). The chapter opens with a review of theories of mental illness, discusses models of care for the mentally ill, surveys Third World experiments in treatment including the use of healing villages, and ends with a discussion of non-medical approaches to prevention.

When I first thought about writing this chapter I had in mind a critique of community mental health services; I thought of looking at the problems of rehabilitation of deinstitutionalized patients and analyzing the failure of public health responses to prevent mental illness. But when I read over the literature on deinstitutionalization it occurred to me that approaches to the treatment of the mentally ill, like approaches to physical illness, vary with theories of disease causation; so we need to examine the concepts of mental disease before we can look at community approaches to methods of treatment or prevention.

Mental illness is a divided, even polarized, field that is vexed by different, competing explanations of the problem. The five theories of disease outlined in chapter one provide a useful way to organize these explanations. The next section reviews the theories briefly with specific reference to mental illness.

Etiological Theories of Mental Illness

According to the germ theory of disease, specific disease agents cause particular conditions, and in this model mental illnesses are caused by disease agents that affect the central nervous system. The agent may attack the central nervous system directly (this is one theory of the cause of Alzheimer's disease [Wurtman 1985]); or it may attack other organs or systems first and reach the central nervous system only in the late stages of disease—for example, *treponema pallidum*, the spirochete responsible for syphilis, causes lesions of the skin and mucous membranes and, in advanced stages, dementia.

The second theory of disease, variously called environmentalism or multifactorial causation, uses concepts of risk factors that include mental as well as physical factors. For example, this theory conceives of cardiovascular disease as caused by a constellation of physical and emotional factors that include personality: Friedman and Rosenman (1974) say that type-A behavior (excessive competitive drive, time urgency, easily aroused hostility) puts one at risk of coronary heart disease. The theory that both physical and mental factors are responsible for disease is less well accepted in explanations of cancer, although some authorities believe that stress plays a definite role in the etiology of at least some cancers.

Multifactorial causation is also used as a model in the explanation of diseases whose manifestations are primarily behavioral; for example, neuroses (anxiety states, reactive depression, hysteria, and obsessional neurosis) are said to be mental illnesses that are influenced by a person's environment. Environmental theories of disease causation have broadened definitions of disease to include conditions previously defined as social. Such deviant behavior as violence and alcoholism now comes within the scope of medicine and is investigated clinically (Lewontin, Rose, and Kamin 1984). The extension is accepted by community mental health workers but it is controversial in some medical and legal circles. Psychiatric social workers, for example, deal with criminal behavior, the physical and sexual abuse of children, wife battering, and rape within marriage, but many psychiatrists believe this behavior does not fall within the purview of mental illness.

Lifestyle theories have less to say about mental illness per se than about behavioral factors in conditions such as cardiovascular disease (Calkins 1987, 63–69). Significantly, researchers using this explanation of mental illness are unable to generate reproducible or precise quantitative data about illness-producing behavior for either the evaluation of intervention strategies or the design of preventive programs.

Genetic theories of disease have made several useful contributions to the field of mental health in research on the genetic basis of mental disorders—for example, on chromosome abnormalities and inborn errors of metabolism. Mental disorders explained by the gene theory include Tay-Sachs (a fatal degenerative disease of the nervous system), Huntington's disease (progressive dementia that becomes apparent after age forty), and Down's Syndrome (trisomy 21, a form of mental retardation).

Some sociobiologists use gene theory to account for criminal behavior, an area of research fraught with controversy. In trying to find a genetic basis for violence and aggression, Price et al. identified men who carry an additional Y chromosome, the so-called XYY supermales discovered in prison populations (cited in Taylor, Walton, and Young 1973, 44–47). Critics Taylor, Walton, and Young charge these researchers with carrying biological reductionism to an extreme and with interpreting biological abnormality in a way that stigmatizes bizarre appearance and behavior. In such positivistic accounts, they note, biological factors enter into crime only indirectly: the crucial unexamined mediation is the interpretation placed on biological characteristics.

In the midst of current trends to explain mental illness genetically, it is important to reaffirm the relevance of culture. The relation of culture (defined broadly as a socioeconomic formation) to health is specific in the social production theory of disease. Explanations of mental illness based on the social production of illness and health rest on Marx's theory of alienation, which "displays the devastating effect of capitalist production on human beings, on their physical and mental states and on the social processes of which they are a part." (Ollman 1976, 131) Alienation concerns four broad relations that cover the whole of human existence: the relation to productive activity, the relation to the product of that activity, and people's relations to each other and to the species.

Marx's theory of alienated labor touches all of these relations: the organization of work, the appropriation and distribution of the fruits of the worker's labor, class conflict, and the dehumanizing, brutalizing effects of work. Because Marx understands causality as a reciprocal relation, it follows that alienation is found in all classes. Capitalists and proletarians are both alienated: workers are alienated when they sell their labor power because they lose control of their time and activity, and the capitalists' treatment of workers as objects of exploitation produces deformity in themselves as well as in their employees (Mandel and Novack 1970, 21; Ollman 1976, 155).

According to Marx, the dealienation of economic life cannot be achieved by the mere abolition of private property or even by its change into state property, for this would not touch the worker's situation. Private property must be transformed into real social property, a process that begins by organizing the whole of social life on the basis of the self-management of the immediate producers; this reorganization must be extended to distribution and consumption (Bottomore 1985, 14). Dealientation is a reunification of splintered human relations (for example, an end to the division of labor), the positive transcendence of all estrangement, and the dissolving of social classes. Critics have dismissed as utopian this promise of mental health, described as a state in which all people fulfill their creative potential as social beings.

Models of Mental Health Care

There are three main models of mental health practice worldwide: the medical model (including biomedical psychiatry, the term used here in preference to western psychiatry), the social model (encompassing traditional medicine), and the public health model (that is, community mental health services based either on the medical model or a combination of the medical and social models). An examination of each of the models shows that the diagnosis and treatment of mental illness are socially determined, just as the symptomatology and diseases of mental illness are.

Medical intervention in mental illness based on the germ theory of disease includes surgical treatment (for example, lobotomy), chemical treatment (the use of psychotropic drugs), and electrical treatment (as in electroconvulsive therapy). Environmental theorists add behavior modification to this range of treatments; it consists of training people with phobias by a system of rewards and punishments to change their responses to certain situations.

Psychiatrists trained abroad and returning to practice in their own countries have tried to adapt biomedical psychiatry to non-European cultures. In a moving personal account, Tsung-yi Lin (1982, 236) describes how the training he received in biomedical psychiatry (in Japan) was useless in his clinical practice in Taiwan; "I often found myself unable to make a clinical judgement with confidence as to whether a patient's behaviour was normal or abnormal." His subsequent research showed that biomedical psychiatric diagnostic criteria of depressive illness misled epidemiologists into documenting low rates of this condition among the Chinese. When different criteria were used, there was a 15 percent increase in the incidence of depressive illness in Taiwan. Lin concludes that problems basic to psychiatry—the identification, diagnosis, and treatment of patients—as well as the perception and conception of mental disease, cannot be divorced from the cultural context in which they occur.

Lin does not offer approaches to treatment that depart radically from biomedical models but, having noted that patient responses to treatment are influenced by culture, he adapted and applied biomedical psychiatry to the Chinese situation. He used his knowledge and understanding of Chinese culture, including medical traditions that inform culture and influence behavior. He proposes (ibid., 243) that "traditional Chinese medical and folk beliefs and the social stigma attached to mental illness in their communities combine to influence the perception of abnormal behaviour and the conception of mental illness, a fact which has pervasive clinical consequences in case finding and diagnosis, and acceptance of and response to treatment."

Arthur Kleinman (1980), a psychiatrist working the same terrain as Lin but with additional training in medical anthropology, urges the introduction of anthropological studies into biomedical and psychiatric training. His idea is that the disciplines of medicine, psychiatry, and anthropology should be mutually informed by each other's paradigm, but that none should adopt the other's framework. Leith Mullings (1984, 198) takes issue with Kleinman, charging him with maintaining a fundamentally idealist conception of culture and failing to investigate the sociohistorical conditions that produce and maintain medical systems.

> By omitting exploration of the extent to which medical systems are influenced by relations of production, by avoiding analysis of medical systems as outcomes of the socioeconomic processes of a world system, medical anthropologists often rely on the concept of culture to explain the diversity of medical systems. They easily fall, as a result, into 'culture of poverty' explanations for disparities in health status, eschewing examination of the realities of domination and subordination.

Interestingly, the mentally ill are frequently segregated and isolated; quarantine, the classic public health approach to contagious disease, is applied to the mentally ill who are institutionalized. The treatment of patients in separate mental hospitals was opposed by several groups during the 1960s, a period of remarkable innovative activity in the field of mental health. One opposing group known broadly as the antipsychiatrists includes Thomas Szasz (1961) in the United States; Ronald Laing (1969), Aaron Esterson (1970), and David Cooper (1972) in Great Britain; Michel Foucault (1965, 1976), Roger Gentis (1971, 1973), and Félix Guattari (1972) in France; and Franco Basaglia (Scheper-Hughes and Lowell 1987) in Italy. The antipsychiatrists attacked then-current theories of mental illness and treatment of the mentally ill, substituting environmental for physical and chemical theories of causation and proposing ex-hospital therapies instead of institutionalization.

The addition of environmental risk factors to the etiology of mental illness allowed these psychiatrists to place mental disorders in an economic, social, and political context. The convictions of many in this group grew out of repugnance for state mental hospitals and observations from their own psychiatric practice. But without doubt their enormous influence in the field of community mental health was assisted by the advent of psychotropic drugs. According to Scull (1984), the main motive for deinstitutionalization was economic: saving the state money was more important than demonstrating a new medical theory.

Critics take the antipsychiatrists to task for their acceptance of the psychiatric terms of the debate and their mirror-image solutions of the problems. The critics say that antipsychiatrists virtually ignore contemporaneous innovations in the related fields of sociology and criminology, which place deviant behavior, not only within the family as the antipsychiatrists do, but within the larger society (Taylor, Walton, and Young 1974).

Laing and Esterson (1970), for example, are best known for their work on schizophrenic families. But they ignore the fact that a diagnosis of schizophrenia is made most often of working-class, inner-city dwellers, least often of middle- and upper-class suburban residents (Lewontin, Rose, and Kamin 1984, 230). Mark Fried (1969, 113) gives a clear picture of the relation between social class and mental illness:

> The evidence is unambiguous and powerful that the lowest social classes have the highest rate of severe psychiatric disorders in our society. Regardless of the measures employed for estimating severe psychiatric disorder and social class, regardless of the region or the date of the study, and regardless of the method of study, the great majority of results all point clearly and strongly to the fact that the lowest social class has by far the greatest incidence of psychoses. It is striking that, despite the strength and consistency of this finding and the infrequency of such results in the social sciences, it remains in the limbo of facts that continue to be understated, challenged, and rarely examined for clarification.

The work of Hollingshead and Redlich (1958) is most often cited in discussions of social class and mental illness. They showed social class biases in the diagnosis of mental problems in the United States; they found that lower-class patients were more likely to be diagnosed as schizophrenic and be hospitalized than upper-class patients, who were less likely to receive such a serious diagnosis and more likely to get therapy in outpatient settings.

Mullings (1984, 197) goes much further than these authors in her analysis of social class and mental therapy:

> any analysis of psychotherapeutic systems must deal with therapies as they are constructed within the context of infrastructural relations. The emergence, persistence, and decline of therapeutic systems are related to the progression and imposition of modes of production, with their accompanying classes, ideologies, and values. Therapies are aligned to specific class interests and ideologies.

In Ghana, Mullings found that traditional therapy seeks to perpetuate an individual as a member of a corporate lineage in a semiegalitarian, agrarian, localized economy. Spiritualist church therapy, in contrast, contributes to the process of producing wage laborers, self-employed informal sector and service workers, whose work relationships are individual and contractual in a capitalist economy. Biomedical psychiatry is not exempt from cultural influence: the dominant forms of psychotherapy perpetuate and rationalize an individualistic social order. Under the guise of rationality, they often obscure basic problems by drawing attention away from the macrosocial relations that produce individual conflicts to the micro expression of them, from the overhauling of society to the increased coping capacity of the individual.

Like social class, race is also strongly associated with treatment for mental illness. Frantz Fanon (1952) and Albert Memmi (1957) both wrote on psychopathology and people of color. Fanon was born in the French colony of Martinique, and he practiced psychiatry in Algeria when it was under French colonial rule. Memmi, a Sephardic Jew, was born in Tunisia when it was a French colony. In *The Colonizer and the Colonized*, Memmi describes the experience of a man of color in a colonized society, opposing assimilation to colonization and rejecting both as resolutions of personal contradictions. He also developed a portrait of colonizers as "disfigured," even "diseased," by their roles in colonial society.

Fanon pointed out that psychoanalytic theory was developed in Europe where children could expect that the laws and values of the families they grew up in were those of the society they would live in as adults. This was not the experience of people of color: when they left home, they experienced themselves as "abnormal" in the eyes of White society. Fanon came to question the validity of psychoanalytic diagnostic criteria in the colonial situation. In 1961, as the Algerian war of liberation was drawing to a close, Fanon wrote specifically about treatment for mental problems in his classic, *The Wretched of the Earth.* How, he asked, can a psychiatrist cure colonized people and return them well-adjusted to a colonial society in which they are systematically rejected and stripped of their humanity?

The work of Fanon and Memmi, who were considered radical in their time, has entered mainstream social psychiatry. In Barbados, Lawrence Fisher (1985) found that 'madness' serves to justify racial and class hierarchies by providing evidence of the inherent weakness of Blacks; 'madness' is not only a response to oppression, it is itself oppressive. In the United States, Simon, Flies, and Gurland (1973) found that race and diagnosis were strongly associated: a diagnosis of schizophrenia rather than affective illness was given more frequently to African-Americans than to Whites. Collins, Rickman, and Mathura (1980) found higher rates of schizophrenia among African-Americans hospitalized in a predominately White institution as compared with rates in a predominately African-American institution and concluded that the race of the diagnostician matters.

The association of sex or gender with mental illness is explicit: in studies of depression in Camberwell, an inner-city, largely working-class area of London, with some pockets of middle-class people, Brown and Harris (1978) showed that about a quarter of working-class women with children were suffering from what they defined as a definite neurosis, mainly severe depression, whereas the incidence among comparable middle-class women was only some 6 percent. A large proportion of these depressed individuals, who if they had attended psychiatric clinics would have been diagnosed as ill and medicated or hospitalized, had suffered severe threatening events in their lives within the past year, such as loss of a husband or of economic security (Lewontin, Rose, and Kamin 1984, 230). Gove (1978) found that women in western industrial societies have higher rates of mental illness than men;

he attributed this sex difference to women's sex and marital roles. Feminists have written extensively about those roles and the psychiatric "careers" to which they lead (Chesler 1973; Showalter 1987).

Third World Experiments in Treatment

Some of the most interesting experiments in community mental health care come from the Third World, where a culture-bound biomedical psychiatry found it had little success. The bulk of the literature in cross-cultural psychiatry consists of anthropological reports on the treatment of mental illness by traditional healers, on the one hand, and of medical reports on the practice of biomedical psychiatry in Third World countries, on the other hand. The anthropological literature is so specific as to be inapplicable to other societies (see Kiev 1964; Salan and Maretzki, 1983), despite the similarities between traditional mental health practice and private psychiatric practice—for example, both function on a fee-for-service basis (the difference is in the world view of traditional practitioners, which is described as holistic [Awanbor 1982; Mullings 1984]). The reports of psychiatric practice in Third World countries are filled with admissions of failure traced to cultural misunderstanding (see, for example, Provencher 1984) or to a lack of adequate resources (see Busnello 1980). My interest is in integrated approaches that blend psychiatry and traditional mental health practice, but reports of such experiments are rare.

The People's Republic of China offers one of the best examples of traditional mental healing practices being revised in the light of biomedical knowledge, and a report from Senegal presents a good example of the adaptation of European hospital-based psychiatry to African cultural traditions.

China has been experimenting with the integration of biomedicine and traditional healing since the 1949 revolution, as well as with a political definition of mental illness (Bermann 1973). The principles of a national health policy were promulgated at the first and second national health conferences in 1950 and 1951. The principles of relevance here are: to emphasize prevention, to integrate traditional healing and biomedicine, and to conduct health work with mass participation (Turshen 1978).

In the 1950s, mental health benefited from general health campaigns such as the eradication of opium addiction, prostitution, and venereal disease (which reduced the incidence of neurosyphilis). In the early 1960s, traditional mental health techniques such as acupuncture, breathing exercises ("Qigong," see Koh 1982), and herbal medication were in use alongside biomedical techniques such as electroshock and insulin shock. During the cultural revolution, psychiatric practice, as did all branches of medicine, placed more emphasis on combining traditional techniques with biomedicine. Hospitals discontinued the use of electroconvulsive and insulin shock treatments and doctors trained in biomedicine revamped their psychiatric services to include a greater emphasis on traditional methods and on political techniques adopted by the society at large (Sidel and Sidel 1982). The major methods used during the early 1980s included drug therapy, acupuncture, "heart-to-heart talks," group discussions, productive labor, follow-up care, and the teachings of Chairman Mao (Thornicroft 1986).[1]

An attempt to adapt a European psychiatric hospital to African culture is reported by Collomb (1973). Understanding that a locked hospital in which patients are isolated and strictly regimented is alien to African village life, psychiatrists at the University of Dakar decided to give the psychiatric hospital a new image. They transformed it from a place where the mentally ill were abandoned to die into an open community where everyone participates in decisions affecting communal life, has a right to speak and a duty to listen. All physical barriers were dropped, traditional African gatherings were substituted for individual interviews and grand rounds in wards, and family members were permitted to accompany patients to hospital and reside there with them. Collomb and his colleagues encountered difficulties in modifying hospital architecture: instead of wards, the psychiatrists wanted small huts to accommodate each patient and a relative. Another problem concerned cooking indoors, which government authorities would not permit.

These changes brought improvements, according to Collomb, but the hospital was still not satisfactory, and the project was too expensive to replicate because Senegal's financial resources are limited and trained personnel are scarce. Thus even a good psychiatric hospital would fail to meet the country's need for mental health services. He therefore turned to the establishment of "healing villages," which he describes as "psychiatry without psychiatrists."

The changes instituted by Collomb and his colleagues transformed the Dakar hospital into a therapeutic community (a therapeutic community can be as small as a psychiatric ward or as large as a town [Jones 1953; 1956]). Four principles guide the creation of therapeutic communities: rehabilitation, which implies the community's dual role as treatment medium and realistic representation of normal life; democratization, which blurs status distinctions so that every community member makes responsible and constructive contributions; permissiveness, which enjoins all community members to tolerate pathological behavior; and communalism, which involves broadly based social interaction to give patients the feeling that they belong to the system (Awanbor 1982).

Therapeutic communities, of which the healing village is one kind, transform the immediate social environment of the mentally ill. In the theoretical terms of the social production of ill health, they transform some of the alienating social relations that produce mental illness. Although they address the treatment of the ill and not the prevention of illness, therapeutic communities are described at length here because they give us some insight into the potential of a reorganized society to create mental health.

Healing Villages

The most creative and innovative of the culture-specific [2] approaches to mental illness is the "healing village," which has a historical tradition in both Europe and Africa. Four variations are discussed here: the traditional approach as exemplified by the Zar cult of Ethiopia; a modified approach introduced by a French psychiatrist in Senegal; another modification implemented by a Nigerian psychiatrist trained in Great Britain; and a European version (probably as old as the Ethiopian) still functioning in Gheel, Belgium.

The Gheel Colony

The origins of this healing village are shrouded in a sixth-century legend of incest: an Irish princess, fleeing from her "possessed" father, took refuge in Gheel but was overtaken and killed by her father's soldiers. Her tomb became a magnet for mental patients, and in 1430 a building called the *Chambre des Malades* was constructed to house the pilgrims. The site was so popular that the overflow of supplicants had to be lodged in private homes; by the seventeenth century, a majority of Gheel's citizens had mental patients living with them. In 1852 psychiatrists formally recognized Gheel as a colony and it became known for its methods of family treatment for the mentally ill. The colony was still flourishing in the 1960s, administered by the Ministry of Family and Public Health and supervised by a state medical director (Muth 1961).

Patients entering Gheel are first observed at the Central Hospital before being placed with families. If in need of active treatment, the sick remain in the hospital until sufficiently recovered to be placed. The proper choice of family placement is important and often difficult. When possible, doctors match patients according to backgrounds (for example, urbanites to city dwellers, rural people to farmers). Doctors see patients on a monthly basis after placement, and professional assistants visit them more frequently (ibid.).

Patients are not confined and are accepted as family members with equal rights. They take their meals with the family and participate in its work and leisure activities. No more than two patients are lodged with a family and each patient has his or her own room. The colony supplies clothes, a bed, medical treatment, and pocket money. The family supplies accommodation, food, and laundry, for which it is paid. Payment depends on the condition of the patient (whether bedridden or ambulatory, disabled or well-bodied) and on the standard of the home and quality of care (ibid.).

Only 26 percent of the 8,358 patients admitted to Gheel between 1926 and 1950 returned to normal life. It is not known whether these results are better than treatment in a mental hospital (ibid.).

I personally observed a second European version of the healing community in Switzerland. In the late 1960s, while employed by WHO in Geneva, I worked on weekends as a volunteer in various mental health services. On one occasion I visited Claire Rival, a self-contained village for about one hundred physically and mentally handicapped people. Residents were distributed among "families" with which they lived and interacted on a daily basis; the "parents" were trained staff members. Everyone in the village was assigned work (baker, butcher, cowherd) according to ability and inclination, and even the most severely retarded participated in village decisions (for example, by contributing sketches for new housing designs).

The protected, caring environment appeared to be the principal therapy; drugs were not used, not even for epileptics who were free of seizures in the calm village atmosphere. The admission of physically handicapped people enabled the village to function smoothly and to be economically self-sufficient by producing food and selling handicrafts throughout Switzerland. Claire Rival conscientiously adhered to the four guiding principles of therapeutic communities. Two drawbacks are that the village was closed, in the sense that it did not interact with surrounding communities, and that it failed to discharge patients, who remained in the village for life.

The Zar Cult

Life membership is a characteristic of the Zar Cult of Ethiopia; no patient is ever discharged as cured, and the cult functions as a form of permanent group therapy. The healing cult is located in Gondar, where the major Zar doctors have their headquarters and their societies of chronic patient-devotees. The mentally ill travel to Gondar and become initiates of the cult; some eventually become doctors. Economic security is provided by employment obtained through the Zar doctor, or by spinning cotton in the doctor's house (Messing 1959).

In the society, patients learn to accept their ailment and come to terms with it. Their new social role within the Zar cult is similar to their position in the social hierarchy of the outside community, but they are no longer lone, unidentified individuals. They now have the backing of the Zar social organization, and group membership offers the sympathy of fellow sufferers. Moreover, every patient is assigned two human protectors, a custom which has its roots in the function of "best man" to the bride in a traditional wedding ceremony (every Ethiopian bride has two "best men" to protect her, even against her own husband). The Zar protectors prevent injury in case of violent outbursts. Part of the healing technique is to channel symptoms in accordance with social and cultural background by "matching" the patient with a Zar spirit of equal social status (ibid.).

Chronic patients benefit as members of the Zar society by calling attention to themselves as individuals and alleviating some of the consequences of low social status in the family or community. Most patients are married women who feel neglected in a man's world in which they serve and in which they are often lonely since they are separated from their families at marriage and reside with their husband's kin. Cult membership is drawn from all the major religious groups; members of the lower classes and minorities find social contact across religious barriers in the cult. Former slaves, many descended from other African nations, are also admitted to full membership in the cult. The aims of the Zar cult are limited, which may account for its success (ibid.).

Aro Village, Nigeria

Probably the best known experiment in combining biomedical psychiatry with indigenous medical culture is the Aro village mental health community in Nigeria (Jegede 1981a). Founded in 1954 by T. A. Lambo (1964), who became deputy director of WHO, Aro village houses 200–400 patients from a wide area who receive biomedical psychiatric diagnosis and treatment in a day hospital. Treatment consists of the use of electroconvulsive therapy, psychotropic drugs, and recreational therapy. Originally, a therapeutic unit was grafted onto four villages in a suburb of Abeokuta; only one village was still functioning in 1981 (Jegede 1981b).

Patients are not accepted alone; they must be in the care of at least one relative who looks after their material needs and escorts them to the hospital each day for treatment. Presumably making the families come prevents their using hospitalization to exclude the sick member, which is how hospitals are frequently used in the United States (Goffman 1961). A nurse is stationed in the village to deal with problems that arise overnight. Even violent patients have been treated successfully in the village.

The ratio of villagers to patients is fixed at three to two. In return for boarding the patients and their relatives, the villagers receive a small payment and loans to build new houses. Participants tend to be the families of nurses and other workers employed in the hospital. Villagers have profited from employment as gardeners and porters in the hospital; they have also benefited from such public health measures as piped water, mosquito eradication, pit latrines, and a clinic. They have a voice in administrative matters through monthly meetings between hospital staff and village elders.

Collaboration with traditional practitioners was a feature of the Aro scheme, but by 1981 traditional healers were no longer involved (Jegede 1981b). Traditional healers were regarded as a source of information about mental illness in the community, (for example, psychosocial causes of neuroses). They were employed under strict supervision to oversee social and group activities and to participate in epidemiological surveys as "contact men."

Social advantages included active involvement of the community in treatment, a feature of therapeutic communities. Medical advantages, according to Lambo, included relatively quick recovery, lessening the risk of social disability, and reduction of problems associated with after-care. Economic advantages included the low cost of running the program.

Eventually, the disposal of patients who did not improve and whose relatives could not continue to stay with them in the village indefinitely became a serious problem. Partial solutions are being worked out by trial and error. Some chronic patients are now living on selected farms; others live near the hospital and earn their keep, but need regular supervision.

A major disadvantage seen by Lambo is that the psychiatric day hospital is seldom possible in the loose-knit, success-oriented societies of industrialized countries, and he feared it would not survive the rapid social change of contemporary underdeveloped societies. In the past, day hospitals have been possible only on a substantial scale that includes a specialized mental hospital and a whole village. The program does not work with occasional mental patients from a general hospital placed in an ordinary village. Sympathetic administration and good public relations are critical to success.

Psychiatric Villages in Senegal

The Aro model was reproduced by Collomb (1978) in Senegal, with less emphasis on the role of the psychiatric hospital and more importance given to the village. Based on his experience at the Fann Hospital Center in Dakar, Collomb opened two psychiatric villages—one in Casamance, southern Senegal, and one in Tambacounda, eastern Senegal. Family members accompanied patients to the village and were expected to contribute to its economic life. Psychiatric personnel lived in the villages, together with the patients and their relatives, occupying twenty-five to thirty houses altogether.

Therapy is "occupational therapy," that is, patients are expected to participate in the usual activities of the village (such as farming and handicraft production). Nursing personnel make a special effort to listen to the patients and encourage them to air their problems. Drugs are used only when needed, and need appears to decrease as patients are incorporated into village social life and as nurses relinquish medical control. A psychiatrist visits the village once a month for a weekend. The obvious advantage is that the cost of village care is fifteen to twenty times less than that of a stay in a classical psychiatric hospital (Collomb 1978).

The Social Production of Mental Illness

Therapeutic communities, even at their best when they embody social rather than biomedical models of disease, do not change the social relations that produce mental illness or label some people as mentally ill. The social production of illness and health theory calls into question the very category of mental illness. Out of the experience of the 1960s came the observation that there is a thin line between insanity, criminality, and political protest; who gets which label depends more on a person's race, gender, and social class than on any objective measure of disease.

A review of judicial practice in many countries suggests that the categories (insanity, criminality, and political protest) are regularly collapsed. Political protesters, for example, are imprisoned together with common criminals; some countries, including the United States, do not recognize the status of political prisoner as distinguished from the common criminal.[3] On the other hand, in the People's Republic of China, political explanations are sometimes used to contextualize both criminality and mental illness (Bermann 1973). In another collapse of these categories, some countries, for example the Soviet Union, treat political prisoners as mentally ill and confine them to psychiatric institutions (Medvedev and Medvedev 1971).

The label "criminally insane" also combines two categories; who gets this double label, as opposed to the single label of criminality, depends in part on social class. Witness the differential treatment of John Hinckley who tried to assassinate President Reagan and Lynnette Fromme who attempted to assassinate President Ford. Ford's assassin is a poor woman who had a court-appointed counsel; she was convicted as a criminal. Reagan's assassin comes from a wealthy family, was able to hire the best available legal counsel, and was declared criminally insane. The sentence passed on Reagan's assassin has prompted a move to redefine the category, which seems to indicate that there is no agreed objective measure of insanity and that the concept of criminal insanity can be redefined politically.

In another example, the Sozialistiches Patienten Kollektiv (S.P.K.), a 500-member socialist patient collective at the University of Heidelberg, was broken up by the German government in 1970 and the patients were dispersed to jail cells as common criminals or political protesters as well as to state mental hospitals (S. P. K. 1972). It seems as though treatment defined the condition, rather than the other way around, and that decisions about treatment were political rather than medical. Apart from issues of labeling, the social production of illness and health theory raises questions about historical time and place, factors that are absent from biomedical constructions of conditions such as schizophrenia. Descriptions of mental illness refer at some point to definitions of normality, which are known to be cultural and temporal. It follows that definitions of mental illness are also bound by time and culture.

Historical time and place give meaning to race, gender, and social class. For example, race is presently highly significant for mental health in South Africa but of little significance in Tanzania. The relation between people in different racial categories is what gives the category meaning in South Africa today. Apartheid is a major source of mental ill health because it destroys family and community support systems through mass uprooting of Blacks, and because it generates stress and tension in the daily lives of millions of Blacks, Indians, and Coloureds through the pervasive insecurity, harassment, and violence that characterize the psychosocial environment of South Africa (WHO 1983, 165).

The relations between people that give meaning to race, gender, and class encompass the organization of work on the job and at home. By the organization of work we mean the division of labor between races, genders, and classes. For example, how work is divided between men and women (the jobs that only men do, the ones only women do, the ones either can do, and so on) and between classes (what owners do, what managers do, and what workers do) defines one aspect of gender and class relations in society.

Relations between people are also defined by the way work is divided between age-groups: what young people do, what old people do, and who is a "productive" member of society (the "productive" category excludes unpaid workers, mainly women volunteers and housewives). In the context of class, race, and gender divisions, age is significant for mental health. It is striking that the "productive" age-group is shrinking all the time in our society; for manual workers it is now between twenty-five and forty-five years of age, which is a very limited time; this is paradoxical when one considers how life expectancy has increased.

In preindustrial societies, all age-groups and both genders worked and contributed to the household; the production unit was the family and the only unproductive groups supported by all others were royalty and, in some cases, the priesthood. In postindustrial America, anyone over the age of fifty who is laid off from one job has difficulty finding another; for the class dependent on wages, the stress of unemployment can lead to mental illness (Colledge and Hainsworth 1982; see also the debates between Eyer 1976a, 1976b and Brenner 1976; Sclar 1980). Elderly women suffer the cumulative effects of lifelong pay discrimination and earn smaller pensions on retirement; the stress of poverty and social isolation in old age can lead to mental breakdown (Dowd 1984). It is hard for teenagers to find any work at all, but unemployment rates in this age-group are highest among African-Americans who also are accused of antisocial behavior (Children's Defense Fund 1985, 64).

If illness and health are both socially produced, then logically the reorganization of society could promote health and reduce ill health, depending on how it is done. Effective social reorganization would include, for example, changes in race relations. It is probably impossible to single out the impact of the 1954 Supreme Court desegregation decision or the 1964 Civil Rights Act, but one wonders whether African-Americans in the United States experience less racism in the 1980s than they did in the 1940s and whether even modest changes in race relations correlate with less stress and less mental illness.

Effective social reorganization would also involve changes in gender relations, which the women's movement has been working for in many countries (Morgan 1984). Again, it is probably impossible to single out the impact of the women's movement, but one wonders whether changes in women's status have altered the incidence of mental illness, psychiatric diagnosis, treatment, or the number of women hospitalized since the 1960s. Gove (1978) thought that higher rates of mental illness among women was related to the stresses associated with the transition in the nature of women's roles in society.

The changes in race and gender relations cited do not involve the sweeping structural revolution that changes in class relations entail. Revolutionary experience comes from the Soviet Union and other socialist economies, but even a few mixed economies (notably Great Britain) have made a conscious attempt to change class relations. This issue is usually ignored in the United States, which defines social class by income and denies the existence of class barriers to social mobility. Thus, despite evidence quoted by Marc Fried, Americans do not give much credence to the problem of social class and mental illness.

An exciting aspect of the approach to mental disorder taken by social production of illness and health theorists is the promised resolution of the mind/body split. According to biomedical models of mental disease, mind and body are two different systems—disease is thought to affect each system separately but in similar ways. Social production theorists do not take that model of disease as given, preferring a holistic model of human health that posits a continuum of physical and mental disease states. Social production theory locates the common source of both physical and mental disease states in social alienation and the experiences of political oppression and economic exploitation. This new approach offers a new set of options for prevention and for nonclinical treatment, but these options are very difficult to realize because they are not medical and involve profound social reorganization.

Chapter 12

AIDS IN AFRICA

AIDS, ACQUIRED IMMUNE DEFICIENCY SYNDROME, has become the preeminent public health problem of the 1980s. Other diseases claim far more lives; for example, in 1985 there were 462,000 deaths from cancer in the United States and 8,430 deaths from AIDS. AIDS cannot be prevented or cured, but that is true of some leading causes of death such as cerebrovascular disease (stroke and Alzheimer's). AIDS is communicable, and the advanced industrial nations have not experienced an episode of infectious disease since the post-World War II epidemics of tuberculosis and poliomyelitis. The rates of many other sexually transmitted diseases are rising, but unlike AIDS they can be treated and are not usually fatal. AIDS appears to be a new disease, so it arouses fears of the unknown; it affects infants and kills adults prematurely, so it shocks nations accustomed to long life expectancies; and it is prevalent in homosexuals and intravenous drug users—two groups that are the object of many social and legal restrictions. Because the prejudices and misconceptions surrounding a disease can be thrown into relief when studied in another context, this chapter examines AIDS in Africa.

AIDS presents many of the public health problems raised in this book. On a practical level, AIDS is interesting to public health because it exposes the limits of clinical medicine, which has little to offer patients dying of AIDS. It challenges the ability of health systems to meet the needs of sick people for equitable and humane treatment. It requires the profit-motivated pharmaceutical industry to make good on promises of research and development of new drugs. It tests the powers of persuasion that health educators claim to have developed. And it poses unique questions of medical ethics regarding confidentiality, social control, and screening for a disease that cannot be cured. This chapter examines these issues in Africa where, under conditions of scarce resources, they become more acute.

AIDS is also interesting at the theoretical level. Germ theorists were quick to claim that they had solved the riddle of the "cause" of the disease when they identified HIV, the human immunodeficiency virus. But as with all infectious diseases, they cannot answer the question of why AIDS does not develop in everyone exposed to the virus. Lifestyle advocates see vindication for their theory in the behavior of the two main groups affected by the disease. When faced with the same disease without the associated behavior in Africa, they level charges of widespread promiscuity and prostitution, distorting the reality of African life to fit their preconceptions. The multifactorialists accept both viral and behavioral etiologies, ignoring prior questions of what causes the behavior or why the disease is occurring at this particular historical conjuncture. Using the theoretical concepts of the social production of illness and health, this chapter examines the political economy of AIDS in Africa.

The Nature of AIDS in Africa

Some 25,000 cases of AIDS—less than 16 percent of the cumulative world total—were reported to WHO from Africa as of 1 May 1989 (WHO 1989). (See table 1). Some reporters think this figure is inaccurate and accuse African governments of underreporting (*Economist,* 21 May 1988, 18). The charge is based on extrapolations from scattered case reports in what may be characterized as the extremely sloppy scientific literature; in many instances no firm diagnosis of AIDS was established (Chirimuuta and Chirimuuta 1987). Generalizations from case reports are impressionistic and cannot be substantiated. Of the 157,191 cases of AIDS recorded worldwide so far, the United States accounts for 92,719 or nearly 60 percent. The rate per 100,000 population in the United States is 10; in Africa it is 2 per 100,000. If diseases are to be given nationalities, AIDS is an American, not an African, disease.

The question of where AIDS originated should not be important but the imputation that the epidemic originated in Africa has ruffled many sensibilities. According to WHO (E. P. Hoare, personal communication, 1988), the first three cases in Africa were documented in South Africa in 1982, at least three years after the disease was reported in the United States. (A further 172 cases in the Americas are attributed to some time prior to 1979; these reports are based on retrospective diagnoses [Haq 1988a, 15].) Tests of older blood samples that were stored, which purportedly show that HIV antibodies circulated in Africa ten years ago, are apparently not as reliable as tests on fresh blood samples and indicate many false positives (Norman 1985, 1141). In all likelihood, AIDS originated in the United States and was transported to Africa, most probably by military personnel.

Epidemiologists claim and many social scientists concur that AIDS is pandemic in Africa (Miller and Rockwell 1988), but it cannot be substantiated at this time. The Oxford English dictionary defines a pandemic as a universal disease affecting an entire population. Sub-Saharan Africa had an estimated population of 450 million in 1986; 25,000 cases of AIDS spread over six years hardly constitute a pandemic, even if this number is underestimated. Compared with 240,000 infant deaths annually from neonatal tetanus (WHO 1987b, 305), a disease easily prevented by inoculating all pregnant women, or an estimated 80 million clinical cases of malaria occurring annually (WHO 1987c, 158), AIDS is not even Africa's number one public health problem.

Nor is there firm evidence that a pandemic will occur in the next few years, although material conditions surely favor an epidemic, which makes preventive measures all the more important. New data from the Congo and Zaire may alter the picture, but currently 56 percent of AIDS cases are in three countries—Kenya, Tanzania, and Uganda—which constituted the old British East African Customs Union. If one adds Rwanda and Burundi, which border on Uganda and Tanzania, the percentage rises to 67, or two-thirds of all reported AIDS cases in Africa. AIDS is not generalized throughout Africa, but is highly concentrated in one region.

Second, as in the United States, AIDS appears to be an urban

TABLE 1.
Cases of AIDS in Africa Reported To WHO

Country	*Number*	*Date Reported*	*1986 Population* in Millions
Algeria	13	26.III.88	22.4
Angola	104	31.XII.88	9.0
Benin	36	31.III.89	4.2
Botswana	49	31.III.89	1.1
Burkina Faso	107	10.II.89	7.1
Burundi	1,408	30.VI.88	4.9
Cameroon	62	3.VIII.88	10.2
Cape Verde	18	4.XI.88	0.3
Central African Republic	662	31.XII.88	2.6
Chad	11	20.X.88	5.1
Comoros	1	28.II.88	0.4
Congo	1,250	31.XII.87	1.8
Côte d'Ivoire	250	20.XI.87	10.2
Djibouti	1	31.XII.88	0.4
Egypt	6	31.XII.88	49.7
Equatorial Guinea	2	3.III.88	0.4
Ethiopia	81	20.XII.88	44.7
Gabon	27	31.XII.88	1.2
Gambia	62	31.XII.88	0.7
Ghana	402	31.I.88	14.0
Guinea	33	30.XI.88	6.2
Guinea Bissau	48	16.I.89	0.9
Kenya	2,732	30.VI.88	21.5
Lesotho	5	28.II.89	1.6
Liberia	2	11.III.88	2.3
Libya	—	31.XII.88	3.9
Madagascar	—	1.II.89	10.3
Malawi	2,586	30.VI.88	7.2
Mali	29	14.I.88	8.3
Mauritania	—	31.XII.88	1.9
Mauritius	2	22.III.89	1.1

Country	*Number*	*Date Reported*	*1986 Population* in Millions
Morocco	27	31.III.89	22.5
Mozambique	29	27.III.89	14.3
Niger	56	31.III.89	6.6
Nigeria	15	31.III.89	98.5
Reunion	20	31.III.89	0.5
Rwanda	1,302	28.II.89	6.3
Sao Tomé and Principe	1	11.II.88	0.1
Senegal	181	9.III.89	6.6
Seychelles	—	20.IV.89	0.1
Sierra Leone	5	31.III.89	3.8
Somalia	—	31.XII.88	5.5
South Africa	226	14.IV.89	33.2
Sudan	88	31.XII.88	22.2
Swaziland	14	16.VI.88	0.8
Tanzania	4,158	31.XII.88	23.3
Togo	2	15.VI.88	3.1
Tunisia	36	31.XII.88	7.3
Uganda	6,772	31.I.89	16.0
Zaire	335	30.VI.87	30.9
Zambia	1,296	31.XII.88	6.9
Zimbabwe	119	30.IV.88	9.1
TOTALS	24,569		559.6

Source: WHO. 1989. "Update: AIDS Cases Reported to Surveillance, Forecasting and Impact Unit, Global Program of AIDS." 1 June. Geneva, mimeo.

disease in Africa. Sample surveys show a significantly higher prevalence of HIV antibodies in urban than rural areas (southwestern Uganda, the only rural area affected so far [Torrey, Way, and Rowe 1988, 37–40], is a densely settled commercial crossroads). This uneven distribution of the virus raises two concerns, one about the possible spread from urban to rural areas, given the historical experience with tuberculosis in Africa, and another about the size of the population at risk in urban areas.

The historical analogy to tuberculosis is not an accurate predictor for the spread of AIDS from urban to rural areas. Tubercular migrant workers were dismissed from their jobs during the colonial era and, untreated, they carried the disease from cities, mines, and plantations back to their villages, creating foci of tuberculosis in the rural areas. Although there is some traffic between urban and rural areas, unless African governments adopt a deliberate policy of sending urban workers, who test positive for HIV antibodies but are free of AIDS disease, back to their villages, my hunch is that the virus will not spread to the rural areas as tuberculosis did, in part because AIDS is not transmitted in the same way.

Tuberculosis is a much more contagious disease than AIDS; in fact, AIDS is difficult to catch. The concept of HIV carrier, the period of communicability (when the virus can be transmitted), and the incubation period (the time from exposure to onset of symptoms) are ill-defined or unknown. Available data from the United States, which are based on studies of homosexuals in San Francisco, may not be applicable to Africa. Because general levels of health, nutrition, and health care are poorer in Africa than the United States, my expectation is that the period from infection to appearance of opportunistic disease is shorter in Africa. My guess is that people sick with AIDS will return to the rural areas only after they have exhausted the greater resources for medical care offered in cities and towns. They will go home to die, and in their morbid state, they are likely to be shunned rather than embraced by villagers. They are unlikely to spread AIDS as returning migrants spread tuberculosis fifty years ago.

The size of the urban population at risk of AIDS is relatively small. Although African cities and towns are growing rapidly, they are still small and contain only a fraction of the population. About 25 percent of the sub-Saharan population lived in urban areas in 1985; in the five East African countries where AIDS is now most prevalent, on average 9.6 percent are urbanites (World Bank 1988, 284–285).[1] Not only is the urban population small, but within that total number it is mainly the even smaller number of young adults who are thought to be at risk of HIV infection

(Haq 1988a). Communicability is generally related to population density, which is very low in Africa—in half of the countries, national averages are under 30 persons per km^2; by contrast, the figure is 384 persons per km^2 in the Netherlands (UN 1987, 134).

The assumed high prevalence of the virus is based on blood tests that failed to distinguish HIV antibodies from those of several other diseases widespread in Africa, such as malaria (Chirimuuta and Chirimuuta 1987, 55; Quinn et al. 1986, 957). The scare of 5 million African asymptomatic HIV carriers quoted by USAID (Merritt, Lyerly and Thomas 1988, 117)[2] is largely based on faulty serological evidence. Much of the epidemiological data published about Africa in 1984 and 1985 has been discarded and recanted because of major serum testing problems (Miller and Rockwell 1988, xxiv; Piot et al. 1988, 574). Most incidence rates for HIV antibodies in urban areas are based on small samples of high risk groups such as prostitutes and cannot be extrapolated to the continent or even to the nation.

Social scientists should not accept uncritically medical reports and epidemiological research findings of AIDS in Africa. They should read the clinical literature and question and interpret medical and epidemiological studies from the vantage point of their knowledge of the economics and politics of African societies. Most physicians and epidemiologists do not encourage such challenges.

Part of the confusion over the scope of the problem lies in the difficulty of diagnosing AIDS in Africa. AIDS, it must be remembered is a syndrome, not a single infection like smallpox. Symptoms of AIDS in Africa—chronic diarrhea, weight loss, and fever of unknown origin—are common and are symptoms of many other conditions. Similarly, the cause of an AIDS death may be a condition that has long been a common cause of death in Africa—for example, meningitis, tuberculosis, or fungal infection. Differential diagnosis is problematic when the best laboratories are available, but with limited funds and equipment, it is extremely difficult. Glatt, Chirgwin, and Landesman (1988) show the wide range of manifestation of AIDS—initially twelve infections and now twice that many—and suggest the difficulty of correct categorization in the United States. The original classification, developed by the Centers for Disease Control, was not applicable in

Third World countries and WHO is revising it.[3] For diagnostic reasons, and because the data are inadequate to distinguish between recent introduction of the virus and recent recognition or awareness of the problem, AIDS may be either underreported or overreported in Africa.[4]

In North America and Europe, the high incidence of AIDS in certain groups—homosexuals and intravenous drug abusers—allows doctors to make a presumptive diagnosis when confronted with these symptoms in persons with these behavioral characteristics. The diagnosis can then be confirmed by laboratory tests. The same cannot be done in Africa where neither homosexuality, nor intravenous drug abuse, nor hemophilia is a factor in the development of the disease. In Africa, AIDS occurs as frequently among women as men.

African women with AIDS are often wrongly characterized as prostitutes (see Biggar, 1988, 4–5; Merritt, Lyerly and Thomas 1988, 120–121). This victim-blaming attitude is common in North America and Europe where first male homosexuals, then intravenous drug abusers, and now prostitutes are accused of spreading the AIDS virus. For purposes of transmission, multiple exposures to an infected partner or frequent contacts with changing sexual partners are at issue, not whether or how the contacts are compensated. Women appear to transmit the virus to men less efficiently than men transmit it to women or other men (Heyward and Curran 1988, 78). The question, "Who is a prostitute in Africa?" is important because USAID appears ready to recommend a roundup of women who sell sexual services as a means of controlling the spread of HIV infection.

Prostitution is not more common in Africa than elsewhere, but rapidly declining economic conditions and lack of security in the war zones have led more women to barter or sell sexual services on occasion in order to meet their basic needs. Brokensha (1988, 169) emphasizes that westerners often use the term "prostitute" loosely and inaccurately in Africa: "Unquestionably, each large city, and many small towns (even some villages) has a group of 'professional' prostitutes who earn their income this way. But many other women 'exchange sexual services' to augment their income, or to meet special needs." In a similar vein, Green (1988, 180) comments,

"Women may be rewarded in cash or gifts for sexual favors, which does not necessarily make them prostitutes. A good deal of female sexual behavior in Africa can be viewed as economic survival and adaptation to patterns of male dominance."

Schoepf et al. (1988) have the most extensive analysis of how the deepening economic crisis in Africa is affecting women's ability to survive. From interviews with women in Zaire they observed that, although the actual monetary value of any single sexual liaison may be very low, poor women who head households offer sexual services when cash is needed to obtain health care for a sick child or to meet social obligations. They conclude that "AIDS now has transformed what appeared to be a survival strategy into a death strategy" (Schoepf et al. 1988, 217).

In contrast, westerners describe African men with AIDS as elites. For example, Piot et al. (1987, 5) write, "The majority of AIDS cases are adults in the most productive stage of life, and in whom the nation has invested in terms of education, health care, etc. This represents a considerable degree of years of potential life lost, and may have far reaching consequences on economic development." Clearly they are not talking about prostitutes. Prompted by reports of premature deaths among (male) cabinet ministers, bankers, surgeons, and high-ranking military officers, aid donors worry about a "hollowing out" or "tunneling" effect on a country's educated leaders (see Merritt, Lyerly and Thomas 1988, 120; Miller and Rockwell 1988, xxv–xxvi). Aside from the obvious sexism in blaming females with AIDS for the deaths of leading men in their prime, this fear strikes me as misplaced for two reasons.

First, I suspect that the elites are no more representative of the majority of those who have died of AIDS in Africa than the highly publicized film stars and fashion designers are of AIDS deaths in the United States. The majority of those who have died of AIDS in North America are working-class homosexuals and poverty-stricken African-American and Hispanic intravenous drug users. Second, I question the emphasis on premature death. Undoubtedly death at age forty shocks in countries that enjoy life expectancies of seventy-four to seventy-eight years, but average life expectancy in sub-Saharan Africa is still under fifty years and only 7 percent of the population is over fifty-five years old (World Bank 1987, 202–203).

The even sexual distribution of AIDS in Africa led to the suggestion that the virus is spread through exotic sexual practices. This imputation is incorrect; the ascribed exoticism is a thinly veiled racist assumption about African culture (Waite 1988, 152–152). The relatively high rates of HIV transmission through heterosexual intercourse appear to be related to the lack of adequate health care for the treatment of syphilis and other venereal diseases, which are widespread. Sexually transmitted diseases enhance susceptibility to the AIDS virus (Allen and Curran 1988, 382; Haq 1988b, 88).

HIV is also commonly transmitted through routine hospital care, especially transfusions of contaminated blood. Illegal abortions, anemia, sickle-cell disease, accidents, and gunshot wounds—common conditions in Africa—often necessitate transfusions. Blood is harder to screen in Africa than in Europe and North America where identified high-risk groups are asked to abstain from donating blood. The costs of screening in Africa are disproportionate to health care budgets. Several African countries have requested assistance for laboratory services from WHO (WHO 1985a, 342).

The reuse of needles and syringes for injections—another reflection of inadequately funded health services—has also been implicated in the transmission of the AIDS virus. The widespread preference for injectable drug administration is a heritage of colonial and missionary medicine. In the current circumstances of insufficient energy resources for sterilization of equipment, this legacy is not benign.

A fourth transmission route for the virus is from mother to child. During pregnancy and childbirth, infected women can pass the virus and its antibodies to their infants. The frequency of transmission is uncertain; studies show a wide range from 20 to 50 percent. Recipients of contaminated blood transfusions after childbirth are in some danger of transmitting the virus through breast-feeding (Allen and Curran 1988, 383). Because African birthrates are higher and the proportion of women with AIDS is larger, the number of pediatric cases is correspondingly greater.

Human Behavior and AIDS

In an age when lifestyle is causally linked to disease, it is not surprising that researchers associate distinct patterns of human behavior with AIDS or that AIDS is categorized primarily as a sexually transmitted, rather than blood-borne, disease. The emphasis on sexual behavior has led some observers wrongly to characterize Africans as highly promiscuous (see Chirimuuta and Chirimuuta 1987, 92, 95). Without a global survey of sexuality, no norm for sexual behavior exists to measure this assertion. What social scientists do know, however, is that migrant labor systems and mobilization of armed forces create concentrations of men without families who are likely to seek female companionship. These workers and soldiers (and the women they partner) are high-risk groups for all sexually transmitted diseases.

Labor migration, which was a colonial institution, continues to be an important although understudied aspect of many African economies. There is a dearth of regional data on East Africa, so evidence of migration and its impact on family life is cited for other regions. Research on nine West African countries found 1.3 million workers migrating across international borders and a further 4.4 million leaving home to search for work elsewhere within their own countries (Zachariah and Condé 1981, xi). Another study, this one of Black labor migration to South Africa, found that 327,000 workers left six states in search of employment, mainly in the South African gold mines (Stahl 1981, 27). Internal displacement is even greater within South Africa: the compulsory contract system under which migrant workers are requisitioned forced nearly 800,000 Black South Africans to leave home in 1984 (Cooper et al. 1986, 145). The government of South Africa does not allow families to accompany either foreign or South African migrants. Most migrant workers are housed in single-sex hostels. Women living in nearby townships find it unsafe to walk about (Wilson 1972, 13).

Mobilization of armed forces is extensive throughout southern Africa because of South Africa's destabilization policies and its repeated murderous incursions into neighboring states. Because these are guerrilla wars, peasant women are especially vulnerable to rape and sexually transmitted disease. An estimated 300,000 men are engaged in fighting in Angola, Mozambique, Namibia and South Africa (*Le Monde Diplomatique,* February 1988, 8). Calculated together, Botswana, Lesotho, Swaziland, Malawi, Zambia, and Zimbabwe maintain standing armies of 80,000 men (ibid.).

In the last decade, wars and drought created unprecedented displacements of people all over Africa; internal dislocation is unparalleled, and the flight of refugees caused massive problems in neighboring countries (U.S. Committee for Refugees 1987). Refugees are more numerous in Africa than elsewhere (except for Afghans in Iran and Pakistan); 3.5 million are known to be in camps (U.S. Committee for Refugees 1988). Again, the problems in southern Africa are the best documented. The South African government has forcibly relocated 3.5 million persons within South Africa since 1961. A total of 1.5 million Mozambicans and 856,000 Angolans were uprooted by war. The total figure for southern Africa (including 34,650 South Africans in external exile, but not those internally relocated) is 2.5 million people uprooted (U.S. Committee for Refugees 1987, 49). Movement on this scale is always a public health concern because, historically, war has created epidemic conditions. In terms of the possible spread of the AIDS virus, this level of population mobility and its circumstances are grave indeed.

Refugee camps pose a particular problem for the spread of sexually transmitted diseases. The majority of adult refugees are women, for whom the camps offer little physical security (UN High Commission for Refugees 1980, 6). Women without male protectors are subject to rape, especially by soldiers (Meijer 1985, 32). When the camps are semipermanent and contact is sustained, a male guard can force a female refugee into concubinage.

Most refugees are destitute, but the lot of many Africans is hardly better. Macroeconomic data suggest that conditions are worsening and the majority are experiencing increasing poverty: in 1986, thirty countries had a gross national product under $500 per person, another seven earned under $1,000, and South Africa, where income distribution is grossly inequitable, and Gabon earned $1,850 and $3,080 respectively (World Bank 1988, 222,

289). Three-quarters of the countries have posted a decline in income since 1980. Double digit rates of inflation troubled twenty countries, and fourteen registered negative growth (ibid.).

The correlation of poverty with disease is well established but its association with AIDS has not been investigated. The increasing number of AIDS cases in poverty-stung inner-city African-American and Hispanic intravenous drug users in the United States suggests that the spread of HIV infection may be linked to the marginalization of the poor. The incidence of some diseases—tuberculosis, pneumonia, and diarrhea, for example—and the outcome of many more, are conditioned by nutritional status, which is often closely tied to economic status. Malnutrition can lower resistance to disease by depressing the immune response (Turshen 1984, 138–139). Common diseases such as tuberculosis can also suppress immune response. Important questions to investigate are whether the poor, sick, and malnourished are more susceptible to HIV infection and whether progression from HIV infection to expression of AIDS is more rapid in malnourished populations or in people with already compromised immune systems.

Studies of survival rates in New York City show that African-American and Hispanic intravenous drug users die far more quickly on average than gay men (*New York Times,* 19 November 1987).[5] This finding suggests that poverty and malnutrition may play a role in the course of the disease. For my purposes, however, the data are confounded by two factors—differences in educational levels and varying economic levels in these two populations, which influence access to, and utilization of, health services. It is possible that the better educated gay population carries health insurance, recognizes early symptoms of disease, presents sooner for treatment, and therefore lives longer.

My concern is that, given the current military and economic situation in Africa, more people are exposed to illness because of increased poverty, exhaustion from overwork, and poorer nutrition. Falling levels of nutrition are suggested by data from eighteen countries that show lower daily calorie supply per person in 1985 than in 1965; for the poor in another nine countries, high rates of inflation probably wiped out any gains in food availability (World Bank 1988, 278). Some of the countries experiencing food emergencies in 1988 are Eritrea, Ethiopia, Sudan, Mozambique,

Angola, Uganda, Chad, Niger, Mali, and Burkina Faso (*Le Monde Diplomatique,* March 1988, 32).

UNICEF (1987) documented a deterioration in child welfare—rising malnutrition, increased incidence of communicable diseases, and higher rates infant and child mortality—in seventeen sub-Saharan nations between 1980 and 1985. Although the agency is mounting special campaigns to combat some health problems such as the dehydration associated with diarrhea, food subsidies and health service budgets in many countries have been cut, usually because the International Monetary Fund made the cuts a condition of so-called "economic adjustment" agreements. In the period 1979–1983, per-person expenditures on health fell in seven of the fifteen countries for which there are data (Andersen, Jaramillo, and Stewart 1987, 74).

When governments are forced to reduce health services, many poor people resort to traditional healers and informal health care. The squeeze on incomes in both formal and informal economic sectors translates into a lack of ready money for health care and has probably led more people to try self-medication with antibiotics sold in marketplaces. (For information on self-medication to treat sexually transmitted diseases and high levels of antibiotic resistant strains of gonorrhea see Barton 1988, 271; Piot et al. 1979; Ratnam et al. 1982.) Synergies of malnutrition and infection combined with indiscriminate use of pharmaceuticals can compromise the immune system and leave people more vulnerable to several communicable diseases, including HIV infection (Haq 1988b, 88).

The Situation in East Africa

All of these problems may be clarified by a more detailed study of East Africa where AIDS is prevalent. In this section of the chapter I outline a scenario of the spread and impact of AIDS in East Africa. I wish to underline the highly speculative nature of this exercise and the circumstantial evidence on which it is based. My purpose is to show the importance of economic, social, political, and military factors to the spread of AIDS.

The background to AIDS in East Africa is a decade of economic crisis, political unrest, and military terror. The specific circumstances differ in each of the countries: in Tanzania, always the poorest member of the East African community, the problems are economic; in Kenya, with its White settler population and close ties to the West, political problems stem from growing economic and social inequality; in Uganda, the problems are consequent upon war, famine, and a succession of coups d'état.

Kenya was the first of the three countries to report AIDS to WHO. The following cryptic notice appeared in the WHO Weekly Epidemiological Record for 20/27 December 1985: "Kenya (17 December 1985).—Ten cases of AIDS, including 4 in persons from 3 other African countries, have been recorded. Eight of the confirmed cases (5 Kenyans and 3 foreigners) have died." The lack of detailed information, such as a history of foreign travel, is frustrating in this and many similar reports.

In trying to establish how AIDS spread in East Africa, one should not overlook the important military relations between Kenya and the United States. According to the Defense and Foreign Affairs Handbook (1988, 520–524, 1067), beginning in the mid-1970s, Kenya expanded and modernized its military forces and forged closer security ties with Great Britain and the United States. In 1980, Kenya and the United States signed an agreement that allows U.S. naval and air forces transit and replenishment privileges at Mombasa's port and airfield as well as at several other airfields scattered around the country. Between 1984 and 1986, the United States gave Kenya $57 million in military assistance. U.S. personnel trained the Kenyan armed forces, upgraded Mombasa's airfield, and dredged Mombasa harbor (this port is useful for maintaining and refueling U.S. Navy ships, even aircraft carriers).

The rate of HIV prevalence in the U.S. military may be gauged from recent studies of service applicants. From October 1985 through March 1986, as part of the medical evaluation of individuals volunteering for military service, the U.S. Department of Defense tested 265,000 men. The mean prevalence of confirmed positive tests was 1.6 per 1,000 (U.S. Department of Health and Human Services 1986). Since 1985, the services have rejected applicants who are HIV positive.

Prostitution provides a link between the appearance of AIDS in Kenya, the expansion of the U.S. military presence in Kenya, and HIV prevalence in the U.S. military. As Gloria Waite (1988, 153) notes, "prostitution thrived in major African cities, particularly for western military visitors." One wants to know how many military men visited Kenya and had sexual encounters there. Investigation of a similar situation in the Philippines, where the U.S. Navy has twice conducted screenings of registered prostitutes and found twenty-six with AIDS, revealed that 2 million men go on shore leave annually at Subic Bay Naval Station; figures for Clark Air Base were not given (*New York Times,* 23 April 1988).

Women who sell sexual services have been named as sources of HIV infection in the United States, but close study of this population suggests that it is mainly the intravenous drug users among them who are infected (Richardson 1988, 42; Rosenberg and Weiner 1988, 418). High rates of venereal disease may account for the comparatively larger number of HIV positive African women who are not intravenous drug users. One study of women who sell sexual services in Nairobi found that up to 70 percent had at least one venereal disease, and a subgroup of ninety-seven women became reinfected with gonorrhea on average twelve days after treatment (D'Costa et al. 1985).

Labor migration may provide the link between the sale of sexual services and the spread of sexually transmitted disease in the general population. In a study of gonorrhea in Kenya, Verhagen and Gemert (1972, 281) found that, whereas 40 percent of male venereal disease patients in large towns were married, as few as 9 percent lived with their wives. Labor migration is a colonial legacy in Kenya; instituted by the British, it continued to affect sex ratios in the cities after independence. In 1969, there were 100 men for every 68 women in Nairobi and 100 men for every 72 women in Mombasa (Robertson 1984, 41).

Men are not now the only labor migrants. Many women who sell sexual services in Kenya come from Uganda and Tanzania, especially from the area around Lake Victoria where the incidence of sexually transmitted disease is historically high and where AIDS in now prevalent (Bennett 1962; Chirimuuta and Chirimuuta 1987, 106; Laurie 1958). In the Kenyan study of gonorrhea, Verhagen and Gemert (1972, 283) found that 15 percent of 1,322 women seen at a clinic for prostitutes in Mombasa were from Uganda. Haq (1988a, 26) suggests this scenario for the heterosexual spread of AIDS:

> Several African studies have shown that seropositive results are often first documented in female prostitutes, especially those in contact with men from other HIV-endemic areas. After rates in prostitutes rise, seropositivity rates in male patients of sexually transmitted disease clinics rise. Subsequently, rates begin to rise in pregnant women, and the general population.

HIV may have been spread in Uganda and Tanzania by returning women who came into contact with their countries' armed forces. Tanzania has a large standing army (the Tanzanian People's Defense Force of 40,000 men maintains security and teaches civilians; in addition there is a Citizens' Militia of 50,000, and a compulsory two-year period of national service for all young men and women with postprimary education; also, workers' militias assist in rural development projects [*Defense and Foreign Affairs Handbook* 1988, 923–924]). Alternatively, the Tanzanian army may have brought the virus back from Uganda after its 1979–1981 invasion of southwestern Uganda to depose Idi Amin.

The spread of AIDS in Uganda seems related to the almost continuous warfare that beset the country; since the early 1970s, 800,000 Ugandans have lost their lives, 200,000 fled into exile, and hundreds of thousands were internally displaced (Watson 1988, 14). Uganda has the highest number of reported AIDS cases in Africa—6,772 in January 1989. Estimates of HIV infection (always questionable) range from under 1 percent in some rural areas to over 80 percent in women who sell sexual services in towns (Haq 1988b, 87). Although the latter suggests that sexual transmission is important, I wonder about the role of blood transfusions and the army's contribution to HIV contamination of blood supplies. I was unable to learn anything about the organization of military medicine for either the regular Ugandan army or the rebels; my suspicion is that both forces and the civilian population relied upon the same government health service and that the health service blood supplies became severely contaminated.

Because continual fighting interrupted agricultural production, malnutrition is rife: 25 percent of Ugandan children surveyed in 1986 were malnourished (Haq 1988b, 87). The health impact of AIDS is grave and complex. Cynthia Haq (ibid., 88), a physician who worked in a rural Ugandan clinic, makes these observations:

> Morbidity from infectious diseases is increased in patients with AIDS, and infections are more likely to be transmitted from them to patients without AIDS. . . . Respiratory infections, including pneumonia and tuberculosis, are common in AIDS patients and may be spread extensively through communities where crowded conditions exist. When access to clean water and effective human waste disposal systems are limited, as in much of rural Africa, exposure to viral, bacterial and amoebic gastrointestinal infections is common in AIDS patients. Once these infections are contracted they readily spread to other persons in the community with or without AIDS.[6]

In response to AIDS the Ugandan government sponsored a well-coordinated multilingual educational program that began in 1985. Tanzania launched its educational program the same year. In mid-1986 the Kenyan Red Cross began to distribute leaflets, posters, and booklets in English and Swahili, and in 1987 the Kenyan government began to screen blood supplies in Nairobi and Mombasa.

The Response from Abroad

The appearance of AIDS in Africa brought out scientists and investigative reporters but little material assistance from the group of governments described loosely as "the North." In this final section of the chapter, I will argue that the character of this response is inappropriate, that the motives for aid are far from altruistic, and that the measures proposed are unlikely to stop the spread of the AIDS virus. I will also suggest what sort of aid would be more helpful in the long run.

A number of authors have commented on the racist character of the North's response to AIDS in Africa. Richard and Rosalind Chirimuuta (1987) and Charles Hunt (1988) feel that racism is the main reason northern researchers ascribed the origin of the AIDS epidemic to Africa. Gloria Waite (1988) finds racist the suggestions of bizarre African sexual behavior and new northern immigration procedures (mainly screening for HIV antibodies) applied to African students and migrant workers. Racism distorts so many aspects of our lives, there was no reason to expect that AIDS research and reporting would be exempt. But other motives are at work here as well.

Thus far, the major financial response of foreign aid donors to African governments is money to buy condoms. Not to be cynical about this strategy, the profits accruing to northern pharmaceutical companies will not be dwelt upon (see Green 1988, 188). Rather, the achievement of the donors's long-term goal to reduce population growth, and thereby control volatile unemployed youth, seems to me a larger and more important motive to consider. USAID is clear about this policy:

> High fertility had become the main factor in extraordinary population growth and also was closely correlated with infant and child mortality. Rapid socioeconomic development had become virtually hostage to the demographic imperatives of rapid growth and high dependency burdens. By 1980 a growing number of public policy advisors in Africa, both indigenous and expatriate, were urging deliberate efforts to induce rapid fertility decline (Merritt, Lyerly, and Thomas 1988, 116).

USAID (ibid., 127) is explicit in insisting that AIDS not deter this endeavor: "Not only is this not the time to diminish family planning efforts, but instead such efforts could be redoubled at this time." Sex education campaigns, sponsored by USAID and WHO, emphasize condom use, although USAID would also like them to stress sexual abstinence by adolescents and marital monogamy (ibid., 126), in keeping with the moral agenda of the Reagan administration, which George Bush promises to honor.

High on USAID's list of priorities is the consolidation of "surveillance so that spread of the disease and evaluation of impact of intervention can be monitored" by the U.S. Bureau of the Census, the U.S. Public Health Services, the Centers for Disease Control, and the National Institutes of Health (ibid.). Between these lines, the following meaning can be read: USAID will establish close working relations with African researchers and their governments. The motive for cooperation is easily discerned; researchers and pharmaceutical companies need experimental populations for clinical trials of drugs and vaccines.[7] Evidence for this assertion is not hard to find. For example, this report appeared in the *New York Times* (19 February 1988): "large-scale tests of potential AIDS vaccines may have to take place in Africa, a senior Federal health official [identified as Dr. Anthony Fauci, director of the National Institute of Allergy and Infectious Diseases] said yesterday, and he has begun discussing the possibility with African officials."

WHO's strategies, in addition to health education, are antibody screening and improvement in blood supply. Aid agencies as well as international organizations are putting considerable pressure on African governments to screen for HIV (Barker and Turshen 1986a, 53). Screening of what is perceived to be a minority health problem by most African governments is expensive. In the United States, each enzyme-linked immunoassay (ELISA) test to screen donated blood costs $3.00 (Eisenstaedt and Getzen 1988). For purposes of protecting the blood supply, a positive result on this test is sufficient reason to discard the donation. For purposes of notifying donors, a repeat ELISA and a Western blot test, which costs $50, are required to eliminate false positives. These costs (even if lower in Africa) are beyond the fiscal capacity of most African governments, which can spend less than $15 per person per year on health care and disease prevention.

AIDS is already distorting African health care. For example, people with AIDS absorb large amounts of scarce resources: they must be treated for intractable forms of common infections such as tuberculosis, requiring more drugs per case, longer stays in the hospital, and more time from skilled medical and nursing personnel. To check the spread of HIV infection by reuse of needles, health services must retrain all health workers in sterilization techniques for needles and other equipment, which removes trainers from other tasks, and governments must divert money to purchases of autoclaves and to pay higher energy bills.

Once again, when confronted with what they perceive as a major problem, northern donors are proposing a vertical solution, that is a set of measures designed to deal only with AIDS. Instead of giving broad aid to upgrade health services to meet all of the population's needs, as originally proposed in the Declaration of Alma Ata on Primary Health Care, some donors are singling out selected services such as blood transfusion and family planning to cope with AIDS. (For a discussion of primary health care versus selected services see Barker and Turshen 1986b.) Yet the situation described by Haq in Uganda demands a horizontal approach based on primary health care.

In addition, as in the response to famine in Africa, nongovernmental organizations (NGOs) are again lining up to play a major role in implementing vertical AIDS programs (see Greeley 1988). The problem with assistance in this guise was posed by Thébaud (1986, 46):

> How can a country construct a coherent health policy on the basis of a national strategy, as WHO recommends, when international experts are placed in ministries, when medical volunteers of more than fifty nationalities are working individually or in organised missions and when the workers of multiple microprojects developed by hundreds of NGOs of different nationalities and different professional, political, and ideological perspectives are all operating in one and the same country?

Foreign aid donors are making no effort to improve general economic conditions in Africa in response to AIDS. On the contrary, the International Monetary Fund and the World Bank continue to impose restrictions on government spending and to resist the recommendations for reform made by Third World states in their UN resolution for a New International Economic Order. Most recently, the United States and other industrial countries insisted that debt-ridden Third World nations applying to the new International Monetary Fund (IMF) loan program, which is designed to help countries hurt by high interest rates, must take increasingly rigorous domestic economic actions under IMF guidance (*New York Times,* 12 April 1988). This new loan program is the first admission that interest rate surges usually flow from economic mismanagement by the industrial countries.

Northern persistence in pursuing demonstrably unsuccessful economic policies in Africa raises questions about underlying motives and strategies. In the nineteenth century, epidemics of infectious disease coincided with attempts by business "to solve its economic problems by creating dramatic gaps between the social needs of an expanding labor force and available goods and services" (Stark 1977, 681). The parallels to the outbreak of AIDS are interesting: present attempts by the North to solve its economic problems have created crises in African agricultural and industrial production, as well as enormous gaps between goods and services and the needs of the rapidly growing African population (Lawrence 1986).

In the past, epidemics were occasions for labor to struggle against injustice, not simply sickness. Epidemics were also occasions for labor to show their capacity for self-organization (as the gay community is showing in response to AIDS). Finally, epidemics were occasions to force authorities to reform fundamentally their organization of work, the market, and social services (Stark 1977, 681). (In the United States, one major question is whether AIDS will hasten or kill initiatives for a national health service.)

Formerly, the government's initial reaction was to delay announcements of the epidemic because officials were afraid to alienate the local business community and they feared their removal from office. (A similar lag was noted in the Reagan administration's response to AIDS.) Once the epidemic was acknowledged, however, police powers to arrest, inspect, and fine were used to repress the rebellious. (Several European governments are invoking police powers to deal with high-risk groups, as well as people infected with the AIDS virus.)

African governments are subject to internal and external pressures: they must respond to domestic crises and maintain good relations with the northern powers upon which they are dependent. If an AIDS epidemic materializes and if history is any predictor of future behavior, combined internal and external pressures may lead governments to cooperate on experimental research (Zaire has already indicated its willingness). Under pressure, African governments may also allow nongovernmental organizations to run AIDS programs in their countries (NGOs should not be surprised if they meet with popular refusal and resistance). Governments may also invoke police powers in an effort to extend their control over their populations. They are likely to join USAID in scapegoating women as the source of the epidemic because this tactic will divide the opposition.

African governments may find willing allies in their male citizenry for measures that increase men's control of women's sexuality. Historically, African women have used their sexuality to assert their freedom and independence from men. Currently, falling prices for primary commodities have made farming unprofitable, forcing women out of the rural areas (Bujra 1986). Both northern and African governments are sensible of the need to increase food production, which in effect means that women must return to the farms and redouble their efforts. An epidemic of a sexually transmitted disease provides the perfect pretext to drive women from cities and towns back to the rural areas.

PART FOUR

Unconventional Wisdom

Chapter 13

ISSUES IN INTEGRATION

PART FOUR, the final section of this book, looks to the future of public health. The issues discussed in chapter thirteen are the need for integration (of several sorts, at many levels); chapter fourteen outlines an agenda for the future. The three issues in integration addressed in this chapter are the integration of services (curative and preventive, public and private), the integrated training of different categories of health personnel (nurses, physicians, and others), and the integration of social science in medical and scientific research.

The first issue, integrated services, arises because of the historical split between preventive health and curative medicine. Public health is usually identified with preventive services and clinical medicine with curative care. This division creates a major obstacle to the improvement of health, especially in underdeveloped countries that cannot afford to duplicate expensive infrastructure. Inherited from the colonial regimes that set up biomedical health care systems in the Third World, this split has proved very costly. I will argue for a need to combine preventive and curative services in the public sector and illustrate that argument with the example of tuberculosis, which shows that separate preventive and curative efforts fail to reduce the incidence of this disease.

The second issue in integration follows from the first: if a country is to offer integrated services it must integrate training so that different categories and levels of personnel understand each other's skills and respect each other's expertise. Currently, most education programs train medical personnel, nursing personnel, and so-called paramedical personnel separately. Health workers are better able to cooperate in providing combined preventive and curative services if they are trained together. I will also argue that all health personnel need training in the social sciences, as well as in biomedical sciences.

The third issue is integrated research, by which I mean the collaboration of medical and non-medical personnel in research projects and the integration of social science in medical and other scientific research. If social and natural scientists are to understand one another's language and discipline, they also need broad training. Of all the health personnel that need to know about social science, public health workers are the first because of their ties to communities. They need training in social science to understand the non-medical aspects of public health including the economic, social, and political organization of the communities in which they work; they also need to understand how sociological information can be used against communities.

Integrated Services

The problem of integration arises both because biomedical practice is organized around single diseases, which often results in vertical public health programs that concentrate resources in an attack on a single problem, and because there is a separation of prevention and cure that is a recent historical phenomenon and not a necessary separation. Dubos (1970, 79) reports that in early Greek writings on the environmental origins of disease, prevention and cure went hand in hand. Following the rise of the germ theory of disease in the nineteenth century and its ascendance in the bacteriological era, cure took precedence over prevention and became separated from it.

The development of vertical public health programs was a logical application of biomedical research. In contrast, horizontal programs are broader and use polyvalent personnel trained to deal with a variety of conditions; these programs are horizontal because they are integrated into the basic health services of the country. When vertical programs are integrated prematurely, as in a situation in which integration is ill-advised, politically or for other reasons, they may suffer; one possibility is that the dominant health program or the dominant medical specialty will take over. In the social sciences, for instance, interdisciplinary research often requires everyone to learn economics, because economics is the dominant discipline. In health care, experience shows that women lose out when maternal and child health services are integrated into primary health care in countries in which the status of women is low, because men with major health problems will be served first, and the preventive aspects of maternal and child care will be pushed aside.

The assumption of preventive functions by the state in the mid-nineteenth century was a historical, political, and economic development, not a scientific or medical choice. State intervention was originally developed to fill gaps in private medical care, which did not provide preventive services, community care, or any service at all for the poor or other specific needy groups. State programs tended to spring up around particular diseases such as tuberculosis or special risk groups such as mothers and children. Because state intervention was a stopgap measure, comprehensive services were never a feature of state programs.

This system—of state provision of preventive services separate from and rarely coordinated with private curative care—was transferred intact from Europe to its colonies, although sometimes the copy looked more like a caricature than the real thing. The transfer resulted in duplication and wasted services, the squandering of scarce trained personnel, and using slender resources at cross purposes. From an administrative and budgetary point of view, the results crippled newly independent Third World governments with very little money to meet the health needs of their people. But there is also the viewpoint of patients who confront a myriad of fragmented services and have no rational way to satisfy their needs.

The imbalance between clinical medicine and preventive health that exists in industrialized countries was also passed on to Third World countries in which as much as 98 percent of the budget is devoted to curative medicine and as little as 2 percent to preventive health. Given the epidemiological picture in these areas, this fiscal division is particularly inappropriate because so many Third World health problems can be addressed more cheaply and more effectively by social policies including public health measures that integrate preventive and curative services.

One would think that, after independence, Third World governments opting for preventive medicine and primary health care would be able to change budgetary priorities, but one observes a curious effect: once clinical services are in place, it is extremely difficult to disestablish them. The Zimbabwe Ministry of Health, in a sectoral review emphasizing equity, insisted that,

> Our emphasis on primary health care and emphasis on rural health care services should not be misinterpreted to mean the urban areas, big central and general hospitals will be neglected. . . . The big central and general hospitals must continue to function smoothly and efficiently. Their specialist role in curative medicine and the training of medical students, nurses etc. must not be allowed to deteriorate (1984, i).

The big central and general hospitals, which are located in the cities where only 24 percent of the people live, absorb 64 percent of the budget, and they do not account for all hospital care in the country (ibid., 33).

Newly independent countries, such as Tanzania and Mozambique, that chose a socialist path found it an economic and political imperative to integrate preventive and curative facilities, to scale down clinical care and its hospital base, and to push primary health care out into the rural areas. The first obstacle Tanzania faced was its own medical staff who were not willing to work in the countryside, in part because the big central and general urban hospitals represent not only the practice of skills they have acquired with great difficulty and sometimes at great expense but also the status and living standard that attracted them to medical careers (Turshen, 1984).

Many Third World countries developed incentive schemes or adopted legislation to require rural service (Israel 1976). Typically, a medical school graduate, equipped with clinical skills but no public health training, is appointed district medical officer to pay off the government's subsidy of his or her medical education, and typically he or she will practice clinical medicine in the provincial hospital center and rarely visit the rural areas to see the satellite stations, let alone oversee public health work. Some graduates buy their way out by paying back medical school fees rather than serve in a rural area.

So the division between public and private services with which we started this book arises again. The government, which is the public sector, pays for medical education in most Third World countries, and it usually provides the infrastructure of medical services including hospitals and primary health care centers. But there is a private medical sector, commonly located in urban areas, and the hemorrhage of people trained in the public sector who go to work in the private sector is massive. Compared with the exodus of people who routinely leave government service to work in the private sector, the "medical brain drain," (the migration of physicians and nurses from the Third World to industrial developed countries), which was a subject of widespread concern several years ago (Mejia, Pizurki, and Royston 1979), is a minor problem. Milton Roemer (1984, 201) suggests that effective tax policies are required to achieve equity in the distribution of health care to all; he notes that industrial countries such as Canada, New Zealand, Sweden, and Great Britain, as well as Third World countries such as Costa Rica, Cuba, Malaysia, and Sri Lanka, have adopted this strategy.

Some countries called for an integration of private services into the public sector but met with enormous resistance from the medical corps, which responded with strikes. Some physicians faced with the public/private choice worked out an individualistic compromise; they would spend half the day in government service and half the day in private practice. What WHO discovered on looking closely at some areas was that the half day in government service was spent recruiting patients for their private practice (Turshen 1980a).

Some governments pushed ahead and outlawed private practice unilaterally, raising fears about black-market medicine. Others decided to scale down the private sector by gradually withdrawing resources from it. For example, Algeria denies licenses to practice a speciality in the private sector; only general practitioners can open private offices. A physician wishing to specialize must work for the government and practice in publicly-owned hospitals in the public sector. This restriction is an example of how the private sector can be cut back, but it does not address the need for integrated preventive and curative services.

Duplication and fragmentation of services, wasted resources, and scarce personnel were also problems in certain industrial market economies in the 1960s. The restrictive policy of the American Medical Association on medical school entrance left the United States with too few American physicians and, some said, too many foreign medical graduates filling so-called less desirable posts in state and county hospitals and "unprofitable" areas of low population density. An increasingly vocal public, alarmed at the difficulty of recruiting staff for rural areas and the public sector, pressed for new solutions to problems of scarcity. In response, medical schools relaxed tight admissions policies, Congress restricted immigration, and training programs increased the number of community health personnel and broadened the training of auxiliaries to include public health skills.

One response to fragmentation of care was rationalization by merging outpatient clinical care in new health maintenance organizations (HMOs), which offered a range of services in one place. From the provider's perspective, HMOs absorbed the physician surpluses created by the overreaction to scarcity. From the user's perspective, HMOs met the varied needs of family members of different ages for curative and preventive medical care, including health education, although that function is declining in the new competitive climate. The fragmentation of service continues in the public sector because the people who use public health services are the poor who have little power to make them respond to their needs.

In response to rising costs of medical care, created mainly by the duplication of increasingly expensive technology and its attendant army of technicians, the 1974 Lalonde report (formally entitled *A New Perspective on the Health of Canadians*) argued for the integration of preventive services. This analysis distinguishes four factors in illness—human biology, environment, lifestyle, and health care organization—and observes that current patterns of morbidity and mortality are not particularly amenable to health care interventions; it therefore suggests that government shift its focus to the other factors, which promise greater returns on the investment of health dollars. The report assumes causal links between lifestyle and health status, which with the exception of smoking are unproven, and relies on individual behavioral change. To modify unhealthy lifestyles or improve environments, health care providers tend to expand intervention by adding clinical services identified as "preventive." Evans (1982, 333) points out the resultant paradox: extended services raise costs, which is the trend that Lalonde set out to reverse, and blur the distinction between prevention and cure.

Evidently integration is not a panacea; it can have positive or negative results. The outcome depends upon how it is carried out, as well as by whom and for whom it is conceived. Certain negative aspects of integration should not be ignored; for example, special programs may disappear or be swallowed up. The dangers as well as the advantages of integration come through clearly in the case study of tuberculosis.

Tuberculosis

Tuberculosis is a chronic, communicable, mycobacterial, pulmonary disease that can spread to other parts of the body. Common symptoms are cough, fatigue, fever, and weight loss. The worldwide incidence is estimated at 3.7 million cases. Despite extensive practical experience with preventive and curative techniques, the rates have not changed in thirty years (Chaulet, Ait Khaled, and Amrane 1983). Tuberculosis is one of the best medical pointers to social inequality, and the trend in its epidemiology one of the best indicators of North-South inequalities (Thébaud and Lert 1985). Not surprisingly, 95 percent of cases are found in the Third World.

Germ theorists describe the disease as caused by the tubercle bacillus; environmentalists attribute it to the bacillus plus poverty, overcrowding, and poor diet; and social production theorists ascribe it to a declining standard of living and stress, which often characterize the situation of migrant workers in market economies. Biomedicine can both cure and prevent TB with effective antibiotics available since the 1950s and a vaccine called BCG after Calmette and Guérin, the Frenchmen who developed it.

However, as the American Public Health Association manual on communicable disease control warns, “a policy of preventive treatment, even of special risk groups, is unrealistic and unsuitable for mass application in a community health program unless the treatment program for patients suffering from infectious tuberculosis is widespread and well organized, and achieves a high rate of cure” (Benenson 1985, 413). Prevention and cure must be integrated if one is to make progress in solving the problem.

Tuberculosis programs are often organized vertically, from the ministry of health on down, using personnel with single purpose training. One way around the disadvantages of vertical organization is to expand the program to include all respiratory diseases, not just TB. But if a TB program is integrated before polyvalent personnel are trained to deal with it or before the country has worked out its program and established procedures, tuberculosis control may drop from sight (preventive care on a community scale will disappear before individual curative work does). One way to prevent vertical programs from being swallowed up, to preserve their unique qualities while avoiding duplication and waste, is to retain a special planning unit at the center in the ministry of health or its equivalent and to decentralize implementation. However, it is a mistake to suggest a single strategy and pretend that one program is equally applicable in countries with different political systems and economic regimes. So, although integration is essential, it cannot just be legislated across the board; it has to be considered in the context of a specific country situation.

Another problem with vertical programs is that they prevent governments from restructuring an inequitable health care system and from creating conditions for the implementation of integrated services. One way to achieve equity is by planning a health service delivery system that is not based on specific disease problems like tuberculosis or on target-group programs such as maternal and child health—a health service system founded on the principles of the nonspecificity of disease.

One service model has the potential to deliver comprehensive preventive and curative services at low cost: the primary health care approach.

Primary Health Care

Primary health care is a community-based service model concerned mainly with the development and extension of a country's existing health and medical services so that care at the primary level (the level of first consultation and the most accessible) is available to all. Nurtured by WHO (1978), the primary health care approach includes the beliefs that health and the improvement of health are related to a whole range of economic, social, and political factors; that governments must distribute whatever resources are available for health care in an equitable manner across geographic regions and social groups; that the health services must use the most appropriate technologies and practitioners (including auxiliary personnel) at each level of health care; and that referral from the primary level to the secondary and higher levels of health care (the hospitals and specialist facilities) must be built into the system and must work in practice. Clearly this model has revolutionary potential, which is probably why USAID has led the attack on its implementation.

Some bilateral aid agencies and several international organizations (other than WHO, notably UNICEF and the World Bank) propose an interim, temporary alternative to primary health care. Rather than provide an integrated system of care, these donors are funding a selective strategy in the Third World. Hotly contested, this approach involves the decision to provide only limited, and usually only preventive, health care (Walsh and Warren 1979). Critics complain that selective care will not improve health, particularly not in the countries normally targeted, where the roots of ill health lie in poverty (Banerji 1984).

Proponents of selective strategies would institute health care directed at preventing or treating the few diseases that are responsible for the greatest loss of life and most illness (but not necessarily the most disability) and for which interventions of proven efficacy exist. They reason that universal primary health care is too expensive for most of the Third World, and they give lower priority to diseases that lack an inexpensive control measure (Bolland and Young 1982). For example, UNICEF would control diarrheal diseases with oral rehydration but ignore pneumonia, tuberculosis, sleeping sickness, and certain parasitic infections. Because the diseases selected are most common among children below the age of three, adults receive little benefit from this program, which stresses a reduction in child mortality as an incentive to plan smaller families and practice birth control. It also stresses the future rather than the present labor force; this bias is contrary to the wishes of many Third World communities, which have high dependency ratios (that is, large numbers of children supported by few adults) and rely heavily on adult labor for survival.

The assumption underlying the selectivist strategy is that a reduction in death rates for a few specific diseases will result in a reduction in the overall death rate of a population; this is the old public health approach of the 1950s, challenged in chapter one. Evidence suggests that mortality is nonspecific and selective strategies ineffective in improving overall health, at least in areas with high levels of poverty and malnutrition. Selectivists mistakenly set priorities from the angle of diseases and take a technocratic approach to complex political problems (Newell 1988). Governments need to plan health care across a different range of categories—manpower training, building planning, and the evaluation of alternative technologies (Barker and Turshen 1986b). They also need to integrate non-medical measures into medical prevention.

Integrated Training

The integration of research and the integration of health services both encounter obstacles from personnel unless educational authorities have integrated their training. Unfortunately few schools or universities offer examples of integrated training below the graduate level. One such program is the University Centre for Health Sciences in Yaoundé, Cameroon (Monekosso and Quenum 1978). This center requires a common core of courses for students of more than one professional group, and it is complemented by specialized courses in various tracks. The Yaoundé center uses team instruction that relies heavily on practical field exercises; the goal of the exercises is to foster mutual trust, respect, and the ability to communicate—capacities essential for effective team functioning and not likely to be learned in the lecture hall.

Some of the country's medical corps resisted the University Centre for Health Sciences because it entailed a radical change in the Cameroonian health service system. The medical profession also opposed the experiment on the grounds that the center would be unable to compete for world standing: that the Cameroons should settle for anything less than a major medical school seemed to many Cameroonians an insult to their country.

The Gondar Health Center in Ethiopia also tried team training between 1954 and 1974 (Turshen 1985). In this center, all community workers were trained together; each team was composed of a sanitarian, a community health nurse, and a health officer. But when health officers were renamed assistant medical officers and some even moved up to become full-fledged doctors (following the creation of the first medical school in Ethiopia), the other members of the team fell correspondingly lower in the inevitable hierarchy. The health officer stood in for the doctor at the head of the team, and the original idea, which was that the teams would train and work together and be of equal status, proved impossible to implement and fell away.

The success of team training appears to depend importantly on an intellectual homogeneity of the faculty that ensures uniform goals and methods. One of the failings in Gondar was the inability of the Ethiopian government to impose standards on the teaching staff, who came from various parts of the world, usually under the auspices of WHO and paid by WHO four times what the local staff earned; the disparity in salaries created animosity between national and international staff. The government was unable to make foreign faculty abide by any single standard or model of health care, so that teachers taught whatever they wanted and the students graduated with a jumble of ideas rather than a kit of integrated concepts that they could apply. In the Cameroons, faculty seemed to be more homogeneous and to share common ideas about the health service model that students were being trained to work in.

Another way to accomplish the goals of mutual trust, respect, and ability to communicate is to require all health personnel to start with the same basic training—for example, all might qualify as nurses before some went on for medical training. Although not expressly planned in Ethiopia, the upgrading of some auxiliary personnel occurred when the medical school opened and several former malaria eradication workers received clinical training. In personal interviews, they frequently mentioned the positive influence of their previous public health experience on their new duties (Turshen 1985).

At the graduate level, schools of public health in the United States that accept students from a variety of backgrounds have experience in integrated training. There is no a priori reason people of different professional backgrounds cannot train together; there is no inherent reason for failure. The question is whether multidisciplinary training can be integrated into other disciplines besides public health. When the United States first established schools of public health in 1916 in response to the need for administrators of the yellow fever and hookworm campaigns (Fenner et al. 1988, 376), only medical doctors qualified for admission; eventually the schools accepted nurses, and some broadened student intake to include all qualified college graduates interested in public health.

Integrated training calls for creative and innovative approaches to teaching. It is not without its hazards, as the following suggests.

Training District Level Managers for Primary Health Care

WHO has identified strong health care management at the district level as essential to the attainment of the goals of Health For All by the Year 2000, which the World Health Assembly adopted following the International Conference on Primary Health Care held at Alma Ata in September 1978. The district level is a crucial link in the chain of command that extends from the ministry of health to the community. The problem for trainers, however, is that all sorts of health professionals function as district level managers; the challenge is to find an efficient way to upgrade their skills and retrain them for their new tasks. In the summer of 1987

I evaluated a five-week course in strengthening health care management at the district level for sixteen participants from seven southern African countries organized by WHO in Zimbabwe. The course illustrates several problems in integrated training, but also the need for it.

The district level course aimed to help practitioners improve their managerial performance through the development of appropriate analytical, managerial, and training skills. The objectives emphasized training in health economics, effective and efficient health care delivery, and techniques for monitoring and evaluating health services. The intention was to focus on the practical application of management concepts and the discussion of real problems faced by participants. WHO assembled an international faculty from its own regional staff, the Zimbabwe Ministry of Health, and the University of Zimbabwe. While well versed in their subjects, most lacked pertinent field experience at the district level.

Most faculty lectured, but didactic lectures are the least effective teaching method because they turn active participants into passive recipients of information and because they tend to convey abstract concepts rather than practical experience. Lectures are particularly unsuited to a mixed group of practicing doctors, nurses, and health inspectors who will not be formally examined and whose absorption of information cannot therefore be measured. The use of a problem-solving approach to the practical difficulties experienced by participants is more consistent with the objectives of a retraining course. The faculty offered no tutorials, which might have assured that participants with widely different educational levels understood the material presented. The use of experienced fieldworkers as faculty can overcome the uneven academic preparation of participants because fieldworkers tend to emphasize the practical application of concepts.

The original intention of the course planners was to train pairs of district level managers and their counterparts at the provincial (or regional) level. The rationale for pairing was that district level workers would find support at the provincial level for the changes they would institute on return if their superiors were trained simultaneously. An alternative approach is to train district level workers together and then invite their provincial counterparts for a one-week consultation in which they try to resolve problems of coordination, but this would reinforce hierarchy rather than break it down.

The WHO course devoted too much time to the functions of training and supervision and not enough to finance and budgeting (critical new district level functions in decentralized systems) and the management of drugs and supplies. Because clinical medical and nursing courses give little instruction in administration, a session on practical administrative techniques, including accounting systems and management of paperwork, would have been useful. Fieldwork is an essential part of any practical training course because it offers participants the opportunity to carry out a community diagnosis, which involves interviews with district administrators, hospital and health service staff, and villagers. The community diagnosis becomes the basis of a district plan of action, which is the culmination of course work. Fieldwork requires local cooperation and can be difficult to arrange. At overused sites, villagers have rehearsed their lines, and course participants encounter uncooperative personnel anxious to resume their normal duties.

Throughout the WHO regional course, discussions suffered from a lack of reality, which was reinforced by the competition among participants to present their country in the best light; the absence of visual images such as slides and films provide; and the artificial environment of the hotel in which the course was conducted, offset by only one day of fieldwork. Faculty avoided discussion of ugly realities such as corruption and nepotism in bureaucracy, theft of drugs, supplies, and equipment, and alcoholism among staff, even when participants raised these issues as problems with which they needed help. Similarly ignored were hard political questions such as the potential of primary health care to empower communities, the ability of communities to bring pressure for change to bear on the health care system, and the bureaucratic resistance that change agents (for example, forward looking district managers) are likely to encounter.

It is questionable whether a regional, as opposed to a national, course is appropriate for the training of district level health workers. A good justification for international exposure is that it expands the range of national alternatives by introducing the experience of other countries. Foreign experience can be applied usefully at the district level when the political and economic contexts of different national alternatives are expressly stated. In this course, lecturers tended to acknowledge cultural differences but to ignore the political and economic diversity of southern Africa. A few examples will suffice to illustrate this point. No one mentioned the constraints on health service delivery caused by South Africa's policy of destabilization, which affects the entire region, nor was there an opportunity to discuss the management of health care for refugees, a critical problem resulting from South Africa's policies. No one talked about the impact on health systems of worsening national economics and economic rationalization imposed by the International Monetary Fund. Finally, despite the region's diversity, faculty presented management theories as politically neutral and equally applicable to free market and centrally planned economies.

In conclusion, integrated training is a desirable educational process that needs careful planning to avoid the problems that arise in groups with disparate backgrounds. But it is essential if multidisciplinary teams of medical, non-medical, and public health workers are to coordinate their interventions.

Integrated Research

This section illustrates the importance of integrating the social sciences in scientific research with case studies of environmental problems in Bhopal, India, and the Kanahaw Valley of West Virginia. The need for integrated research is as great as the need for new and broader theories of disease causation. Much environmental research concentrates narrowly on biological causes, using multifactorial, lifestyle, and germ theories of disease. Working alone, biologically trained environmentalists cannot carry out adequate research on disease causation, and the use of techniques such as recombinant DNA does not improve their research ability in this sense. They need to cooperate with public health workers, sociologists and anthropologists, demographers, political scientists, economists, and others; but there is always a danger that social information about a community will be used against its members, often to blame the victims of some health crisis and tighten social control of the work force. Public health is involved in the integration of research because some environmentalists are employed in the public sector and because other public health workers are regularly called in to monitor the spread of diseases linked to environmental exposure and to help stop or slow epidemics.

Bhopal

The industrial accident that occurred in Bhopal, India, in December 1984 illustrates the need to integrate social science in the pure and applied physical sciences. Most scientific research in the chemical industry concentrates on the discovery of profitable products. Industrial chemists leave to toxicologists the problem of evaluating a product's hazards to human beings, usually after the fact. Even then, the primary concern is with occupational hazards to workers rather than harm to the general public or the environment. Both groups of researchers study a product's physical properties only, rather than the economic, social, and political climate in which products are made, used, and disposed of.

The events at Bhopal can be told briefly. The accident occurred at a $25 million pesticide plant coowned by the government of India and Union Carbide, a multinational corporation that has its headquarters in Connecticut (Weir 1987, 31). The release of an intermediate, methyl isocyanate (MIC), used to formulate the pesticide *Sevin* caused the tragedy when water leaked into an MIC storage tank and produced an uncontrollable or runaway reaction. During the night of December 2–3, a toxic cloud covered several *bastis*—poor, densely populated, residential areas—killing thousands of people and injuring hundreds of thousands.

The official death toll, believed to be an underestimate, stands at 2,850 and is still rising, allegedly at the rate of one death per day (Bhopal Action Resource Center 1988). Few autopsies are performed because Bhopal's large Muslim population does not allow them, so no one can be sure how many people died and are still dying of MIC poisoning. The number of injuries is unknown—200,000 is the figure usually cited, based on the number of people who went to hospitals for treatment. Also unknown is the number of permanently disabled—the visually impaired, breathless, malformed, and genetically damaged.

Reports of long-term effects of the injuries are disputed. Initially, Union Carbide stated that they expected no sequelae and that MIC affected eyes, skin, and lungs only. Recent reports suggest that the chemical affects other organs throughout the body and that gynecological complications have occurred (Ramana Dhara, personal communication 1988). The corporation continues to deny that cyanide was released, the gas some medical scientists claim is responsible for most of the long-term effects (Kurzman 1987, 100–102). Doctors working in Bhopal are struck by the wide variety of symptoms reported by their patients (Bhopal Group for Information and Action 1986, 6). Laboratory studies of MIC were not designed to predict its effects on poor, chronically malnourished people.

The problem is that chemists and toxicologists work in a closed experimental environment, without reference to the real world in which their research will be applied. The argument against positivist science is basic: science does not end with the publication of a discovery and scientists cannot divorce themselves from the uses to which their ideas are put. From the protest of physicists who developed the atomic bomb to the movements for socially responsible science and medicine, demands to include social science concerns in the curriculum of science courses and in public and private research laboratories are a fundamental response to current environmental crises.

In Bhopal's tense, politically charged atmosphere of billion dollar lawsuits and demonstrations by victims demanding compensation, researchers have carried out a number of studies seeking to place blame for the accident on Union Carbide, the Indian government, or individual workers. Most investigations concentrate on technical matters and try to explain the failures of plant design, safety engineering, and training of workers in safe procedures—or how one or more workers might have sabotaged the operation. A few journalistic reports discuss economic relations between multinational corporations and Third World nations, the double standards for safety at home and abroad, the technology of the green revolution that created the market for which *Sevin* was formulated, and the social relations of production—the structure of decision-making in the corporation, its relations with the community, and the domestic situation of its workforce (Everest 1985; Kurzman 1987; Weir 1987).

Several Indian groups composed of doctors, scientists, and activists who united around the tragedy are calling for structural reforms. They are asking for a review of state occupational safety and health legislation, including laws on industrial zoning and workers' compensation, with a view to drafting uniform, nationwide regulations. They want to know about company liability in relation to residents living near factories as well as the work force. And then, because these groups are well-informed about developments in advanced industrial countries such as the United States, they want a right-to-know law that would give workers and communities the right to know about the dangerous properties of chemicals handled by companies. One of the ironies of Bhopal is that, although *Sevin* was used on commercial crops, many people thought of pesticides as healthful products—medicines for crops—because Union Carbide sought to associate its products with the green revolution and the expanded production of food. Companies jealously guard proprietary information about their products, but the lack of precise knowledge of MIC especially among doctors in Bhopal's hospital emergency rooms may have raised the death toll because few medics knew how to respond beyond symptomatic treatment.

Kanahaw Valley, West Virginia

Let us now compare the Kanahaw Valley in West Virginia to see how much the fact that India is a Third World country mattered in the Bhopal tragedy. In the late 1970s I worked with a group of activists at Highlander, an adult education center in Tennessee, on environmental problems in Kingsport, Tennessee, one of three study sites. The second was in Cabin Creek, Kentucky, an investigation of community health problems related to coal production; and the third was in the Kanahaw Valley, an investigation of health consequences of chemical and coal production. Whereas we were able to do a lot in Kingsport on chemical pollution, and whereas some interesting findings came out of Kentucky, the chemical industry and the coal companies managed to stymie Highlander's efforts to organize communities in the Kanahaw Valley.

Highlander activists compare the history of Appalachian poverty to the Third World colonial experience of underdevelopment (Lewis, Johnson, and Askins 1978). Coal and chemical companies, bankers, and other investors reduced the once proud, self-sufficient farming and hunting communities of Appalachia to penury by stripping them of their natural resources and leaving behind an environmental shambles. Despite the passage of protective environmental legislation such as the law requiring the rehabilitation of mountainsides strip-mined for coal, undoing the damage is complicated because economic and political power resides mainly with companies headquartered outside the region. Major multinational corporations such as Oxy Petroleum (which owns Consolidated Coal) mine in the region and Union Carbide, Eastman Kodak, American Cyanamid, Velsicol, and others have large chemical plants along the river valleys.

Highlander's activities are to me the essence of integrated, nonmedical, public health work, especially public health education. The first step in this project was to organize communities and teach people how to do their own research—from land deeds (to figure out who owns what in their communities), major health problems, pollutants in air and water, and chemicals in landfills, to companies, company ownership, future development plans, and company health and safety records. Each community undertook to study its own problems, and Highlander pooled the findings so that a regional picture could emerge. The second step was to study federal and state laws and county and municipal regulations to figure out how people with illnesses and diseases living in polluted areas could respond within the law, using legislation to their own advantage. One obstacle that communities encountered was the inability of scientists to provide the scientific information needed in legal suits; for example, researchers had studied the effects of mercury discharges on fish and knew what levels were safe for pisciculture but not how much mercury contamination could be tolerated by human beings drinking polluted water. When communities called in scientists from the local universities to help them, even those scientists who were willing to cooperate (very few were) could not help because they did not know what tests to make. So Highlander taught people to be scientists by using questionnaires, interviewing one another, keeping health diaries, and talking to pharmacists, doctors, and hospitals. Their research was unsophisticated, but it was purposeful and sound enough to persuade government agencies to carry out epidemiological studies (Highlander Research and Education Center 1980).

Clearly the people of West Virginia have more power and more resources than the people of Bhopal. They are better educated, they have a higher standard of living, and they do not have the same level of ill health as many people in Bhopal. West Virginian workers are more often unionized—not that unions do not exist in India; they do, but we are talking about the relative power of people. A basic difference in the two situations is the relationship between the companies and governments. The United States government is in a stronger position to control Union Carbide (should it wish to do so) than the Indian government is—and the relative power of the Indian and American work forces and communities to oppose Union Carbide management follows from this. The Indian government attempted to gain some control by arranging coownership of the Bhopal plant, which has so complicated any resolution of the tragedy.

If we talk about public health as an instrument of empowerment, then we have to talk about moving outside of laboratories and into communities, working with people on their own terms, teaching them how to use the resources of their own community to their own benefit, and sometimes taking on even the scientists as well as the corporations that are the systemic sources of their illness. This integration can take place: witness the current movement for socially responsible science that includes such groups as Physicians for Social Responsibility opposed to the development and use of nuclear weapons, which last year won the Nobel Peace Prize.

The integration of social science in medical research is needed to solve complex contemporary public health problems such as environmental pollution. Interdisciplinary research presumes the integrated training of health personnel: the training of medical scientists in social science and the joint training of teams of health workers with different responsibilities (for example, nursing, epidemiology, and sanitation). With integrated training, there is hope that preventive and curative health services will be integrated in the public sector and that public health programs will no longer be based on single diseases but on broad health and social problems.

Chapter 14

AN AGENDA FOR ACTION

THE OLD PUBLIC HEALTH agenda pits private medicine against community care in the public sector. The arguments are that public health solutions are cheaper and reach more people, they alleviate much illness and accompanying stress because they prevent the conditions that private medicine treats, and they are more democratic because access does not depend upon the ability to pay. The logic of public health activists is not wrong, but their premise is wrong because it is futile to polarize the choice between private medicine and public health. Curative care has to be offered together with preventive health services if either is to be successful. How to finance public health is a separate issue; it is not a question of choosing between different forms of health care delivery but of setting national budgetary priorities for welfare, defense, and economic development.

Public health activists are constantly defending government intervention, even when they themselves question the value of some of the programs. For example, food stamps are nutritional Band-Aids that in no way solve problems of malnutrition in the United States, but in the absence of other reforms, public health workers feel compelled to advocate maintenance of the program. Overseas famine relief workers recognize the limits of handouts, and the musicians' coalition that raised money for Ethiopians in 1986 punned correctly in calling themselves Band-Aid.

While energy is dissipated holding the line against cutbacks, public attention is diverted from issues of capitalist development, which are at the root of so many health problems here and abroad. Private interests triumph when the public demands solutions in the public health arena to health problems that are essentially political. Should activists abandon the line and devote their energies to other causes? It is an old debate, but the logic of new descriptions of health and illness dictates new resolutions.

If mortality is nonspecific, if even the eradication of a disease merely means that people will die of something else, then we need a radical transformation of public health work and the epidemiology that supports it so that it is no longer oriented to the control of single diseases. Concepts of complex social prevention in place of medical prevention, the integration of social science in medicine, concepts of social class, knowledge of political economy, and the goals of equity and access must inform public health work and education in the health professions. The need for structural reform, if embraced by public health workers, will generate conflicts between public health and private industry because structural reforms change the nature of economic activity and transform social relations. The successful implementation of this public health agenda for the year 2000 depends upon the mass mobilization of people and their empowerment.

Background to the Current Health Crisis

From the 1950s, with cheap oil expropriated from the Middle East, backed by imperialist foreign policy and pro-business domestic policy (which in the United States helped Senator Joseph McCarthy decimate trade union leadership), the international petroleum industry fueled an era of unexampled corporate prosperity and environmental deterioration. The source of both that prosperity and that deterioration is the way work is organized under capitalism, and it is the organization of work that has created the health crisis. The petroleum industry comprises eight branches: inorganic chemicals, dyes, and explosives; organic chemicals; fertilizers; plastics, rubbers, nuclear materials, vegetable and animal oils and fats; synthetic fibers and resins; pharmaceuticals and cosmetics; soaps, polishes, inks, matches, candles, and pesticides; and paints, varnishes, and lacquers. Together they account for most of the toxic wastes, noxious emissions, and hazardous occupational exposures associated with the precipitous rise in deaths from cancers (Epstein 1979). Accelerated exploitation of the labor force correlates with high rates of heart disease, still the number-one killer in industrial countries. From the 1950s, patients with these chronic conditions swamped hospitals and insurance systems designed to handle only surgery and acute episodes of disease.

Although some historians characterize the 1950s as "silent," the repressive decade brewed an explosive response. Africans successfully fought their European colonial masters and joined Latin Americans and Asians as citizens of independent nations. In the United States, African-Americans created the Civil Rights Movement and struggled for a political voice that would empower them to wrest improved living and working conditions from the system. Strikes, student unrest, and urban riots exerted pressure for change in over seventy countries throughout the 1960s and 1970s.

In 1962 Rachel Carson published *Silent Spring* and set off a cannonade of demands for environmental rescue that still reverberates more than twenty-five years later. Environmental action groups organized investigations, clean-ups, and lobbies in many countries; some groups grew into political parties (called everywhere the "greens"), others formed international ties. One official response was a world conference on the environment held in Stockholm in 1972 and the creation of the United Nations Environment Program. The new ecological political parties propelled many countries to establish environment ministries to centralize the operations of local units, to plan the use of natural resources, and to coordinate their efforts with other nations. Many more governments adopted new or stricter legislation on pollution.

In the United States, business and government responded with new laws. In 1963, Congress adopted the first clean air act and in 1965, a stronger water quality act; it passed civil rights legislation in 1964; the 1969 Mine Safety Act was followed in 1970 by the Occupational Safety and Health Act (OSHA), the Environmental Policy Act (EPA), and the Toxic Substances Control Act (TOSCA). In 1965, at the height of the Great Society, the American people won, not a national health service, which the British have enjoyed since 1948, not national health insurance, which has been on our national agenda since World War I, but Medicare and Medicaid, two pieces of legislation ostensibly designed to provide access to health care for the aged and indigent, but in fact destined to become the gateway for the entry of private corporations into the health care industry.

The 1973–1975 worldwide recession began in the United States as the result of the combined effects of the Vietnam War and overseas investment and competition (with European and Japanese industry recovered from World War II and with newly industrialized Asian nations). The recession heightened contradictions in the world capitalist economy and eventually prompted the International Monetary Fund to press debt-ridden Third World countries to cut social services. While the momentum for stronger environmental legislation and for the enforcement of occupational safety and health laws continued into the 1980s, multinational corporations began to contest new regulations in court as part of a wider plan to protect profits. Strong job safety and health rules undoubtedly benefit unionized workers, yet union members helped return conservative administrations to office. With the election of Ronald Reagan to the U.S. presidency in 1980, business sought to end government intervention (except in the defense sector) and to implement deregulation and a supply-side strategy that favored competition in a profit-making health care industry.[1]

The corollary to public rollbacks is the expansion of the private market, which the World Bank encourages everywhere. In the new for-profit health care industry, national corporations purchase hospitals and run them like hotel chains from a central office, depriving communities of locally responsive institutions; nonhospital services are delivered in for-profit "emergicenters" and "urgicenters" located in suburban shopping malls; these centers operate like muffler and brake shops designed to fix specific parts of cars and offer no continuity of care. In the United States, health maintenance organizations (HMOs), which were originally nonprofit, prepaid group plans staffed by salaried doctors who emphasized prevention, are now profit-making corporations (some HMOs are financed by insurance companies), aggressively competing for healthy, young, white patients and avoiding the poor, the elderly, and patients with AIDS.

Building an International Public Health Movement

A movement for public health relies crucially on a global understanding of what causes illness and why only some people fall ill and die prematurely. The most exciting developments in public health in the past decade are a new definition of health and illness and a new comprehension of the economic, social, and political determinants of health and health care. In the 1970s, a handful of people scattered around the world began to explore health and health care from a Marxist perspective and to exchange ideas in a series of biennial conferences. Since then the analysis has developed and the handful has grown. The Socialist Caucus of the American Public Health Association has over one thousand members (in an association that has thirty thousand members). We have forged links with progressive health groups in Europe, Asia, Latin America, and Africa; and we have expanded our concerns to include women's health, occupational and environmental health, and human rights.

The new definition of health and illness emerging from Marxist analyses shifts attention away from medical explanations of *how* disease develops and toward the socially important and historically specific questions of *why* disease develops. The new definition also switches from a mechanical, biomedical model of disease to a holistic concept of health that considers the emotional as well as the physical aspects of illness.

Marxists recognize that health and illness are products of the global organization of society and of the way subsistence and surplus are produced and distributed internationally among society's members. Health and illness are products of complicated power relationships between national producers and, often, multinational owners, and between producers and distributors. They are also products of the way reproduction is organized, not only childbearing, but also child rearing. Health and illness are social products of the specific historical circumstances and relations.

A growing number of Marxist and socialist studies of First and Third World people demonstrate the dynamics of economic, social, and political determinants of health and health care. Research in South Africa shows the pervasive, negative impact of racism on health (de Beer 1986; WHO 1983); studies in Great

Britain show the destructive health effects of poverty and class (Townsend and Davidson 1982); feminists in the United States demonstrate the erosion of women's health and health care in a sexist and ageist society (Ehrenreich and English 1979; Minkler and Estes 1984); in Brazil there is an impressive and thoughtful body of literature on malnutrition and the role of the food industry in its etiology (da Conceição 1981; De Castro 1977; Linhart 1980); and work in India (Bang and Patel n.d.) and Zimbabwe (Davies and Sanders 1987), for example, explores the legacy of colonialism and the impact of imperialism on health. All of these studies explore the dialectical relationship of health and illness to economic, social, and political organization. These are selected examples, by no means an exhaustive list.

Socialist studies of health care explain the unequal geographical distribution of medical services (for example, in Nigeria there are fewer physicians in rural than urban areas) and the unequal distribution among classes (the working class, the poor, and minorities in the United States have the fewest services), as well as the paucity of preventive care almost everywhere. Studies range from muckraking accounts of scandals in the medical-industrial complex and the pharmaceutical industry in France (Dupuy and Karsenty 1974; Polack 1972) to Marxist analyses of health care and family planning services in Puerto Rico (Wessman 1981) and Namibia (Lindsay 1986; Lobstein 1984). Marxists have looked at almost every aspect of work and the environment, from the health effects of the business cycle and shift work to reproductive occupational hazards and the health consequences of nuclear war. The outstanding achievement of this body of literature is the documentation of the social—as opposed to individual—origins of disease.

In the late nineteenth-century, physicians used the germ theory to attribute diseases such as smallpox to discrete, specific, and external causal agents for processes that they thought were acute, self-limiting, and short-lived. The germ theory was never discarded (it is the basis for current research on a viral cause of cancer, for example), but most mainstream research today is based on the belief that disease has multiple causes, some of which are due to lifestyle (a convenient way to blame the victim).

Once illness is lifted from the victim-blaming ethic of individual responsibility, women and men can find the common origins of their illness (for example, company doctors regularly diagnosed asthma before miners realized that coal dust causes black lung disease). With a common cause identified, people can join together in combating disease-producing environments (as British miners did when they demanded nationalization of the mines and mine safety and health laws). Although it is clear that health services do not and cannot produce health (at best, good medical care can relieve pain or restore a person to health), the fight for better, more humane, and more accessible services is an integral part of progressive struggles.

New Opportunities Presented by the Crisis

The first line of defense against ill health in a capitalist society is income-producing employment in a workplace that has a strong union to protect workers' health on the job and to negotiate benefits for them and their families. Conservative policies have undermined that defense by attacking unions and promoting irresponsible corporate behavior. Among the specific consequences affecting health are: unfavorable wage rates, so that some full-time workers live below the poverty line; negligible job creation, so that teenagers and dislocated older workers find work only in the minimum-wage service sector; the erosion of trade union bargaining power, which has forced some workers to accept reduced wages and benefits; unhealthy and unsafe working conditions and increased air and water pollution, both of which are related to the unions' weakened position.

The second line of defense, when the first has failed, is a welfare state to supply life's essentials—the food, clothing, shelter, and medical care that the unemployed no longer have the income to purchase. By reversing social legislation, which in some countries dates from the 1850s, conservative governments expose vulnerable members of society—the unemployed, children and the women who rear them on their own, the elderly, immigrants, and minorities—to poverty, malnutrition, and homelessness, as well as to inadequate medical care.

The privatization of health care severely limits access to medical services for the poor and minorities. One consequence is that sick people wait longer for help; for some diseases such as cancer, this delay can mean the difference between effective treatment and death. The rates of deaths resulting from cancer are routinely higher among African-Americans, who receive treatment later because the system does not facilitate their access to care. Another consequence is a lack of prenatal care for pregnant women resulting in higher maternal death rates in childbirth. Current estimates of maternal mortality range from 500,000 to 1 million deaths worldwide. Reduced social services also affect infant and child mortality rates, which are rising in a number of Third World countries: for example, Ethiopia, Tanzania, and Uganda.

Thirty-five to 40 million Americans now lack health insurance; many are employed full-time or part-time in small businesses. Because insurance is a benefit of year-round full-time employment in the primary labor market, this number will climb to 65 or 70 million when the country experiences the next serious economic recession. Defining lack of insurance as a public health problem biases the argument for corporate responsibility. The number of people theoretically insured but to whom no health services are available is much larger worldwide. Will the health crisis combined with an economic crisis reopen the debate on national health care?

National health insurance is a mechanism of payment (for example, a social security tax on employers) adopted by every country—except the United States and South Africa—which does not have a national health service. Devised by Bismarck in the aftermath of the 1848 uprisings to curb the enthusiasm for German socialism, national health insurance merely increases access to inequitable health care systems. In 1911, when British workers won it, national health insurance still seemed like a good idea. It was on the U.S. agenda in World War I, but Congress scuttled it when a worldwide pandemic of influenza took hundreds of thousands of lives and overwhelmed health facilities. Perhaps an AIDS epidemic in the next decade will overwhelm health services and accelerate the conservative trend to privatization, which is endangering national health insurance systems.

Because it is inferior to a national health service, national health insurance is not a progressive choice; however, some people support it as the realistic alternative to a national health service. Usually identified with Great Britain, nationalized health services treat 33 percent of the world's population in fourteen countries (Terris 1978). They are financed by taxation and employ salaried physicians and other health personnel in government-owned hospitals and health centers. The British NHS is remarkably effective in controlling the rising costs that trouble countries with large private medical sectors, and it avoids the waste, oversupply, and unnecessary treatment characteristic of fee-for-service medicine (Higgins 1988, 236).

Socialized medicine, which is controlled by local communities, is preferable to nationalized health care, which is controlled by physicians and bureaucrats. It seems to me that the first opportunity opened by the health care crisis is for socialized health programs, to replace national health insurance systems and to reverse the regressive trend toward privatization. The second opening is for special-interest groups—women, unions, environmentalists—to press their demands. The international women's health movement, represented by such groups as the Women's International Health Network and the Women's Global Network on Reproductive Rights, has a long list of accomplishments to its credit. In the 1990s, it will tackle the problems of infertility, maternal and infant mortality, and birth defects. Women will join coalitions to obtain the improved living and working conditions, as well as greater access to medical care, that will result in better pregnancy outcomes.

Unions play a critical role in the struggle for better working and living conditions. Ten years ago, the Oil Chemical and Atomic Workers International Union (OCAW) started a coalition of unionists and environmentalists to campaign for legislation that would guarantee workers in the United States the right to know the hazardous nature of the materials they work with. Adopted first by the city of Philadelphia in 1981, right-to-know acts have been implemented in at least thirteen states and thirty-five cities. Workers in every country need this protection. The next step is legislation that would give communities the right to know the hazardous nature of the materials manufactured in their neighborhoods, a need that the Bhopal disaster tragically demonstrated. Communities surrounding plants also need the protection of workers who have the right to act—to shut down a dangerous operation, for example. Companies are resisting right-to-act legislation because it gives workers the powers that are tightly held prerogatives of management. OCAW, which represents workers in a West Virginian plant similar to the one in Bhopal, is working closely with groups in India such as Medico Friend Circle and the Bhopal Group for Information and Action for international legislation to control multinationals such as Union Carbide.

The environmental movement has grown from a fringe protest to an international force for improved air and water quality. It has confronted major transnational corporations and achieved significant reforms in national legislation and local enforcement. It has also survived corporate attempts to divide it from workers, its natural constituency, who were told that costly environmental controls would shut down plants and eliminate jobs. However, militant grass-roots efforts are fragmented and defensive, leading to piecemeal solutions, while international organizations such as the Sierra Club are easily outspent and outmaneuvered by government and industry (Freudenberg 1984, 250-257). To achieve the major demand on the environmental agenda for the 1990s—the right to participate in decision-making that affects our environment, including the decisions made by private corporations—we need to build strong international coalitions.

More has been accomplished in the past decade by coalitions than by single-interest lobbies acting alone. We need to build international coalitions, not only to recoup our losses under conservative administrations, not only to continue to press for socialized health systems, but also to address the unresolved health problems of neglected groups such as migrant laborers, Third World women, and ethnic minorities. Short of revolution, international coalition-building offers the most promising way forward to a solution of the global health crisis.

NOTES

NOTES TO INTRODUCTION

[1] The term "Third World" refers to the underdeveloped countries of Asia, Africa, and Latin America. It excludes countries such as South Africa that are highly developed; but it includes countries such as Angola and Algeria that have oil as sources of income but still remain relatively underdeveloped. The term was originally coined by a Frenchman who recalled that in the French Revolution the first estate was the clergy, the second estate was the nobility, and the third estate was the common people; poverty was the common unifying force of the third estate in the revolution. By analogy today, the First World comprises the advanced industrialized market economies, the Second World includes the industrial socialist countries, and the Third World is composed of the poor underdeveloped countries.

NOTES TO CHAPTER 1

[1] Geographers note that, in addition to the East-West divide between the First and Second Worlds, there is a North-South divide between the First and Second Worlds (North) and the Third World (South). The Brandt Commission popularized the terms North-South in the dialogue it advocates. The international Mason-Dixon line runs below the United States, across the Atlantic and through the Mediterranean and the Black Sea, below the Soviet Union and Japan, and drops south to loop around Australia and New Zealand.

NOTES TO CHAPTER 2

[1] J. D. Bernal (1954) traced somewhat mechanistically the history of science in his four-volume study. For a more sophisticated but incomplete account see the pages of *Radical Science Journal.*
[2] David Hume (1711–1776) was a skeptic who believed human knowledge was restricted to experience of ideas and impressions; he denied the possibility of obtaining any ultimate verification of truth.
[3] See Stephen J. Gould's (1981, 234–320) brilliant critique of factor analysis, developed by Spearman and Burt for the purpose of evaluating human intelligence.

NOTES TO CHAPTER 3

[1] Paul Starr (1982, 180ff), in his book *The Social Transformation of American Medicine*, describes the split between prevention and cure as the work of general

practitioners who believed their incomes were lowered by the free medical care available through the public dispensaries that provided teaching material for specialists; private practitioners sought to close the dispensaries and establish preventive service as the limit of public health. Starr, who devotes only 18 pages to public health in a book of 500 pages, not only confuses the issues of public health as free medical care (that is, paid for by the government) and public health as community health services, but also misses the point about the larger economic forces that were decisive in determining the direction of American medicine. His thesis is that an autonomous medical profession shaped the medical system; and he limits economic forces to the economics of illness and medical care.

[2] Medicine's immense psychological influence is tempered only by growing dissatisfaction with treatment and outcomes (Corea 1985; Ribicoff 1972).

[3] Edgar Sydenstricker is my nominee for great heroes of public health. Trained as a political economist as well as a statistician, he designed the epidemiological studies carried out over a period of three years. I think he was more brilliant than Joseph Goldberger (the physician who carried out the medical examinations), although Goldberger is credited with discovering the cause of pellagra and is considered the hero in the public health literature.

Notes to Chapter 4

[1] Some contrasts in Indian and White attitudes toward the natural world are reflected in this passage from a letter written in 1855 by the Dwamish chief Seattle of Washington Territory to President Franklin Pierce:

> There is no quiet place in the white man's cities. No place to hear the leaves of spring or the rustle of insect's wings. But perhaps because I am a savage and do not understand, the clatter only seems to insult the ears. The Indian prefers the soft sound of the wind itself cleansed by a mid-day rain, or scented with a piñon pine. The air is precious to the red man. For all things share the same breath—the beasts, the trees, the man (Nabakov 1978, 108).

[2] Stacey (1985, 293), in her study comparing women's health care in the United States and the United Kingdom, points out an interesting paradox: in Great Britain, so long as women's health problems are recognized, the best available methods can be prescribed for any woman regardless of race, class, or financial means; but if women's problems are not acknowledged it is much harder to find a way out—there is little or no space for the U.S.-style demonstration project.

[3] Occupational health services are mandatory in Belgium, France, the Netherlands, and Sweden; Italy and the Federal Republic of Germany have separate medical inspectorates, generally staffed by doctors, to conduct industrial hygiene inspections and medical examinations (Ashford 1976, 502, 507). For additional information on occupational health services in the Federal Republic of Germany, Finland, German Democratic Republic, Sweden, the United Kingdom, and the United States see Elling (1986).

[4] The first fee-for-service hospital opened in Moscow in the Fall of 1987; the 7-story facility has 120 beds, 22 physicians, 4 departments (gynecology, neurology, otolaryngology, and therapeutics), and costs 5 to 6 rubles per day plus meals

(Trehub 1987). About 20 fee-for-service polyclinics exist in Moscow but, overall, fee-paying services represent only 0.4 percent of all medical services in the Soviet Union.

NOTES TO CHAPTER 5

[1] Comprehensive data on health and nutrition status are hard to come by for underdeveloped countries. Even United Nations agencies have difficulty gathering current information. UNICEF reached this conclusion in a major study carried out to assess the impact of national and international economic policies on children; a considerable amount of "bitty data" was used because country studies are by their nature intermittent (Cornia, Jolly, and Stewart 1987, 261).

[2] Forced labor was abolished in 1946 but persisted till 1960 when the independent government took control of labor migration to the Ivory Coast; it banned the old colonial recruiting agency made up of an association of Ivorian planters because of documented complaints of the continuing practice of forced labor (Songre 1973, 202–203).

[3] The economic reality behind such "natural" explanations of drought and desertification is described by Touré (1988) in an article on the settlement of neighboring Senegalese pastoralists around the boreholes drilled by French colonialists; these boreholes enabled the French to commercialize cattle production, which is the main reason for the disappearance of long-distance transhumance.

[4] Of the paid labor force—mainly urban, white-collar workers in government employ—12,000 workers are organized in forty trade unions (Kurian 1978, 1514–1515). According to Taylor (1981, 104) the unions are strong: in 1966 they brought down the unpopular and authoritarian Yameogo regime, and in 1975 they prevented then-president Lamizana from setting up a one-party system.

[5] For a more positive assessment see Murphy and Sprey (1980).

[6] Steven Feierman (personal communication, 1984) suggests that the economic basis of traditional medicine within any one country ranges from totally commoditized practice to medical practice embedded in kinship reciprocity and therefore in the network of use values.

[7] The government plans to immunize all women delivered in rural maternity wards against tetanus (World Bank 1982, 18), but there is no plan to immunize girls before clitoridectomy.

[8] Seventy percent of health development expenditure is from external donors (ILO 1982, 94). Government expenditure on health declined by an average 1.5 percent per annum between 1973 and 1979, a trend that continued during the 1980s, whereas total government expenditure rose from 4 to 36 percent during those years (ibid., 310). Both the lack of morbidity data and the corresponding availability of health service data are indicative of this dependency, which is not only financial but also scientific and technological.

[9] Under European systems of social security, which resemble national health insurance rather than public welfare, enterprises sponsor sociomedical centers and the state reimburses private medical practitioners who serve in the centers through the mechanism of employer and worker contributions.

Notes to Chapter 6

[1] There are seventy-four chlorinated dioxins (the substances take hexa, hepta, and octa forms), including twenty-one tetrachloro species (abbreviated TCDD). The most poisonous is 2,3,7,8-tetrachlorodibenzo-p-dioxin, a contaminant created by intense heat in the manufacture of trichlorophenol, which is the basis of 2,4,5-T, silvex, and hexachlorophene, once a widely used bactericide. With current technology, there is no way to avoid creating 2,3,7,8-TCDD or to eliminate it completely from final products (Turshen 1979).

[2] For an account of the health impacts of 2,4,5-T herbicides, see Cook and Kaufman (1982).

Notes to Chapter 7

[1] The mid-nineteenth-century famine in Ireland, which produced one million emigrants for the English and American labor forces, owes as much to British colonial control as to agricultural organization. Marx showed that the system of absentee landlords upheld by British colonialism continually increased its extortion of rents from the Irish peasantry and reduced their diet to a single staple, the potato (Marx and Engels 1972, 74–76). Blight brought about the famine in which 1.5 million people starved to death between 1846 and 1851 (Susser, Watson, and Hopper 1985, 14–15).

[2] The diet of English peasants before the industrial revolution, according to Braudel (1967, 132), included fresh food in the summer and salt beef in winter. Braudel (ibid., 143–144) also comments on the adulteration of milk in London, which he calls a "gigantic fraud." See also Thompson (1968, 350) on adulteration.

[3] A number of great Victorian novels are devoted to the threat of worker revolts and the plight of the poor, rural and urban: for example, Elizabeth Gaskell's *North and South*; Benjamin Disraeli's *Sybil or The Two Nations*; George Eliot's *Felix Holt*; and Harriet Martineau's *Deerfield*.

Notes to Chapter 8

[1] Historians Francis Parkman and Howard Peckman describe plans made in 1763 by General Jeffrey Amherst and Colonel Henry Boquet of the British Army to present smallpox infested blankets to Senecas and Cayugas along the western frontiers of Pennsylvania, Maryland, and Virginia (cited in Johansen and Maestas [1979, 241]; see also Pinkney [1972, 102]). It is not clear how widespread this practice was.

[2] Ackerknecht (1945, 59) argues that malaria was imported into the United States; there is no evidence that Native Americans had any experience with the disease.

[3] Chemists developed DDT in 1874 but it was first used as an insecticide in World War II (Graham 1970, 65).

NOTES TO CHAPTER 9

[1] Sickle-cell trait should be distinguished from sickle-cell anemia in which the capacity of the blood to transport oxygen is lowered (a condition called hemolytic anemia). Sickle-cell trait is of little medical significance (comparable to rhesus negative blood type); sickle-cell anemia is associated with infections, internal bleeding, and pain and may result in early death.

NOTES TO CHAPTER 10

[1] There is a large bibliography linking agribusiness to food consumption and nutrition. The classic is De Castro (1977). Some books in the muckraking tradition are George (1976), Kotz (1971), Lappé and Collins (1978), Lerza and Jacobson (1975), and Silverstein (1984).
[2] Food chemists in private and state employ have developed methods to extract edible oil from cotton seed, but even when the seed is processed locally, the cooking oil produced is exported, not consumed domestically.
[3] The trend is to more aid and fewer purchases, indicative of sub-Saharan Africa's declining purchasing power.
[4] Hunger is defined by the Physician Task Force as mild or moderate malnutrition with a multiplicity of health outcomes—for example, low birth weight, children's failure to thrive (too short, too thin), and deficiency diseases in the elderly. The Task Force gathered data from field investigations in Alabama, Illinois, Mississippi, Missouri, New Mexico, North Carolina, Tennessee, and Texas. A detailed statewide study in New Jersey found 600,000 hungry people (7.7 percent of the state's population), largely confirming the findings of the Physician Task Force (Colman 1986).

NOTES TO CHAPTER 11

[1] On a trip to China in the summer of 1982 with the Harvard School of Public Health, I observed health care in the Beijing and Shanghai regions. Although mental health services were not the focus of my tour, I did visit both traditional and biomedical services. With the exception of acupuncture used to anesthetize patients undergoing certain types of surgery (thyroidectomy, for example), traditional techniques were not integrated into biomedical practice. My general impression was that the Chinese people preferred traditional to biomedical care, judging by the heavy use of traditional services and the empty beds and waiting rooms in the biomedical sector.
[2] As interpreted here, culture-specific approaches to mental health are those which adapt biomedical psychiatry to non-European cultures and those which revise traditional mental health practice in the light of biomedical knowledge.
[3] The United States does not recognize the category "political prisoner." When Andrew Young visited South Africa as U.S. Ambassador to the United Nations during the Carter administration, he spoke about Black political prisoners in the United States; his remarks so outraged some Americans that critics demanded his recall. Recently, a federal district judge ordered the Bureau of Prisons to transfer into regular cells two women held in an isolation unit because of their

radical political beliefs; Judge Parker said that "consigning anyone to a high-security unit for past political associations they will never shed unless forced to renounce them is a dangerous mission for this country's prison system to continue" (*New York Times*, 17 July 1988).

Notes to Chapter 12

[1] The World Bank (1988, 304) warns that national definitions of what is "urban" differ, and cross-country comparisons should be interpreted with caution. Only four sub-Saharan African cities have one million or more inhabitants: Addis Ababa, Kinshasa, Lagos, and Nairobi (according to 1987 estimates).

[2] All three authors work in USAID's Bureau for Africa, Washington, D.C. Their paper describes USAID policy and plans, although it carries the usual disclaimer, "The views expressed herein are entirely those of the authors and do not necessarily represent those of the Agency for International Development."

[3] A WHO-sponsored Workshop on AIDS in Central Africa held in October 1985 adopted a uniform case definition to be applied in the absence of laboratory diagnosis (WHO 1986c, 71). AIDS in an adult is defined by the presence of at least two of the major signs (weight loss >10 percent of body weight, chronic diarrhea >1 month, and prolonged fever >1 month) and one of the minor signs (persistent cough >1 month, recurrent herpes zoster, generalized pruritic dermatitis, chronic progressive and disseminated herpes simplex, oropharyngeal candidiasis, and generalized lymphadenopathy). Initial experience with the new definition in Zaire indicates overreporting in about 40 percent of cases (Haq 1988a, 14).

[4] These difficulties are not exclusive to African countries. In July 1988 the New York City Health Department reduced its estimate of 400,000 people infected with the AIDS virus to a range of 149,000–225,000. According to the *New York Times* on July 22, 1988, virtually all the key statistics on AIDS—number infected, number of deaths, number of cases—are suffused with uncertainty.

[5] The survival figures broken down by ethnic group are: 411 days for Whites, 325 days for African-Americans, and 320 days for Hispanics. Broken down by risk group, the figures are 400 days for homosexuals and 318 days for intravenous drug users (*New York Times,* 19 November 1987).

[6] According to Glatt, Chirgwin, and Landesman (1988, 1439), based on work in the United States, "the only HIV-associated infections that can readily be communicated are tuberculosis, herpes zoster, and perhaps salmonellosis." However they add that "the observed frequency of certain fungal or parasitic infections depends on the prevalence of asymptomatic infection with these pathogens in the local population."

[7] Some of the pharmaceutical companies involved in AIDS research are Burroughs Wellcome, Genentech, Schering-Plough, Bristol-Myers, Eli Lilly, Imreg, ICN Pharmaceuticals, Amgem, Genetics Institute, Repligen, Merck, Microgenesis, Chiron, Ciba-Geigy, Imre, Cambridge Bioscience, Baxter Travenol, and Hoffmann-La Roche (*New York Times,* 1 April 1988).

Notes to Chapter 14

[1] Paradoxically, U.S. government intervention in the form of new hospital billing procedures for Medicare patients based on diagnostic related groups (DRGs) instead of length of stay (which often results in the premature discharge of very sick people) represents the single biggest blow to the twenty-year free ride that the government gave to the private sector. At the same time, the government reduced Medicaid and Medicare benefits and allowed public hospitals to decline. These are features of the deliberate shrinkage of the public sector, which serves mainly the poor, the elderly, and minorities.

BIBLIOGRAPHY

Ackerknecht, Erwin H. 1945. *Malaria in the Upper Mississippi Valley 1760–1900*. Baltimore: The Johns Hopkins Press.

Afonja, Simi. 1986. "Land Control: A Critical Factor in Yoruba Gender Stratification." In *Women and Class in Africa,* edited by Claire Robertson and Iris Berger, 78–91. New York: Africana Publishing Company.

Akerele, O., A. Dhalla, and Q. Qhobela. 1978. "Country Health Profile: United Republic of Tanzania." Dar es Salaam: World Health Organization, mimeo.

Allen, J. R. and J. W. Curran. 1988. "Prevention of AIDS and HIV Infection: Needs and Priorities for Epidemiologic Research." *American Journal of Public Health* 78(4):381–386.

Amin, Samir. 1973. *Neo-Colonialism in West Africa*. New York: Monthly Review Press.

Andersen, P., M. Jaramillo, and F. Stewart. 1987. "The Impact on Government Expenditure." In *Adjustment with a Human Face: Protecting the Vulnerable and Promoting Growth*, edited by G. A. Cornia, R. Jolly, and F. Stewart, 73–89. Oxford: Clarendon Press.

Anderson, Richard F. 1987. "Solid Waste and Public Health." In *Public Health and the Environment: The United States Experience,* edited by Michael R. Greenberg, 173–204. New York: Guilford Press.

Andrae, Gunilla and Bjorn Beckman. 1985. *The Wheat Trap: Bread and Underdevelopment in Nigeria*. London: Zed Books.

Apthorpe, R. 1977. "The Cooperatives' Poor Harvest." *New Internationalist* 48:4–6.

Artaud, Antonin. 1970. *The Theatre and Its Double*. London: John Calder.

Ashford, Nicholas. 1976. *Crisis in the Workplace: Occupational Disease and Injury*. Cambridge: MIT Press.

Awanbor, David. 1982. "The Healing Process in African Psychotherapy." *American Journal of Psychotherapy* 36(2):206–213.

Bach, D. 1982. "L'insertion dans les rapports internationaux." In *État et Bourgeoisie en Côte-d'Ivoire,* edited by Y.-A. Fauré and J.-F. Médard, 89–121. Paris: Karthala.

Bahry, Donna and Carol Nechemias. 1981. "Half Full or Half Empty? The Debate Over Soviet Regional Equality." *Slavic Review* 40(3):366–383.

Baker, Dean. 1980. "The Use and Health Consequences of Shift Work." *International Journal of Health Services* 10(3):405–420.

Banerji, Debabar. 1984. "Primary Health Care: Selective or Comprehensive?" *World Health Forum* 5:312–315.

Bang, Abhay and Ashvin J. Patel. n.d. *Health Care: Which Way to Go?*. Pune, India: Medico Friend Circle.

Bannerman, Robert H., John Burton, and Ch'en Wen-Chieh. 1983. *Traditional*

Medicine and Health Care Coverage: A Reader for Health Administrators and Practitioners. Geneva: World Health Organization.

Barker, C. and M. Turshen. 1986a. "AIDS in Africa." *Review of African Political Economy* 36:51–54.

Barker, C. and M. Turshen. 1986b. "Primary Health Care or Selective Health Strategies." *Review of African Political Economy* 36:78–85.

Barraclough, Solon. 1982. *A Preliminary Analysis of the Nicaraguan Food System*. Geneva: United Nations Research Institute for Social Development.

Barton, Tom. 1988. "Sexually-related Illness in Eastern and Central Africa: A Selected Bibliography." In *AIDS in Africa: The Social and Policy Impact*, edited by N. Miller and R. C. Rockwell, 269–291. Lewiston, N.Y.: The Edwin Mellen Press.

Bay, E.C. 1982. "Introduction." In *Women and Work in Africa,* edited by E. C. Bay, 1–18. Boulder, Colo.: Westview Press.

Béhar, Moisés. 1976. "European Diets vs. Traditional Foods." *Food Policy* 1(5):432–435.

Belden, Joseph N. 1986. *Dirt Rich, Dirt Poor*. New York: Routledge & Kegan Paul.

Benenson, Abram S. ed. 1985. *Control of Communicable Diseases in Man*. Washington, D.C.: American Public Health Association. (Fourteenth edition.)

Benería, Lourdes. 1981. "Conceptualizing the Labor Force: The Underestimiation of Women's Economic Activities." In *African Women in the Development Process,* edited by Nici Nelson, 10–28. London: Frank Cass.

Bennett, F. J. 1962. "The Social Determinants of Gonorrhea in an East African Town." *East African Medical Journal* 39(6):332–342.

———. 1987. "AIDS as a Social Phenomenon." *Social Science & Medicine* 25(6):529–539.

Berliner, Howard S. 1985. *A System of Scientific Medicine: Philanthropic Foundations in the Flexner Era*. New York: Tavistock.

Berliner, Howard and J. Warren Salmon. 1976. "Swine Flu, the Phantom Threat." *The Nation* September 25: 269–272.

Bermann, Gregorio. 1973. *La Santé Mentale en Chine*. Paris: François Maspero.

Bernal, J. D. 1954. *Science in History*. New York: Cameron Associates.

Berthelot, Jacques and François de Ravignan. 1980. *Les Sillons de la Faim*. Paris: Editions L'Harmattan.

Bessis, Sophie. 1979. *L'Arme Alimentaire*. Paris: François Maspero.

Bhaskar, Roy. 1979. "On the Possibility of Social Scientific Knowledge and the Limits of Naturalism." In *Issues in Marxist Philosophy,* edited by John Mepham and D.-H. Ruben, 107–139. Brighton: Harvester Press.

Bhatia, S. 1983. "Traditional Practices Affecting Female Health and Survival: Evidence from Countries of South Asia." In *Sex Differentials in Mortality: Trends, Determinants, and Consequences,* edited by A. D. Lopez & L. T. Rudicka, 165–177. Canberra: Australian National University Press.

Bhopal Action Resource Center. 1988. "Interim Relief for the Bhopal Victims: So Near and Yet So Far?" BARC Briefing Paper #8, New York, mimeo.

Bhopal Group for Information and Action. 1986. *Bhopal* No. 2, July, mimeo.

Biggar, Robert J. 1988. "Overview: Africa, AIDS, and Epidemiology." In *AIDS in Africa: The Social and Policy Impact*, edited by N. Miller and R. C. Rockwell, 1–8. Lewiston, N.Y.: The Edwin Mellen Press.

Blane, David. 1982. "Inequality and Social Class." In *Sociology as Applied to Medicine,* edited by Donald L. Patrick and Graham Scambler, 113–124. London: Bailliere Tindall.

Bohmer, C. 1980. "Modernization, Divorce and the Status of Women: Le Tribunal Coutumier in Bobodioulasso." *African Studies Review* 23(2):81–90.

Bolland, R. and M. Young. 1982. "The Strategy, Cost and Progress of Primary Health Care." *Bulletin of the Pan American Health Organization* 16(3):233–241.

Boserup, Ester. 1970. *Women's Role in Economic Development.* New York: St. Martin's Press.

Bottomore, Tom, ed. 1985. *A Dictionary of Marxist Thought.* Oxford: Blackwell.

Bottomore, T. B. and Maximilien Rubel. 1963. "Introduction." *Karl Marx: Selected Writings in Sociology and Social Philosophy.* Harmondsworth: Penguin Books.

Bradford Hill, A. 1961. *Principles of Medical Statistics.* London: The Lancet.

Brain, J. L. 1976. "Less Than Second-class: Women in Rural Resettlement Schemes in Tanzania." In *Women in Africa,* edited by N. J. Hafkin & E. G. Bay, 205–232. Stanford: Stanford University Press.

Braudel, Fernand. 1967. *Capitalism and Material Life 1400–1800.* New York: Harper & Row.

Brenner, M. Harvey. 1976. "Reply to Mr. Eyer." *International Journal of Health Services* 6(1): 149–155.

Brokensha, David. 1988. "Overview: Social Factors in the Transmission and Control of African AIDS." In *AIDS in Africa: The Social and Policy Impact,* edited by N. Miller and R. C. Rockwell, 167–173. Lewiston, N.Y.: The Edwin Mellen Press.

Brown, E. Richard. 1984. "Medicare and Medicaid: Band-Aids for the Old and Poor." In *Reforming Medicine: Lessons of the Last Quarter Century,* edited by Victor W. Sidel and Ruth Sidel, 50–76. New York: Pantheon Books.

Brown, G. W. and T. Harris. 1978. *Social Origins of Depression: Study of Psychiatric Disorder in Women.* London: Tavistock.

Bryceson, D. F. 1980. "Changes in Peasant Food Production and Food Supply in Relation to the Historical Development of Commodity Production in Precolonial and Colonial Tanganyika." *Journal of Peasant Studies* 7(3):281–311.

Bryceson, D. F. and M. Mbilinyi. 1978. "The Changing Role of Tanzanian Women in Production: From Peasants to Proletarians." Dar es Salaam: Bureau of Resource Assessment and Land Use Planning Service Paper no. 78/5.

Bujra, Janet. 1986. " 'Urging Women to Redouble Their Eforts . . . ': Class, Gender, and Capitalist Transformation in Africa." In *Women and Class in Africa,* edited by C. Robertson and I. Berger, 117–140. New York: Holmes & Meier.

Bull, David. 1982. *A Growing Problem: Pesticides and the Third World Poor.* Oxford: Oxfam.

Burenkov, Sergei. 1985. "Soviet Health Care." In *Medicine and Health Care in the USSR,* edited by Sergei Burenkov, 3–16. New York: International Universities Press.

Busnello, Ellis D'A. 1980. "Psychiatry for the Underdeveloped or Underdeveloped Psychiatry?" *Bulletin of the Pan American Health Organization* 14(3):224–228.

Butler, Judy et al. 1978. "Dying for Work: Occupational Health and Asbestos." *NACLA Report on the Americas* 12(2):21–29.

Calkins, Beverly M. 1987. "Life-style and Chronic Disease in Western Society." In *Public Health and the Environment: The United States Experience,* edited by Michael R. Greenberg, 25–75. New York: Guilford Press.

Caplan, Arthur L., ed. 1978. *The Sociobiology Debate: Readings on Ethical and Scientific Issues*. New York: Harper & Row.

Capra, Fritjof. 1983. *The Turning Point: Science, Society, and the Rising Culture*. New York: Bantam Books.

Carson, Rachel. 1965. *Silent Spring*. Harmondsworth: Penguin Books.

Cassel, John and Herman A. Tyroler. 1961. "Epidemiological Studies of Culture Change: Health Status and Recency of Migration." *Archives of Environmental Health* 3:31–39.

Castleman, Barry and Vicente Navarro. 1987. "International Mobility of Hazardous Products, Industries, and Wastes." *International Journal of Health Services*. 17(4):617–633.

Ceesay-Marenah, Coumba. 1982. "Women's Cooperative Thrift and Credit Societies: An Element of Women's Programs in the Gambia." In *Women and Work in Africa,* edited by Edna G. Bay, 289–295. Boulder, Colo.: Westview Press.

Cerruti, Giovanni. 1977. "Cent Jours à la Dioxine." In *Survivre à Seveso?* par une équipe de scientifiques, de militants et de journalistes italiens, 9–19. Paris: François Maspero.

Chapin, Georganne and Robert Wasserstrom. 1981. "Agricultural Production and Malaria Resurgence in Central America and India." *Nature* 293:181–185.

Chaulet, P., N. Ait Khaled, and R. Amrane. 1983. "Problèmes Posés par la Tuberculose dans le Monde en 1982." *Revue Française de Maladies Respiratoires* 11:79–110.

Checkland, S. G. and E. O. A. Checkland, eds. 1974. *The Poor Law Report of 1834.* Harmondsworth: Penguin Books.

Chen, Edwin. 1979. *PBB: An American Tragedy*. Englewood Cliffs, N.J.: Prentice-Hall, Inc.

Chesler, Phyllis. 1973. *Women and Madness*. New York: Avon Books.

Chetley, Andy. 1979. *The Baby Killer Scandal: A War on Want Investigation into the Promotion and Sale of Powdered Baby Milks in the Third World*. London: War on Want.

Children's Defense Fund. 1985. *Black and White Children in America: Key Facts*. Washington, D.C.: Children's Defense Fund.

Chirimuuta, Richard C. and Rosalind J. Chirimuuta. 1987. *Aids, Africa and Racism*. Bretby, U.K.: published by the authors.

Christiani, David C. 1984. "Workers' Health on the New 'Long March': Occupational Health in the People's Republic of China." *International Journal of Health Services* 14(4):605–618.

Cleaver, Harry. 1977. "Malaria, the Politics of Public Health and the International Crisis." *Review of Radical Political Economics* 9(1):81–103.

Clegg, I. 1971. *Workers' Self-Management in Algeria.* London: Allen Lane.

Cliff, Julie and Abdul Razak Noormahomed. 1988. "South African Destabilization and Health in Mozambique." *Review of African Political Economy* 42:76–81.

Cloudsley-Thompson, J. L. 1976. *Insects and History.* New York: St. Martin's Press.
Cohen, Dennis L. and John Daniel, eds. 1981. *Political Economy of Africa: Selected Readings*. London and New York: Longman.
Colledge, Malcolm and Michael Hainsworth. 1982. "Death on the Dole? The Impact of Unemployment on Health." *Medicine in Society* 8(2):15–22.
Collins, J. L., L. E. Rickman and C. B. Mathura. 1980. "Frequency of Schizophrenia and Depression in a Black Inpatient Population." *Journal of the National Medical Association* 72(9):851–856.
Collomb, H. 1973. "Rencontre de deux systèmes de soins. A propos de thérapeutiques des maladies mentales en Afrique." *Social Science and Medicine* 7:623–633.
———. 1978. "L'économie des villages psychiatrique." *Social Science and Medicine* 12C:113–115.
Colman, Penny, ed. 1986. *Hunger: Report and Recommendations of the New Jersey Commission on Hunger*. Trenton: N.J. State.
Commoner, Barry. 1968. "Failure of the Watson-Crick Theory as a Chemical Explanation of Inheritance." *Nature* 220:334–340.
Connelly, Mark Thomas. 1984. "Prostitution, Venereal Disease, and American Medicine." In *Women and Health in America,* edited by Judith Walzer Leavitt, 196–221. Madison: The University of Wisconsin Press.
Conti, A. 1979. "Capitalist Organization of Production through Non-Capitalist Relations: Women's Role in a Pilot Resettlement in Upper Volta." *Review of African Political Economy* 15/16:75–92.
Conway, Mimi. 1979. *Rise Gonna Rise: A Portrait of Southern Textile Workers*. New York: Doubleday.
Cook, Judith and Chris Kaufman. 1982. *Portrait of a Poison: The 2,4,5-T Story*. London: Pluto Press.
Cooper, C. et al. 1986. *Race Relations Survey 1985*. Johannesburg: South African Institute of Race Relations.
Cooper, David. 1972. *The Death of the Family*. Harmondsworth: Penguin Books.
Cooper, Richard and Arthur Schatzkin. 1982. "The Pattern of Mass Disease in the USSR: A Product of Socialist or Capitalist Development?" *International Journal of Health Services* 12(3):459–480.
Cordell, D. D. & J. W. Gregory. 1982. "Labour Reservoirs and Population: French Colonial Strategies in Koudougou, Upper Volta, 1914 to 1939." *Journal of African History* 23:205–224.
Corea, Gena. 1985. *The Hidden Malpractice: How American Medicine Mistreats Women*. New York: Harper & Row.
Corn, Jacqueline. 1987. "Protective Legislation for Coal Miners, 1870–1900: Response to Safety and Health Hazards." In *Dying for Work: Workers' Safety and Health in Twentieth Century America,* edited by David Rosner and Gerald Markowitz, 67–82. Bloomington: Indiana University Press.
Cornia, G. A., R. Jolly, and F. Stewart, editors. 1987. *Adjustment with a Human Face: Protecting the Vulnerable and Promoting Growth.* Oxford: Clarendon Press.
Coulson, A., ed. 1979. *African Socialism in Practice: The Tanzanian Experience*. Nottingham: Spokesman.
Coulson, A. 1982. *Tanzania: A Political Economy.* Oxford: Clarendon Press.

Coye, Molly Joel, Mark Douglas Smith, and Anthony Mazzocchi. 1984. "Occupational Health and Safety: Two Steps Forward, One Step Back." In *Reforming Medicine: Lessons of the Last Quarter Century*, edited by Victor W. Sidel and Ruth Sidel, 79–106. New York: Pantheon Books.

Croll, Elisabeth. 1982. *The Family Rice Bowl: Food and the Domestic Economy in China*. Geneva: United Nations Research Institute for Social Development.

Da Conceição, Manuel. 1981. *Cette terre est à nous: La vie d'un paysan du Nordeste brésilien*. Paris: François Maspero.

Danielson, David and Arthur Mazer. 1986. "The Massachusetts Referendum for a National Health Program." *Journal of Public Health Policy* 7(2):161–173.

Davies, J. N. P. 1959. "James Christie and the Cholera Epidemics of East Africa." *East African Medical Journal* 36:1–6.

Davies, Rob and David Sanders. 1987. "Stabilisation Policies and the Effects on Child Health in Zimbabwe." *Review of African Political Economy* 38:3–23.

Davis, C. and M. Feshbach. 1980. *Rising Infant Mortality in the USSR in the 1970s*. Washington, D.C.: U.S. Bureau of the Census.

Davis, Karen and Cathy Schoen. 1978. *Health and the War on Poverty: A Ten-Year Appraisal.* Washington, D.C.: The Brookings Institution.

D'Costa, L. J. et al. 1985. "Prostitutes are a Major Reservoir of Sexually Transmitted Disease in Nairobi, Kenya." *Sexually Transmitted Disease* 12(2):64–67.

de Beer, Cedric. 1984. *The South African Disease: Apartheid Health and Health Services*. Trenton, N.J.: Africa World Press.

De Castro, Josué. 1977. *The Geopolitics of Hunger*. New York: Monthly Review Press.

Defense and Foreign Affairs Handbook 1987–88. Washington, D.C.: The Perth Corporation.

Defoe, Daniel. 1970. *A Journal of the Plague Year*. Harmondsworth: Penguin Books. (First published 1722.)

DeMaeyer, E. M. 1976. "Protein-Energy Malnutrition." In *Nutrition in Preventive Medicine,* edited by G. H. Beaton and J. M. Bengoa, 23–53. Geneva: World Health Organization.

Desplanques, Guy. 1984. "L'inégalité sociale devant la mort." *Economie et Statistique* 162:29–50.

Doniger, David. 1978. *The Law and Policy of Toxic Substances Control: A Case Study of Vinyl Chloride.* Baltimore: Johns Hopkins University Press.

Donzelot, Jacques. 1979. *The Policing of Families*. New York: Pantheon Books.

Dowd, James J. 1984, "Mental Illness and the Aged Stranger." In *Readings in The Political Economy of Aging,* edited by Meredith Minkler and Carroll L. Estes, 94–116. Farmingdale, N.Y.: Baywood Publishing.

Dubos, René J. 1950. *Louis Pasteur: Free Lance of Science*. Boston: Little, Brown and Co.

———. 1959. *Mirage of Health: Utopias, Progress, and Biological Change*. New York: Harper & Row.

———. 1968. *Man, Medicine, and Environment*. Harmondsworth: Penguin Books.

Dumont, R. 1981. "Haute-Volta." In *Pauvreté et Inégalités Rurales en Afrique de l'Ouest Francophone*, edited by R. Dumont et al., 1–19. Geneva: International Labour Organisation.

Dumont, René and Nicholas Cohen. 1980. *The Growth of Hunger: A New Politics of Agriculture*. Salem, N.H.: Marion Boyars.

Dupuy, Jean-Pierre and Serge Karsenty. 1974. *L'Invasion Pharmaceutique.* Paris: Éditions du Seuil.

Eberstadt, Nicholas. 1981. "The Health Crisis in the USSR." *New York Review of Books* February 19:23–31.

Egger, Philippe. 1986. "Banking for the Rural Poor: Lessons from Some Innovative Savings and Credit Schemes." *International Labour Review* 125(4):447–462.

Ehrenreich, Barbara and Deirdre English. 1979. *For Her Own Good: 150 Years of the Experts' Advice to Women.* New York: Doubleday.

Ehrlich, Paul. 1968. *The Population Bomb.* New York: Ballantine Books.

Eisenstaedt, R. S. and T. E. Getzen. 1988. "Screening Blood Donors for Human Immunodeficiency Virus Antibody: Cost-Benefit Analysis." *American Journal of Public Health* 78(4):450–454.

Elling, Ray H. 1986. *The Struggle for Workers' Health: A Study of Six Industrialized Countries.* Farmingdale, N.Y.: Baywood Publishing Company.

el Saadawi, Nawal. 1980. *The Hidden Face of Eve: Women in the Arab World.* London: Zed Press.

Encyclopaedia Britannica. 1984. Chicago: Helen Hemingway Benton, Publisher.

Engels, Frederick. 1969. *The Condition of the Working Class in England.* Frogmore: Panther Books. (First published in English in 1892.)

Enzensberger, Hans Magnus. 1974. "A Critique of Political Ecology." *New Left Review* 84:3–31.

Epstein, Samuel S. 1979. *The Politics of Cancer.* New York: Doubleday.

Erickson, Jon and Charles Wilhelm, eds. 1986. *Housing the Homeless.* New Brunswick, N.J.: Center for Urban Policy Research.

Esterson, Aaron. 1970. *The Leaves of Spring.* London: Tavistock.

Evans, Robert. 1982. "A Retrospective on the 'New Perspective'." *Journal of Health Politics, Policy and Law* 7(2):325–344.

Everest, Larry. 1985. *Behind the Poison Cloud: Union Carbide's Bhopal Massacre.* Chicago: Banner Press.

Eyer, Joseph. 1976a. "Review of Mental Illness and the Economy." *International Journal of Health Services* 6(1):139–148.

———. 1976b. "Rejoinder to Dr. Brenner." *International Journal of Health Services* 6(1):157–168.

Eyer, Joseph and Peter Sterling. 1977. "Stress-Related Mortality and Social Organization." *Review of Radical Political Economics* 9(1):1–44.

Fanon, Frantz. 1952. *Peau Noire, Masques Blancs.* Paris: Editions du Seuil.

Fanon, Frantz. 1961. *Les Damnés de la Terre.* Paris: François Maspero.

Farid, M. A. 1980. "The Malaria Programme—From Euphoria to Anarchy." *World Health Forum* 1(1,2):8–33.

Feierman, E. K. 1981. "Alternative Medical Services in Tanzania: A Physician's View." *Social Science & Medicine* 15B:399–404.

Feldman, Moshe and Ernest R. Sears. 1981. "The Wild Gene Resources of Wheat." *Scientific American* 244(1):102–112.

Fenner, F. et al. 1988. *Smallpox and its Eradication.* Geneva: World Health Organization.

Fisher, Lawrence E. 1985. *Colonial Madness: Mental Health in the Barbadian Social Order.* New Brunswick: Rutgers University Press.

Flew, Anthony, ed. 1970. *Malthus: An Essay on the Principle of Population*. Harmondsworth: Penguin Books.

Flinn, M. E., ed. 1965. *Report on the Sanitary Condition of the Labouring Population of Great Britain by Edwin Chadwick* [1842]. Edinburgh: The University Press.

Fooden, Myra, Susan Gordon, and Betty Hughley. 1983. *Genes and Gender IV: The Second X and Women's Health*. New York: Gordian Press.

Foucault, Michel. 1965. *Madness and Civilization. A History of Insanity in the Age of Reason*. New York: Pantheon Books.

———. 1976. *Mental Illness and Psychology*. New York: Harper & Row.

Frank, Andre Gunder. 1971. *Sociology of Development and Underdevelopment of Sociology*. London: Pluto Press.

Franke, R. W. and B. Chasin. 1980. *Seeds of Famine*. Montclair, N.J.: Allenheld, Osmun.

Fredrickson, George M. 1981. *White Supremacy: A Comparative Study in American and South African History*. New York: Oxford University Press.

Fried, Marc. 1969. "Social Differences in Mental Health." In *Poverty and Health: A Sociological Analysis,* edited by John Kosa, Aaron Antonovsky, and Irving Kenneth Zola, 113–167. Cambridge: Harvard University Press.

Friedman, Meyer and Ray H. Rosenman. 1974. *Type A Behavior and Your Heart*. New York: Fawcett Crest.

Freudenberg, Nicholas. 1984. *Not in Our Backyards! Community Action for Health and the Environment*. New York: Monthly Review Press.

Fuller, John G. 1977. *The Poison that Fell from the Sky*. New York: Random House.

Geiger, S. 1982. "Umoja wa Wanawake wa Tanzania and the Needs of the Rural Poor." *African Studies Review* 25(2 & 3):45–65.

Gentis, Roger. 1971. *Guérir la Vie*. Paris: François Maspero.

———. 1973. *La Psychiatrie doit être faite/défaite par Tous*. Paris: François Maspero.

George, Susan. 1976. *How the Other Half Dies: The Real Reasons for World Hunger*. Harmondsworth: Penguin Books.

Gèze, François et al. 1984. *L'état du Monde 1984*. Paris: Editions la Découverte.

———. 1987. *L'état du Monde 1987–1988*. Paris: Editions la Découverte.

Gillett, J. D. 1975. "Mosquito-borne Disease: A Strategy for the Future." *Scientific Progress, Oxford* 62:395–414.

Gish, Oscar. 1978. "A Comment on 'Malaria and the Political Economy of Health.' " Ann Arbor: University of Michigan School of Public Health, mimeo.

Glatt, A. E., K. Chirgwin, and S. H. Landesman. 1988. "Treatment of Infections Associated with Human Immunodeficiency Virus." *New England Journal of Medicine* 318(22):1439–1448.

Goffman, Erving. 1961. *Asylums: Essays on the Social Situation of Mental Patients and Other Inmates*. New York: Doubleday.

Goldsmith, Frank E. 1980. "Occupational Health in the Soviet Union." *Occupational Health and Safety* June: 50–54.

Goodman, Neville M. 1971. *International Health Organizations and Their Work*. Edinburgh: Churchill Livingstone.

Gotsch, Audrey R. and Clarence E. Pearson. 1987. "Education-for-Health:

Strategies for Change." In *Public Health and the Environment: The United States Experience,* edited by Michael R. Greenberg, 293–330. New York: Guilford Press.

Gottfried, Robert S. 1983. *The Black Death: Natural and Human Disaster in Medieval Europe*. New York: Free Press.

Gottlieb, M. S. et al. "Pneumocystis Pneumonia—Los Angeles." *Morbidity and Mortality Weekly Report* 30(21):250–251.

Gough, Ian. 1979. *The Political Economy of the Welfare State*. London: Macmillan.

Gough, Michael. 1986. *Dioxin, Agent Orange: The Facts*. New York: Plenum Press.

Gould, Carol C. 1980. *Marx's Social Ontology*. Cambridge: MIT Press.

Gould, Stephen J. 1978. "Biological Potential vs. Biological Determinism." In *The Sociobiology Debate: Readings on Ethical and Scientific Issues*, edited by Arthur L. Caplan, 343–351. New York: Harper & Row.

———. 1979. *Ever Since Darwin: Reflections in Natural History*. New York: W. W. Norton & Company.

———. 1981. *The Mismeasure of Man*. New York: W. W. Norton & Company.

Gove, Walter R. 1978. "Sex Differences in Mental Illness among Adult Men and Women: An Evaluation of Four Questions Raised Regarding the Evidence on the Higher Rates of Women." *Social Science and Medicine* vol. 12B, 187–198.

Graham, Frank. 1970. *Since Silent Spring*. Greenwich, Conn.: Fawcett.

Grainger, Alan. 1982. *Desertification: How People Make Deserts, How People Can Stop Them, and Why They Don't*. London: Earthscan.

Greeley, Edward H. 1988. "The Role of Non-governmental Organizations in AIDS Prevention: Parallels to African Family Planning Activity." In *AIDS in Africa: The Social and Policy Impact*, edited by N. Miller and R. C. Rockwell, 131–144. Lewiston, N.Y.: The Edwin Mellen Press.

Green, Edward C. 1988. "AIDS in Africa: An Agenda for Behavioral Scientists." In *AIDS in Africa: The Social and Policy Impact*, edited by N. Miller and R. C. Rockwell, 175–195. Lewiston, N.Y.: The Edwin Mellen Press.

Green, Jeremy. 1983. "Detecting the Hypersusceptible Worker: Genetics and Politics in Industrial Medicine." *International Journal of Health Services* 13 (2), 247–264.

Greenberg, Michael R. 1987. "Health and Risk in Urban-Industrial Society." In *Public Health and the Environment: The United States Experience,* edited by Michael R. Greenberg, 3–24. New York: Guilford Press.

Gregory, J. W. 1979. "Underdevelopment, Dependence and Migration in Upper Volta." In *The Politics of Africa: Dependence and Development,* edited by T. M. Shaw and K. A. Heard, 73–94. London: Longman & Dalhousie University Press.

Guattari, Félix. 1972. *Psychanalyse et Transversalité*. Paris: François Maspero.

Guyer, Jane I. 1984. "Women in the Rural Economy: Contemporary Variations." In *African Women South of the Sahara,* edited by Jean Hay and Sharon Stichter, 19–32. London and New York: Longman.

Hammoud, E. I. 1977. "Sex Differentials in Mortality. An Enquiry with Reference to the Arab Countries and Others." *World Health Statistics Report* 30(3):174–206.

Hanft, Ruth. 1981. "Health Manpower." In *Health Care Delivery in the United*

States, by Steven Jonas with contributors, 61–95. New York: Springer Publishing Company.

Haq, Cynthia. 1988a. "Data on AIDS in Africa: An Assessment." In *AIDS in Africa: The Social and Policy Impact*, edited by N. Miller and R. C. Rockwell, 9–29. Lewiston, N.Y.: The Edwin Mellen Press.

———. 1988b. "Management of AIDS Patients: Case Report from Uganda." In *AIDS in Africa: The Social and Policy Impact*, edited by N. Miller and R. C. Rockwell, 87–95. Lewiston, N.Y.: The Edwin Mellen Press.

Harding, Sandra. 1986. *The Science Question in Feminism*. Ithaca: Cornell University Press.

Harrington, Charlene. 1984. "Public Policy and the Nursing Home Industry." In *Readings in the Political Economy of Aging,* edited by Meredith Minkler and Carroll L. Estes, 144–154. Farmingdale, N.Y.: Baywood Publishing Company.

Harsch, Ernest. 1988. "A Revolution Derailed." *Africa Report* January-February: 33–39.

Hart, Nicky. 1985. *Sociology of Health and Medicine*. Ormskirk, U.K.: Causeway Press.

———. 1986. "Inequalities in Health: The Individual versus the Environment." *Journal of the Royal Statistical Society* Series A 149(3):228–246.

Hatch, John W. and Eugenia Eng. 1984. "Community Participation and Control: Or Control of Community Participation." In *Reforming Medicine: Lessons of the Last Quarter Century,* edited by Victor W. Sidel and Ruth Sidel, 223–244. New York: Pantheon Books.

Hemmings-Gapihan, G. S. 1982. "International Development and the Evolution of Women's Economic Roles: A Case Study from Northern Gulma, Upper Volta." In *Women and Work in Africa*, edited by E. G. Bay, 171–189. Boulder, Colo.: Westview Press.

Henderson, Donald A. 1976. "The Eradication of Smallpox." *Scientific American* 235(4): 25–33.

Henn, Jeanne K. 1984. "Women in the Rural Economy: Past, Present, and Future." In *African Women South of the Sahara,* edited by Jean Hay and Sharon Stichter, 1–18. London and New York: Longman.

Heyward, W. L. and J. W. Curran. 1988. "The Epidemiology of AIDS in the U.S." *Scientific American* 259(4): 72–81.

Higgins, Joan. 1988. *The Business of Medicine: Private Health Care in Britain*. London: Macmillan Education.

Highlander Research and Education Center. 1980. *We're Tired of Being Guinea Pigs: A Handbook for Citizens on Environmental Health in Appalachia*. New Market, Tenn.: Highlander.

Hightower, Jim. 1975. *Eat Your Heart Out: Profiteering in America*. New York: Crown Publishers.

Himmelfarb, Gertrude. 1985. *The Idea of Poverty: England in the Early Industrial Age*. New York: Vintage Books.

Hinman, Alan R. et al., eds. 1982. "Health Services in Shanghai County." *American Journal of Public Health* 72 (Supplement): 1–95.

Hobsbawm, Eric J. 1962. *The Age of Revolution, 1789–1848*. New York: New American Library.

Hobsbawm, Eric, ed. 1969. *Frederick Engels, The Condition of the Working Class in England* [1845]. St Albans: Panther Books Ltd.

Hobsbawm, Eric J. 1975. *The Age of Capital 1848–1875*.New York: Charles Scribner's Sons.

———. 1987. *The Age of Empire*. New York: Pantheon Books.

Hollingshead, A. B. and F. C. Redlich. 1958. *Social Class and Mental Illness: A Community Study*. New York: John Wiley and Sons.

Holtzman, Neil A. 1979. "Prevention: Rhetoric and Reality." *International Journal of Health Services* 9(1):25–39.

Howard-Jones, Norman. 1975. *The Scientific Background of the International Sanitary Conferences, 1851–1938*. Geneva: World Health Organization.

Hubbard, Ruth. 1979. "Have Only Men Evolved?" In *Women Look at Biology Looking at Women: A Collection of Feminist Critiques,* edited by Ruth Hubbard, Mary Sue Henifin, and Barbara Fried, 7–35. Boston: G.K. Hall.

Hubbard, Ruth. 1982. "The Theory and Practice of Genetic Reductionism—from Mendel's Laws to Genetic Engineering." In *Towards a Liberatory Biology,* edited by Steven Rose, 62–78. London: Allison and Busby Limited.

Hubbard, Ruth and Mary Sue Henifin. 1985. "Genetic Screening of Prospective Parents and of Workers: Some Scientific and Social Issues." *International Journal of Health Services*. 15(2):231–251.

Hunt, Charles W. 1988. "Africa and AIDS: Dependent Development, Sexism, and Racism." *Monthly Review* 39(9):10–22.

Hunt, Morton. 1986. "The Total Gene Screen" *New York Times Magazine* January 19: 33 ff.

ILO. 1977. *Poverty and Landlessness in Rural Asia*. Geneva: International Labour Office.

———. 1982. *Basic Needs in Danger: A Basic Needs Oriented Development Strategy for Tanzania*. Addis Ababa.

Innes, D. 1984. *Anglo American and the Rise of Modern South Africa*. New York: Monthly Review Press.

International Nuclear Safety Advisory Group. 1986. *Summary Report on the Post-accident Review Meeting on the Chernobyl Accident*. Vienna: International Atomic Energy Agency.

Irvine, John, Ian Miles, and Jeff Evans, editors. 1979. *Demystifying Social Statistics*. London: Pluto Press.

Israel, E. 1976. "Incentives offered to Civil Servants in the Medical Fields for Services in Remote, Semi-rural and Rural Areas." WHO/SHS/76.1. Geneva: World Health Organization, mimeo.

Jamison, Dean T. 1985. "China's Health Care System: Policies, Organization, Inputs and Finance." In *Good Health at Low Cost,* edited by Scott B. Halstead, Julia A. Walsh, and Kenneth S. Warren, 21–32. New York: The Rockefeller Foundation.

Jaumont, Bernard, Daniel Lenegre, and Michel Rocard. 1971. *Le Marché commun contre l'Europe*. Paris: Editions du Seuil.

Jegede, R. Olukayode. 1981a. "Aro Village System of Community Psychiatry in Perspective." *Canadian Journal of Psychiatry* 26:173–177.

———. 1981b. "Nigerian Psychiatry in Perspective." *Acta psychiatrica scandinavia* 63:45–56.

Johansen, Bruce and Roberto Maestas. 1979. *Wasi'chu: The Continuing Indian Wars*. New York: Monthly Review Press.

Joint Programme Committee. 1980. "Socioeconomic Development Aspects: Upper Volta." Yamoussoukro: Onchocerciasis Control Programme in the Volta River Basin Area. Unpublished conference document.

———. 1981. "Report on the Socioeconomic Development of the Zones Cleared of Onchocerciasis in Upper Volta." Geneva: Onchocerciasis Control Programme in the Volta River Basin Area. Unpublished document.

Jonas, Steven. 1981. *Health Care Delivery in the United States*. New York: Springer Publishing Company.

Jonas, Steven and David Banta. 1981. "Government in the Health Care Delivery System." In *Health Care Delivery in the United States,* by Steven Jonas with contributors, 313–351. New York: Springer Publishing Company.

Jones, M. 1953. *The Therapeutic Community*. New York: Basic Books.

———. 1956. "The Concept of a Therapeutic Community." *American Journal of Psychiatry* 1:25.

Kabone, B. A. n.d. "Upper Volta." Tri-regional Seminar. Tunis, October 30–November 3. WHO unpublished document c. 1978. TR/SEM.PHY.POP.CH.

Kacha, F., A. Ouchfoun, and A. Yaker, 1983. "Bilan de l'Action Sanitaire." Séminaire sur le développement d'un système national de santé: l'expérience Algérienne, Alger 7–8 avril 1983, mimeo.

Kasius, R.V. ed. 1974. *The Challenge of Facts: Selected Public Health Papers of Edgar Sydenstricker*. New York: Prodist.

Kass, Edward H. 1979. "Review of *The Swine Flu Affair*" *The Lancet* 300(13):740–741.

Kazis, Richard and Richard L. Grossman. 1982. *Fear at Work: Job Blackmail, Labor and the Environment*. New York: Pilgrim Press. Lawrence & Wishart.

Kenney, Martin. 1986. *Biotechnology: The University-Industrial Complex*. New Haven: Yale University Press.

Kershaw, David N. 1972. "A Negative-Income-Tax Experiment." *Scientific American* 227(4):19–25.

Khatibi, Abdel Kebir. 1983. *Maghreb Pluriel.* Paris: Éditions Denoël.

Kiev, Ari, ed. 1964 *Magic, Faith, and Healing: Studies in Primitive Psychiatry Today*. New York: The Free Press.

Kjekshus, H. 1975. "The Elected Elite: A Socioeconomic Profile of Candidates in Tanzania's Parliamentary Election, 1970." Uppsala: Scandinavian Institute of African Studies Research Report no. 29.

Kleinman, Arthur. 1980. *Patients and Healers in the Context of Culture: An Exploration of the Borderland between Anthropology, Medicine, and Psychiatry*. Berkeley: University of California Press.

Knowles, John. 1977. "The Responsibility of the Individual." *Daedalus* Winter:57–80.

Koh, T. C. 1982. "Qigong—Chinese Breathing Exercise." *American Journal of Chinese Medicine* 10(1–4):86–91.

Kokuhirwa, H. n.d. "Towards the Social and Economic Promotion of Rural Women in Tanzania." Dar es Salaam: Institute for Adult Education.

Kosminskii, Evgenii Alekseevich. 1971. "The Plague Deemphasized." In *The Black Death: A Turning Point in History?,* edited by William H. Bowsky, 38–46. New York: Holt, Rhinehart and Winston.

Kotz, Nick. 1971. *Let Them Eat Promises: The Politics of Hunger in America*. Garden City, N.Y.: Doubleday.

Koutaissoff, Elisabeth. 1986. "Environmental Problems in Eastern Europe and the Soviet Union: Review of Recent Studies." *Environmental Conservation* 13(1):4–6.

Kurian, G.T. 1978. *Encyclopedia of the Third World*. New York: Facts on File.

Kurzman, Dan. 1987. *A Killing Wind: Inside Union Carbide and the Bhopal Catastrophe*. New York: McGraw-Hill.

Laing, R. D. 1969. *The Politics of the Family and Other Essays*. New York: Pantheon Books.

Laing, R. D. and A. Esterson. 1970. *Sanity, Madness and the Family: Families of Schizophrenics*. Harmondsworth: Penguin Books.

Lalonde, Marc. 1974. *A New Perspective on the Health of Canadians: A Working Document*. Ottawa: Ministry of National Health and Welfare.

Lambo, T. A. 1964. "Patterns of Psychiatric Care in Developing African Countries." In *Magic, Faith, and Healing,* edited by Ari Kiev, 443–453. New York: The Free Press.

Langer, William L. 1976. "Immunization against Smallpox before Jenner." *Scientific American* January, 112–117.

Lappé, Frances Moore and Joseph Collins. 1978. *Food First: Beyond the Myth of Scarcity*. New York: Ballantine Books.

Laurie, William. 1958. "A Pilot Scheme of Venereal Disease Control in East Africa." *British Journal of Venereal Disease* 34:16–21.

Lawrence, Peter, ed. 1986. *World Recession and the Food Crisis in Africa*. London: James Currey.

Leacock, Eleanor Burke, ed. 1971. *The Culture of Poverty*. New York: Simon and Schuster.

Leavitt, Judith W. 1976. "Politics and Public Health." *Bulletin of the History of Medicine* 50:553–568.

Lerza, Catherine and Michael Jacobson, eds. 1975. *Food for People Not for Profit: A Sourcebook on the Food Crisis*. New York: Ballantine Books.

Levins, Richard, and Richard Lewontin. 1985. *The Dialectical Biologist*. Cambridge: Harvard University Press.

Lewis, H. M., L. Johnson, and D. Askins. 1978. *Colonialism in Modern America: The Appalachian Case*. Boone, N.C.: The Appalachian Consortium Press.

Lewis, R. A. 1952. *Edwin Chadwick and the Public Health Movement 1832–1854*. London: Longmans, Green & Co.

Lewontin, R. C., Steven Rose, and Leon J. Kamin. 1984. *Not in Our Genes: Biology, Ideology, and Human Nature*. New York: Pantheon Books.

Lin, Tsung-yi. 1982. "Culture and Psychiatry: A Chinese Perspective." *Australian and New Zealand Journal of Psychiatry* 16:235–245.

Lindsay, Jenny. 1986. "The Politics of Population Control in Namibia." *Review of African Political Economy* 36:58–62.

Linhart, Robert. 1980. *Le sucre et la faim: Enquête dans les régions sucrières du Nord-Est brésilien*. Paris: Les Edition de Minuit.

Lisitsin, Y. 1972. *Health Protection in the USSR*. Moscow: Progress Publishers.

Lobstein, Tim. 1984. *Namibia: Reclaiming the People's Health*. London: AON Publications, Namibia Support Committee.

Lopez, A. D. 1983. "The Sex Mortality Differential in Developed Countries."

In *Sex Differentials in Mortality: Trends, Determinants, and Consequences,* edited by A. D. Lopez & L. T. Rudicka, 53–120. Canberra: Australian National University Press.

Louis, M.-V. 1982. "Les Algériennes, la Lutte." *Les Temps Modernes* 432–433; 152–193.

Lubin, Nancy. 1984. *Labour and Nationality in Soviet Central Asia*. Princeton: Princeton University Press.

Luria, S. E. 1974. "What can Biologists Solve?" *New York Review of Books* 21(1):27–28.

Macleod, R. M. 1967. "The Frustration of State Medicine, 1880–1899." *Medical History* 11:15–40.

Management Committee. 1987. "China Introduced Water Law to Protect Limited Water Resources." *Environmental Conservation* 14(4):370.

Mandel, Ernest and George Novack. 1970. *The Marxist Theory of Alienation*. New York: Pathfinder Press.

Martinez, Lindsay. 1988. "Progress in Malaria Antigen Work." *TDR Newsletter* 26:5.

Marx, Karl and Frederick Engels. 1972. *Ireland and the Irish Question*. New York: International Publishers.

May, Jacques. 1954. "The Cultural Aspects of Tropical Medicine." *American Journal of Tropical Medicine* 3(3):422–430.

Mazzocchi, Tony. 1984. "A Decade of Genetic Struggle." *International Journal of Health Services*. 14(3):447–451.

McKeown, Thomas. 1971. "A Historical Appraisal of the Medical Task." In *Medical History and Medical Care,* edited by Gordon McLachlan and Thomas McKeown. London: Oxford University Press for the Nuffield Provincial Hospitals Trust.

———. 1976. *The Role of Medicine: Dream, Mirage, or Nemesis?* London: The Nuffield Provincial Hospitals Trust.

McKeown, T. and R. G. Record. 1962. "Reasons for the Decline of Mortality in England and Wales during the Nineteenth Century." *Population Studies* XVI (2) Part 2:94–122.

McKinlay, John B. 1977. "The Business of Good Doctoring or Doctoring as Good Business: Reflections on Freidson's View of the Medical Game." *International Journal of Health Services* (7)3:459–483.

McKinlay, John B. and Sonja M. McKinlay. 1977. "The Questionable Contribution of Medical Measures to the Decline of Mortality in the United States in the Twentieth Century." *Milbank Memorial Fund Quarterly* 405–428.

McNeill, William H. 1976. *Plagues and Peoples*. New York: Doubleday.

Medvedev, Roy A. and Zhores A. Medvedev. 1971. *A Question of Madness*. New York: Alfred A. Knopf.

Meijer, Marijke. 1985. "Oppression of Women and Refugee Status." In *Proceedings of the International Seminar on Refugee Women*, 30–38. Amsterdam: Dutch Refugee Association.

Mejia, Alfonso, Helena Pizurki, and Erica Royston. 1979. *Physician and Nurse Migration: Analysis and Policy Implications*. Geneva: World Health Organization.

Memmi, Albert. 1957. *Portrait du Colonisé précédé du Portrait de Colonisateur*. Paris: Editions Buchet.

Mendelievich, Elias. 1980. *Le Travail des Enfants*. Geneva: International Labour Office.
Merkle, A. 1983. "Upper Volta: What can be done?" *World Health Forum* 4(3):195–199.
Mernissi, Fatima. 1975. *Beyond the Veil: Male-Female Dynamics in a Modern Muslim Society.* Cambridge, Mass.: Schenkman Publishing Co.
Merritt, Gary, William Lyerly, and Jack Thomas. 1988. "The HIV/AIDS Pandemic in Africa: Issues of Donor Strategy." In *AIDS in Africa: The Social and Policy Impact*, edited by N. Miller and R. C. Rockwell, 115–129. Lewiston, N.Y.: The Edwin Mellen Press.
Messing, Simon. 1959. "Group Therapy and Social Status in the Zar Cult of Ethiopia." In *Culture and Mental Health,* edited by M. K. Opler, 319–332. New York: Macmillan.
Mihyo, P. 1975. "The Struggle for Workers' Control in Tanzania." *Review of African Political Economy* 4:62–84.
Miles, Ian. 1985. *Social Indicators for Human Development.* London: Frances Pinter.
Miller, Norman and Richard C. Rockwell, eds. 1988. *AIDS in Africa: The Social and Policy Impact*. Lewiston, N.Y.: The Edwin Mellen Press.
Millington, A. and S. Mutiso. 1986. "Appropriate Technology—The Political Economy of Technical Choice in African Agriculture." Paper presented at the Review of African Political Economy Conference on Popular Struggles in Africa, Liverpool, U.K. 26–27 September.
Minkler, Meredith and Carroll L. Estes, editors. 1984. *Readings in the Political Economy of Aging.* Farmingdale, N.Y.: Baywood Publishing Company, Inc.
Molyneux, M. 1981. "Women in Socialist Societies: Problems of Theory and Practice." In *Of Marriage and the Market: Women's Subordination in International Perspective,* edited by K. Young, C. Wolkowitz, and R. McCullagh, 167–202. London: CSE Books.
Monekosso, G. L. and Comlan A. Quenum. 1978. "The University Centre for Health Sciences, Yaoundé, United Republic of Cameroon: Training the Health Team." In *Personnel for Health Care: Case Studies of Educational Programmes,* edited by F. M. Katz and T. Fulop, 185–207. Geneva: World Health Organization.
Montagu, Ashley. 1968. *The Natural Superiority of Women.* New York: Collier Books.
Morgan, Robin. 1984. *Sisterhood is Global: The International Women's Movement Anthology*. New York: Doubleday.
Morton, A. L. 1974. *A People's History of England.* London: Lawrence & Wishart.
Muller, Mike. 1982. *The Health of Nations: A North-South Investigation*. London: Faber and Faber.
Mullings, Leith. 1984. *Therapy, Ideology, and Social Change: Mental Healing in Urban Ghana.* Berkeley: University of California Press.
Murphy, J. and L. H. Sprey. 1980. "The Volta Valley Authority: Socio-Economic Evaluation of a Resettlement Project in Upper Volta." West Lafayette, Ind.: Purdue University Department of Agricultural Economics.
Muth, Lee T. 1961. *Community Treatment of Mental Illness: A World Survey*. Huntington, W. Va: Veterans Hospital.

Myrdal, Gunnar. 1969. *Objectivity in Social Research*. New York: Pantheon Books.

Nabakov, Peter, ed. 1978. *Native American Testimony. An Anthology of Indian and White Relations: First Encounter to Dispossession*. New York: Harper & Row.

Navarro, Vicente. 1976. *Medicine Under Capitalism*. New York: Prodist.

———. 1977. *Social Security and Medicine in the USSR: A Marxist Critique*. Lexington, Mass.: D. C. Heath and Company.

Nectoux, François, John Lintott, and Roy Carr-Hill. 1980. "Social Indicators: For Individual Well-Being or Social Control?" *International Journal of Health Services* 10 (1):89–113.

Neustadt, Richard E. and Harvey V. Fineberg. 1978. *The Swine Flu Affair: Decision-making on a Slippery Disease*. Washington, D.C.: U.S. Department of Health, Education, and Welfare.

Newell, Kenneth W. 1988. "Selective Primary Health Care: The Counter Revolution." *Social Science & Medicine* 26 (9):903–906.

Nichols, T. 1979. "Social Class: Official, Sociological, and Marxist." In *Demystifying Social Statistics,* edited by J. Irvine et al., 152–171. London: Pluto Press.

Noble, Charles. 1986. *Liberalism at Work: The Rise and Fall of OSHA*. Philadelphia: Temple University Press.

Norman, Colin. 1985. "Politics and Science Clash on African AIDS." *Science* 230:1140–1142.

Novicki, Margaret A. 1986. "Josephine Ouédraogo, Minister of Family Affairs and National Solidarity, Burkina Faso." *Africa Report* November-December, 26–30.

Nyerere, Julius K. 1967. *Freedom and Unity*. London: Oxford University Press.

Ollman, Bertell. 1976. *Alienation: Marx's Conception of Man in Capitalist Society*. Cambridge: Cambridge University Press.

Omari, C. K. 1987. "Some Problems Facing Health Delivery System in Tanzania: Prospects and Future." International and Comparative Studies, University of Iowa, mimeo.

Oren, Laura. 1973. "The Welfare of Women in Laboring Families: England, 1860–1950." *Feminist Studies* 1(3–4):107–125.

Ouédraogo, J. and J.-P. Ouédraogo. 1983. "Impact des migrations sur le rôle et le statut des femmes en Haute Volta." Geneva: UN Research Institute for Social Development, unpublished provisional report.

Paddock, William and Paul Paddock. 1967. *Famine, 1975! America's Decision: Who Will Survive?*. Boston: Little Brown.

Payer, Cheryl. 1982. *The World Bank: A Critical Analysis*. New York: Monthly Review Press.

Perrow, Charles. 1984. *Normal Accidents: Living with High-Risk Technologies*. New York: Basic Books.

Pfeifer, K. 1981. "Algeria's Agrarian Transformation." *Merip Reports* 99:6–14.

Physician Task Force on Hunger in America. 1985. *Hunger in America: The Growing Epidemic*. Middletown, Conn.: Wesleyan University Press.

Pinkney, Alphonso. 1972. *American Way of Violence*. New York: Random House.

Piot, P. et al. 1979. "Antibiotic Susceptibility of Neisseria Gonorrhea Strains for Europe and Africa." *Antimicrobial Agents and Chemotherapy* 15(4):535–539.
———. 1987. "AIDS in Africa: a Public Health Priority." *Journal of Virological Methods* 17:1–10.
———. 1988. "AIDS: An International Perspective." *Science* 239:573–579.
Piven, Frances Fox and Richard A. Cloward. 1971. *Regulating the Poor: The Functions of Public Welfare*. New York: Vintage Books.
Polack, Jean-Claude. 1971. *La Médecine du Capital*. Paris: François Maspero.
Pomata, Gianna. 1979. "Seveso—Safety in Numbers?" *Radical Science Journal* 9:69–81.
Popper, Frank J. 1985. "The Environmentalist and the LULU." *Environment* 27(2):6–11, 37–40.
Porter, Theodore M. 1986. *The Rise of Statistical Thinking 1820–1900*. Princeton, N.J.: Princeton University Press.
Poulantzas, Nicos. 1973. "On Social Classes." *New Left Review* 78:27–54.
Powles, John. 1973. "On the Limitations of Modern Medicine." *Science, Medicine and Man* 1(1):1–30.
Proctor, J. H. editor, 1971. *The Cell System of the Tanganyika African National Union*. Dar es Salaam: Tanzania Publishing House.
Prothero, R. Mansell. 1965. *Migrants and Malaria*. London: Longmans.
Provencher, Ronald. 1984. " 'Mother Needles': Lessons on Interethnic Psychiatry in Malaysian Society." *Social Science and Medicine* 18(2):139–146.
Puffer, R. R. and C. V. Serrano. 1973. "Patterns of Mortality in Childhood." Washington, D.C.: Pan American Health Organization, Scientific Publication no. 202.

Qu Geping. 1982. "Environmental Protection in China." *Environmental Conservation* 9(1):31–33.
Quine, W. V. O. 1953. *From a Logical Point of View*. Cambridge, Mass.: Harvard University Press.
Quinn, T. C. et al. 1986. "AIDS in Africa: An Epidemiologic Paradigm." *Science* 234:955–962.

Raikes, Philip. 1986. "Flowing with Milk and Money: Food Production in Africa and the Policies of the EEC." In *World Recession and the Food Crisis in Africa* edited by Peter Lawrence, 160–176. London: Review of African Political Economy and James Currey.
Ratnam, A. V. et al. 1982. "Penicillinase-producing Gonococcal Strains in Zambia." *British Journal of Venereal Disease* 58:29–31.
Rejsner, Marc. 1986. *Cadillac Desert: The American West and Its Disappearing Water*. New York: Viking.
Renaud, Marc. 1975. "On the Structural Constraints to State Intervention in Health." *International Journal of Health Services* 5(4);559–571.
République Algérienne. 1976. *Charte Nationale*. Alger.
Reyna, S. P. 1983. "Dual Class Formation and Agrarian Underdevelopment: An Analysis of the Articulation of Production Relations in Upper Volta." *Canadian Journal of African Studies* 17(2):211–233.
Reynolds, D. R. 1975. "An Appraisal of Rural Women in Tanzania." Washington, D.C.: U.S. Agency for International Development, unpublished document.

Ribicoff, Abraham. 1972. *The American Medical Machine*. New York: Harper & Row.

Richardson, Diane. 1988. *Women and AIDS*. New York: Methuen.

Ridgeway, James. 1971. *The Politics of Ecology*. New York: E. P. Dutton.

Ringen, Knut. 1979. "The 'New Ferment' in National Health Policies: The Case of Norway's Nutrition and Food Policy." *Social Science and Medicine* 13C:33–41.

Robertson, Claire. 1984. "Women in the Urban Economy." In *African Women South of the Sahara,* edited by M. J. Hay and S. Stichter, 33–50. London: Longman.

Roemer, Milton I. 1976. *Health Care Systems in World Perspective*. Ann Arbor: Health Administration Press.

———. 1982. *An Introduction to the U.S. Health Care System*. New York: Springer Publishing Company.

———. 1984. "Private Medical Practice: Obstacle to Health for All." *World Health Forum* 5:195–201.

Rose, Steven, editor. 1982. *Against Biological Determinism. The Dialectics of Biology Group*. London: Allison & Busby.

———. 1982. *Towards a Liberatory Biology. The Dialectics of Biology Group*. London: Allison & Busby.

Rosen, George. 1958. *A History of Public Health*. New York: MD Publications.

Rosenberg, M. J. and J. M. Weiner. 1988. "Prostitutes and AIDS: A Health Department Priority?" *American Journal of Public Health* 78(4):418–423.

Rosner, David and Gerald Markowitz, eds. 1987. *Dying for Work: Workers' Safety and Health in Twentieth Century America*. Bloomington: Indiana University Press.

Rothman, Kenneth J. 1982. "Causation and Causal Inference." In *Cancer Epidemiology and Prevention,* edited by David Schottenfeld and Joseph F. Fraumeni, 55–22. Philadelphia: Saunders.

Ryan, William. 1976. *Blaming the Victim*. New York: Vintage Books.

Salan, R. and T. Maretzki. 1983. "Mental Health Services and Traditional Healing in Indonesia: Are the Roles Compatible?" *Culture, Medicine and Psychiatry* 7:377–412.

Salmon, J. Warren. 1984. *Alternative Medicines: Popular and Policy Perspectives*. New York: Tavistock Publications.

Scheper-Hughes, Nancy and Anne M. Lovell, eds. 1987. *Psychiatry from Inside Out: Selected Writings of Franco Basaglia*. New York: Columbia University Press.

Schoen, Cathy. 1977. "Case Study 3. Program Evaluation Studies: The Office of Economic Opportunity Neighborhood Health Centers" *Kapitalistate* 6:176–180.

Schoepf, B. G. et al. 1988. "AIDS and Society in Central Africa: A View from Zaire." In *AIDS in Africa: The Social and Policy Impact,* edited by N. Miller and R. C. Rockwell, 211–235. Lewiston, N.Y.: The Edwin Mellen Press.

Schuyler, George W. 1980. *Hunger in a Land of Plenty*. Cambridge: Schenkman Publishing.

Sclar, Elliott D. 1980. "Community Economic Structure and Individual Well-Being: a Look Behind the Statistics" *International Journal of Health Services* 10(4):563–579.

Scott, Wolf. 1981. *Concepts and Measurement of Poverty*. Geneva: UN Research Institute for Social Development.
Scull, Andrew. 1984. *Community Treatment and the Deviant—a Radical View*. New Brunswick: Rutgers University Press.
Seddon, David. 1986. "Bread Riots in North Africa: Economic Policy and Social Unrest in Tunisia and Morocco." In *World Recession and the Food Crisis in Africa,* edited by Peter Lawrence, 177–192. London: Review of African Political Economy and James Currey.
Selden, Mark. 1971. *The Yenan Way in Revolutionary China*. Cambridge: Harvard University Press.
Selye, Hans. 1956. *The Stress of Life*. New York: McGraw Hill.
Sen, Amartya. 1982. *Poverty and Famines: An Essay on Entitlement and Deprivation.* Oxford: Clarendon Press.
Sen, Gita and Caren Grown. 1987. *Development, Crises, and Alternative Visions*. New York: Monthly Review Press.
Sharma, V. P. and K. N. Mehrotra. 1986. "Malaria Resurgence in India: A Critical Study." *Social Science & Medicine* 22(8):835–845.
Sheridan, David. 1981. *The Desertification of the United States*. Washington, D.C.: Council on Environmental Quality.
Showalter, Elaine. 1987. *The Female Malady: Women, Madness, and English Culture, 1830–1980*. New York: Penguin Books.
Sidel, Ruth. 1986. *Women and Children Last: The Plight of Poor Women in Affluent America*. New York: Viking Penguin.
Sidel, R. and V. W. Sidel. 1982. *The Health of China: Current Conflicts in Medical and Human Services for One Billion People.* Boston: Beacon Press.
Sidel, Victor W. and Ruth Sidel. 1977. *A Healthy State: An International Perspective on the Crisis in United States Medical Care*. New York: Pantheon Books.
———. 1984. *Reforming Medicine: Lessons of the Last Quarter Century*. New York: Pantheon Books.
Sigerist, Henry E. 1943. *Civilization and Disease*. Chicago: University of Chicago Press.
Silverstein, Brett. 1984. *Fed Up! The Food Forces That Make You Fat, Sick and Poor*. Boston: South End Press.
Simon, R. J., J. L. Flies, and B. J. Gurland. 1973. "Depression and Schizophrenia in Hospitalized Black and White Mental Patients." *Archives of General Psychiatry* 28:509–512.
Smith, Barbara Ellen. 1981. "Black Lung: The Social Production of Disease." *International Journal of Health Services* 11:343–359.
Solagral. 1984. *L'Aide Alimentaire*. Paris: Syros.
Solimano, Giorgio and Peter Hakim. 1979. "Nutrition and National Development: The Case of Chile." *International Journal of Health Services* 9(3):495–510.
Songre, A. 1973. "Mass Emigration from Upper Volta: the Facts and the Implications." In *Employment in Africa: Some Critical Issues*, 199–215. Geneva: International Labour Organisation.
S. P. K. 1972. *Psychiatrie Politique: L'Affaire de Heidelberg*. Paris: François Maspero.
Stacey, Margaret. 1985. "Women and Health: the United States and the United Kingdom Compared." In *Women, Health, and Healing: Toward a New Perspec-*

tive, edited by Ellen Lewin and Virginia Olesen, 270–303. New York and London: Tavistock.

Stahl, C. W. 1981. "Migrant Labour Supplies, Past, Present and Future; with Special Reference to the Gold-mining Industry." In *Black Migration to South Africa: A Selection of Policy-oriented Research,* edited by W. R. Bohning, 7–44. Geneva: International Labour Office.

Stark, Evan. 1977. "The Epidemic as a Social Event." *International Journal of Health Services* 7:681–705.

———. 1982. "What is Medicine?" *Radical Science Journal* 12:46–89.

Starr, Paul. 1982. *The Social Transformation of American Medicine.* New York: Basic Books.

Stavenhagen, Rodolfo, ed. 1970. *Agrarian Problems and Peasant Movements in Latin America.* Garden City, N.Y.: Doubleday.

Stock, Robert. 1988. "Environmental Sanitation in Nigeria: Colonial and Contemporary." *Review of African Political Economy* 42: 19–31.

Stokinger, H. E. and L. D. Scheel. 1973. "Hypersusceptibility and Genetic Problems in Occupational Medicine—a Consensus Report." *Journal of Occupational Medicine* 14:564–573.

Strasser, Alexander L. 1984. "Genetic Screening Can Be a Useful Tool to Promote Safety" *Occupational Health and Safety* January 29.

Suret-Canal, J. 1971. *French Colonialism in Tropical Africa, 1900–1945.* New York: PICA Press.

Susser, Mervyn, William Watson, and Kim Hopper. 1985. *Sociology in Medicine.* New York: Oxford University Press.

Szasz, Thomas. 1961. *The Myth of Mental Illness.* New York: Harper & Row.

Szentes, Tamas. 1971. *The Political Economy of Underdevelopment.* Budapest: Akademiai Kiado.

Szymanski, Albert. 1982. "On the Uses of Disinformation to Legitimize the Revival of the Cold War: Health in the USSR." *International Journal of Health Services* 12(3):481–496.

Tahon, M.-B. 1982. "L'emploi des Femmes en Algérie." *Canadian Journal of African Studies* 16(19):43–66.

Taylor, B. 1981. " 'Democracy' in Upper Volta." *Review of African Political Economy* 21:102–109.

Taylor, Ian, Paul Walton, and Jock Young. 1974. *The New Criminology: For a Social Theory of Deviance.* New York: Harper & Row.

Terris, Milton, ed. 1964. *Goldberger on Pellagra.* Baton Rouge: Louisiana State University Press.

Terris, Milton. 1978. "The Three World Systems of Medical Care: Trends and Prospects." *American Journal of Public Health* 68(11): 1125–1131.

Tesh, Sylvia. 1988. *Hidden Arguments: Political Ideology and Disease Prevention Policy.* New Brunswick: Rutgers University Press.

Thébaud-Mony, A. 1980. "Besoins de Santé et Politique de Santé." Paris: Université Paris V René Descartes, doctorat d'état inédit.

Thébaud, Annie. 1986. "Aid Games." *Review of African Political Economy* 36:43–49.

Thébaud, Annie and France Lert. 1985. "Maladie Subie, Maladie Dominée, Industrialisation et Technologie Médicale: Le Cas de la Tuberculose." *Social Science and Medicine* 21(2):129–137.

Thomas, I. D. and A. C. Mascarenhas, 1973. *Health Facilities and Population in Tanzania*. Dar es Salaam: Bureau of Resource Assessment and Land Use Planning Research Paper no. 21.
Thomas, Lewis. 1974. *The Lives of a Cell*. New York: Viking Press.
Thompson, E. P. 1968. *The Making of the English Working Class*. Harmondsworth: Penguin Books.
Thompson, Janna L. 1982. "Human Nature and Social Explanation." In *Against Biological Determinism. The Dialectics of Biology Group*, edited by Steven Rose, 30–49. London: Allison & Busby.
Thornicroft, Graham. 1986. "Contemporary Psychiatry in China." *British Medical Journal* 292:813–815.
Thunhurst, Colin. 1982. *It Makes You Sick: The Politics of the NHS*. London: Pluto Press.
Titmuss, Richard M. 1968. *Commitment to Welfare*. New York: Pantheon Books.
Torrey, B. B., P. O. Way, and P. M. Rowe. 1988. "Epidemiology of HIV and AIDS in Africa: Emerging Issues and Social Implications." In *AIDS in Africa: The Social and Policy Impact,* edited by N. Miller and R. C. Rockwell, 31–54. Lewiston, N.Y.: The Edwin Mellen Press.
Touré, Oussouby. 1988. "The Pastoral Environment of Northern Senegal" *Review of African Political Economy* 42:32–39.
Townsend, Peter and Nick Davidson. 1982. *Inequalities in Health: The Black Report*. Harmondsworth: Penguin Books.
Trehub, Aaron. 1987. "First Fee-for-service Hospital in USSR to Open in Moscow." Radio Liberty, September 14, mimeo.
Traoré, A. 1981. "L'accès des femmes ivoiriennes aux ressources— les femmes et la terre en pays Adioukrou." Dakar: Séminaire Régional Tripartite du BIT pour l'Afrique, Développement Rural et la Femme, mimeo.
Triendregeogon, A. 1982. "Female Circumcision in Upper Volta." In *Traditional Practices Affecting the Health of Women and Children*, 360–362. Alexandria, Egypt: WHO/EMRO Technical Publication vol. 2, no. 2.
Turshen, Meredeth. 1975. *The Political Economy of Health with a Case Study of Tanzania*. Unpublished Ph. D. Dissertation. Brighton, U.K.: University of Sussex.
———. 1977. "The Political Ecology of Disease." *Review of Radical Political Economics* 9(1):45–60.
———. 1978. "Women and Health in China." *Antipode* 10(1):51–63.
———. 1979. "Dioxin: Dow Fights Back Against the EPA Ban." *The Elements: A Journal of World Resources* 52:3–6.
———. 1980a. "Analytical Review of the WHO Health Manpower Development Programme, 1948–1978: Survey of the Literature of Six Countries." Geneva: World Health Organization. Unpublished report.
———. 1980b. "Carcinogens and Workers' Evidence." *Hastings Center Report* February, 44–45.
———. 1982. "Health Hazards in Pharmaceutical Production: A Review of the Literature." Paper presented at the Conference on Problems of Modernization and Occupational Health, July 19–20, 1982, Shanghai First Medical College, People's Republic of China.
———. 1984. *The Political Ecology of Disease in Tanzania*. New Brunswick: Rutgers University Press.

Turshen, Meredeth. 1985. "Medical Aid to Ethiopia, 1950–1970." *Northeast African Studies* 7(1):49–61.

———. 1986. "Food and Hunger in Ciskei." In *World Recession and the Food Crisis in Africa,* edited by Peter Lawrence, 275–282. London: Review of African Political Economy and James Currey.

Turshen, Meredeth and Carol Barker. 1986. "The Health Issue." *Review of African Political Economy* 36:1–6.

Turshen, Meredeth, Carol Barker, and Phil O'Keefe. 1988. "Editorial: The African Environment." *Review of African Political Economy* 42: 1–4.

Turshen, Meredeth and Annie Thébaud. 1981. "International Medical Aid." *Monthly Review* 33(7):39–50.

UN. 1983. *Demographic Yearbook 1981*. New York: United Nations.

———. 1987. *United Nations Demographic Yearbook 1985*. New York: United Nations.

UNDP/World Bank/WHO. 1985. *Tropical Disease Research: Seventh Programme Report, 1 January 1983–31 December 1984*. Geneva: World Health Organization.

———. 1986. *Newsletter* No.23. Geneva: Special Programme for Research and Training in Tropical Diseases.

UN Economic Commission for Africa, 1976. Report on the Workshop on Food Preservation and Storage, Kibaha, Tanzania. Addis Ababa.

UN High Commission for Refugees. 1980. *News from the UNHCR*. 2:6

UNICEF. 1987. *Adjustment with a Human Face: Protecting the Vulnerable and Promoting Growth*. Oxford: Clarendon Press.

———. 1988. *The State of the World's Children*. New York: Oxford University Press.

United Republic of Tanzania, 1972. *The Economic Survey 1971–71*. Dar es Salaam: Government Printer.

U.S. Bureau of the Census. 1987. *Statistical Abstract of the United States 1988*. Washington, D.C.

U.S. Committee for Refugees. 1987. *World Refugee Survey: 1986 in Review*. Washington, D.C.

———. 1988. *World Refugee Survey: 1987 in Review.* Washington, D.C.

U.S. Department of Agriculture. 1981a. *Food Problems and Prospects in Sub-Saharan Africa: The Decade of the 1980s*. Washington, D.C.

———. 1981b. *Agricultural Situation: Africa and the Middle East. Review of 1980 and Outlook for 1981.* Washington, D.C.

U.S. Department of Health and Human Services, Public Health Service. 1986. "Human T-Lymphotropic Virus Type III/Lymphadenopathy-Associated Virus Antibody Prevalence in U.S. Military Recruit Applicants." *Mortality and Morbidity Weekly Review* 35(26):421–424.

U.S. National Commission on State Workmen's Compensation Laws. 1973. *Report*. Washington, D.C: U.S. Government Printing Office.

van den Bosch, Robert. 1978. *The Pesticide Conspiracy*. New York: Doubleday.

van Etten, G. M. 1976. *Rural Health Development in Tanzania.* Assen: Van Gorcum.

van Ginneken, W. 1976. *Rural and Urban Income Inequalities*. Geneva: International Labour Organisation.

Verhagen, R. and W. Gemert. 1972. "Social and Epidemiological Determinants

of Gonorrhea in an East African Country." *British Journal of Venereal Disease* 48:277–286.
Virchow, Rudolf. 1985. *Collected Essays on Public Health and Epidemiology.* N.Y.: Amerind Publishing Co.
von Freyhold, M., K. Sawaki, and M. Zalla, 1973. "Moshi District." In *The Young Child Study in Tanzania.* Dar es Salaam: UNICEF Liaison Office.

Wain, Harry. 1970. *A History of Preventive Medicine.* Springfield, Ill.: Charles C. Thomas Publisher.
Waite, Gloria. 1988. "The Politics of Disease: The AIDS Virus and Africa." In *AIDS in Africa: The Social and Policy Impact*, edited by N. Miller and R. C. Rockwell, 145–162. Lewiston, N.Y.: The Edwin Mellen Press.
Waldron, I. 1976. "Why Do Women Live Longer than Men?" *Social Science & Medicine* 10:349–362.
Walsh, Julia A. and Kenneth S. Warren. 1979. "Selective Primary Health Care—An Interim Strategy for Disease Control in Developing Countries." *New England Journal of Medicine* 301(18):967–974.
Watkins, Alfred J. and David C. Perry. 1977. "Regional Change and the Impact of Uneven Urban Development." In *The Rise of the Sunbelt Cities,* edited by David C. Perry and Alfred J. Watkins, 19–54. Beverly Hills: Sage Publications.
Watson, Catharine. 1988. "Ending the Rule of the Gun." *Africa Report.* January-February, 14–17.
Weir, David. 1987. *The Bhopal Syndrome.* San Francisco: Sierra Club Books.
Weir, David and Mark Schapiro. 1981. *Circle of Poison: Pesticides and People in a Hungry World.* San Francisco: Institute for Food and Development Policy.
Wessen, Albert F. 1986. "Introduction: Resurgent Malaria and the Social Sciences." *Social Science & Medicine* 22(8):III-IV.
Wessman, James. 1981. "Neo-Malthusian Ideology and Colonial Capitalism: Population Dynamics in Southwestern Puerto Rico." In *And the Poor Get Children: Radical Perspective on Population Dynamics,* edited by Karen L. Michaelson, 194–220. New York: Monthly Review Press.
Whiteside, Thomas. 1979. *The Pendulum and the Toxic Cloud: The Course of Dioxin Contamination.* New Haven: Yale University Press.
WHO. 1962. *Expert Committee on Malaria: Ninth Report.* Geneva: Technical Report Series No. 243.
———. 1967. *Handbook for Smallpox Eradication Programmes in Endemic Areas.* Geneva: World Health Organization.
———. 1976. *Treatment and Prevention of Dehydration in Diarrhoeal Diseases.* Geneva: World Health Organization.
———. 1978. "Declaration of Alma Ata." In *Report of the International Conference on Primary Health Care.* Geneva: World Health Organization.
———. 1980. *Sixth Report on the World Health Situation: Part Two, Review by Country and Area.* Geneva: World Health Organization.
———. 1981. "Infant and Juvenile Mortality at Algiers." *World Health Statistics Quarterly* 34(1):44–63.
———. 1983. *Apartheid and Health.* Geneva: World Health Organization.
———. 1985a. Scientific Working Group on the Chemotherapy of Malaria: Third Programme Review. Document TDR/CHEMAL/3RD REVIEW/85.3. Geneva: World Health Organization.

WHO. 1985b. *Weekly Epidemiological Record* No. 44.
———. 1986a. *Evaluation of the Strategy for Health for All by the Year 2000*. Seventh Report on the World Health Situation. Volume 5, European Region. Copenhagen: WHO Regional Office for Europe.
———. 1986b. *The Work of WHO 1984–1985*. Geneva: World Health Organization.
———. 1986c. *Weekly Epidemiological Record* No. 10.
———. 1987a. *Weekly Epidemiological Record* No. 49.
———. 1987b. *Weekly Epidemiological Record* No. 41.
———. 1987c. *Weekly Epidemiological Record* No. 22.
———. 1988. *Weekly Epidemiological Record* No. 45.
———. 1989. "Update: AIDS Cases Reported to Surveillance, Forecasting, and Impact Unit, Global Programme on AIDS." 1 June. Geneva: World Health Organization. Mimeo.
Wilson, E. O. 1975. *Sociobiology: The New Synthesis*. Cambridge: Harvard University Press.
———. 1978. *On Human Nature*. Cambridge: Harvard University Press.
Wilson, Florence A. and Duncan Neuhauser. 1987. *Health Services in the United States*. Cambridge, Mass.: Ballinger Publishing Company.
Wilson, Francis. 1972. *Migrant Labour in South Africa*. Johannesburg: South African Council of Churches.
Wolf, Eric R. 1973. *Peasant Wars of the Twentieth Century*. London: Faber and Faber.
World Bank. 1981. *Accelerated Development in Sub-Saharan Africa*. Washington, D.C.: The World Bank.
———. 1982. "Upper Volta: Health and Nutrition Sector Review." Washington, D.C.: unpublished document.
———. 1987. *World Development Report 1987*. New York: Oxford University Press.
———. 1988. *World Development Report 1988*. New York: Oxford University Press.
Wright, Erik Olin. 1978. *Class, Crisis and the State*. London: New Left Books.
Wurtman, Richard J. 1985. "Alzheimer's Disease." *Scientific American* January, 62–74.

Young, K. 1979. "Editorial." *IDS Bulletin* 10(3):1–4.
Young, K., C. Wolkowitz, and R. McCullagh. 1981. *Of Marriage and the Market: Women's Subordination in International Perspective*. London: CSE Books.
Young, Mary E. and André Prost. 1985. "Child Health in China." World Bank Staff Working Papers Number 767. Washington, D.C.: The World Bank.
Yoxen, Edward. 1983. *The Gene Business: Who Should Control Biotechnology?* New York: Oxford University Press.

Zachariah, K. C. and J. Condé. 1981. *Migration in West Africa: Demographic Aspects*. New York: Oxford University Press.
Zalaquett, José. 1981. *The Human Rights Issue and the Human Rights Movement*. Geneva: World Council of Churches.
Zimbabwe Ministry of Health. 1984. *Planning for Equity in Health: A Sectoral Review and Policy Statement*. Harare: Government of the Republic of Zimbabwe.

INDEX